SCOTTISH COLONIAL SCHEMES

A Facsimile Reprint
of the 1922 Glasgow Edition

Published 2004

American History Imprints
Nashville Tennessee

Visit us on the Internet and explore our
extensive catalog listing thousands of titles
of interest to the genealogist and historian.

www.Americanhistoryimprints.com
www.genealogyinprint.com

ISBN 0-9753667-1-8

Printed in the United States of America

ILLUSTRATIONS

	PAGE
SIR WILLIAM ALEXANDER, EARL OF STIRLING	*frontispiece*
FACSIMILE TITLE PAGE OF LOCHINVAR'S "ENCOURAGEMENTS"	96
SEAT OF THE SCOTTISH-QUAKER PROPRIETORS OF EAST JERSEY	160

(*From Whitehead's "East Jersey under the Proprietary Governors."*)

PRINCIPAL WILLIAM DUNLOP - - - - - - 208

(*From portrait in Senate Room of Glasgow University.*)

SCOTTISH COLONIAL SCHEMES

1620-1686

BY

GEORGE PRATT INSH, M.A., D.Litt.

GLASGOW
MACLEHOSE, JACKSON & CO.
PUBLISHERS TO THE UNIVERSITY
1922

TO MY MOTHER

PREFACE

In revising for publication my essay on "Scottish Colonial Schemes Prior to the Union," which was awarded the Carnegie Essay Prize for the year 1920-1921, I felt that both historical and artistic unity demanded that the smaller and comparatively unknown enterprises preceding the Darien Scheme should be dealt with by themselves, and that the manifold activities of the "Company of Scotland Trading to Africa and the Indies" should form a separate study. In this volume I have traced the history of Scottish colonial enterprise from the days of the Nova Scotia scheme of Sir William Alexander down to the destruction of the outpost of the Scottish Covenanters in South Carolina: I have in preparation a volume dealing with the Darien Scheme.

To the Carnegie Trust for the Universities of Scotland I am indebted not only for a grant in aid of the publication of this volume, but also for the encouragement of research connoted by the offer of their Essay Prize. To my old University of Glasgow, which has set the seal of its approval on my historical work by the award of the degree of Doctor of Letters, I am indebted for permission to reproduce the portrait of Principal William Dunlop, who took the chief part in the settlement of the Scottish Covenanters at Stuart's Town in South Carolina.

GLASGOW, *April*, 1922.

CONTENTS

	PAGE
INTRODUCTION	1

CHAPTER
I. NEWFOUNDLAND	27
II. NOVA SCOTIA	40
III. NEW GALLOWAY (CAPE BRETON ISLAND)	91
IV. "THE YEARS BETWEEN"	113
V. EAST NEW JERSEY	145
VI. STUART'S TOWN, SOUTH CAROLINA	186

APPENDICES

A. FRENCH PROTEST AGAINST SCOTTISH EXPEDITION OF 1623	212
B. DATE OF SETTLEMENT OF SCOTS AT PORT ROYAL IN ACADIE	214
C. "A NOTE OF ALL SUCHE THINGS AS THE COMPANY HATH IN CANADA"	227
D. BARBADOS CORRESPONDENCE CONCERNING SCOTTISH SETTLERS	229
E. (a) BROADSIDE BY ROBERT BARCLAY	233
(b) LETTERS FROM SCOT OF PITLOCHIE'S "MODEL"	237
F. PROPOSALS BY WALTER GIBSON	278
INDEX	280

SCOTTISH COLONIAL SCHEMES

INTRODUCTION

FOR many a year the call of the West, the summons to the new lands beyond the Atlantic, evoked from Scotland no response; the lure of strange landfalls, the wonders and the wealth of the great New Continent, failed to stir the imagination either of the douce traders north of the Tweed, or of adventurous wanderers setting out from the shores of Scotland. In Danzic or in Campvere the Scottish merchant still drove his trade, ignorant of, or indifferent to, the fabled riches of the New World: on the banks of the Seine, or amid the polders of the Netherlands, the Scottish soldier of fortune still sought an employer for his sword.

When the Elizabethan age of voyaging and discovery was succeeded by the Stuart era of settlement and consolidation, the part played by Scotland in these latter activities was at first insignificant. For England the seventeenth century was a time of energetic and progressive Colonial expansion. "The years of our settlement," writes a distinguished American historian, "were a romantic period, a time of energy and heroism, of bold ventures at sea and exploration on the land, when island and continental colony in that wonderful region of Florida and the West Indies were planted in insecurity, and like the frontier posts of Western America were maintained amid the constant perils of existence. Along the coast of the Atlantic, from Hudson Bay on the north to the Amazon on the south, royalist and parliamentarian, Anglican and Puritan, feudal lord and democratic radical, sea rover and buccaneer, sought to establish settlements that would directly enhance their own fortunes or furnish them with homes, and indirectly redound to the glory of God, the discomfiture of the enemy, and the good of the realm, and serve as strategic centres in the conflict for supremacy with the other pioneers of Europe."[1] The tale of effective English settlement begins in 1607 with the plantation of Jamestown in Virginia by the London Virginia Company. In 1612 the island of Bermuda, discovered three years previously by Sir George Somers, was added by a charter to Virginia, but was later formed into a separate colony. On the reorganization of the Plymouth Virginia Company as the New England Council, followed the gradual settlement of the coast well to the north of Virginia: the decade 1620-1630 saw in its opening year the landing of the Pilgrims at Plymouth; in its closing year it witnessed the migration of the Massachusetts Bay Company to Salem. In the Caribbean Islands English settlers had, within the same decade, made a joint occupation of St. Christopher's with the French, and had begun the plantation of Nevis and Barbados. In the following decade, Connecticut and Rhode Island were established; Maine was granted to Sir Ferdinando Gorges; the foundation of New Hampshire was laid by Captain John Mason; and Leonard Calvert, brother of the second Lord Baltimore, conducted a band of emigrants to Maryland.

Some of these settlements owed their origin to the political strife between the early Stuart Kings and those who opposed them either on political or on religious grounds: others, again, were founded by courtiers who saw in the undeveloped lands beyond the Atlantic an opportunity of establishing a new feudalism. By absorbing the energies of Cavalier and Parliamentarian the Civil War brought to a close the first epoch of English colonial progress. The second epoch opened with the capture of Jamaica in 1655 by the expedition under Admiral Penn and General Venables, sent out by Cromwell. The decade following the Restoration saw the grant of a Charter to the Lords Proprietors of Carolina; the capture of New Amsterdam from the Dutch, followed by the grant of New Jersey to Carteret and Berkeley; the founding of a

[1] C. M. Andrews, *The Colonial Period*, p. 10.

company for the development of the Bahamas. The next two decades saw the development of East and West Jersey, under Proprietary governments, in which Quaker influence was latterly to become very strong, and this led up naturally to the establishment in 1681 of the Quaker colony of Pennsylvania. The establishment of Georgia in 1732 stands outside the general range of English colonial expansion; it owed its origin partly to the nascent philanthropic tendencies of the eighteenth century, partly to political considerations; designed by Oglethorpe as a colony of refuge for men who had suffered imprisonment for debt, Georgia commended itself both to the American colonists and to the Imperial government as a barrier against Spanish aggression.

To the history of English colonial expansion during the seventeenth century the record of Scottish colonial enterprise in the days before the Union of 1707 offers a striking contrast. Virginia had struggled successfully through its critical early years, and the Pilgrims had crossed the Atlantic before Sir William Alexander received in 1621, from King James, the charter that conveyed to him the grant of Nova Scotia, to be holden of the Crown of Scotland. The expedition that sailed from Kirkcudbright in the summer of 1622 did not even reach the shores of Sir William's new domain, but was obliged to winter at Newfoundland; the relief expedition dispatched in 1623 did indeed explore a part of the coast of Acadie, but did not effect a settlement. Thereafter the project languished for some years, but in 1629[1] a small Scottish colony was established at Port Royal on the Bay of Fundy: its brief and precarious existence was terminated by the Treaty of St. Germain-en-Laye in 1632. In 1629, too, a small Scottish colony was planted by Lord Ochiltree on one of the coves of the Cape Breton coast: after an existence of a few months it was broken up by a French raiding force. Half a century after these fruitless efforts to establish Scottish colonies, two attempts were made to form Scottish settlements within the territories occupied by the English colonists: the Quaker Scottish settlement of East Jersey met with considerable success; but after a very brief and very troubled existence

[1] For this date, see Appendix B.

the small Presbyterian colony of Stuart's Town in South Carolina was destroyed by a Spanish force from St. Augustine. The ever-growing desire of the Scottish merchants to have a colony of their own, to have a market for the goods produced by the factories that began to spring up in Scotland during the closing decades of the seventeenth century, found expression in the eagerness with which Scottish investors entrusted their carefully garnered savings to the Directors of the Company of Scotland Trading to Africa and the Indies : and never was more tragic contrast than that between the anticipations roused by the Darien Scheme and the tale of disaster that is the record of the Darien expeditions.

Yet though the history of Scottish colonial enterprise reveals but a meagre record of actual achievements, that history is invested with a romantic interest that renders it more akin, in its essential aspects, to the story of French colonial activities in North America than to the somewhat prosaic annals of the English settlements along the Atlantic sea-board. When the Scots came into conflict in North America with their Ancient Ally, the course of events seemed to threaten the very existence of the French power, not only in Acadie, where Port Royal was effectively occupied by the Master of Stirling, but also along the St. Lawrence valley : the security of the ocean gateway to that region was menaced by Ochiltree's fortalice on Cape Breton Island : in 1629 Champlain surrendered his fort and habitation of Quebec to Captain Kirke, who was operating in connection with the Scots : the thistle had for the moment triumphed over the fleur-de-lys. It is not wholly chimerical to imagine that if Nova Scotia and the St. Lawrence valley had not been surrendered by Charles I. in 1632, the feudal organization designed for Sir William Alexander's province and the adventurous life that Canadian lake and forest and river opened up to the daring pioneer would have offered to the Scottish military adventurer a congenial sphere of activity and a life quite as attractive as that of a career of arms in Sweden or in Muscovy. And the student of military history who remembers that on the Cape Breton coast, near the spot where Ochiltree's fortalice was razed to the ground, there was erected a French fort that grew ultimately into the mighty citadel of Louisbourg, will not be unwilling to concede that the Scottish station might well have played an important part in colonial naval and military strategy.

And at the mention of Darien what romantic visions rise before one : of the *St. Andrew* and her consorts threading their way among the Carribean Islands and piloted to the Main by a grizzled buccaneer ; of the huts and battery of New Edinburgh looking across the narrow channel of Caledonia Bay to the rugged jungle-clad Cordillera, whence Bilbao had gazed down on the distant shimmering radiance that was the South Sea ; of Scottish claymore and Indian machete flashing together in the tropical sunshine as Captain Campbell of Fonab charged the entrenchments of Toubacante. By many who were well acquainted with West Indian and Central American affairs the Scottish project was considered to stand more than a fair chance of success. And if Scotland had made good her footing on the Isthmus. . . .

The latent possibilities of these Scottish schemes adds interest to the problem of why the Scots, who took a leading part in the colonial activities of the eighteenth and nineteenth centuries, achieved so little in the way of acquisition of colonies during the seventeenth century. The failure of the Scottish schemes was due mainly to the persistence of certain national tendencies, military, economic and religious, and it will be not unprofitable to discuss these before we take up the history of the various schemes.

I.

" The contempt of commerce entertained by young men having some pretence to gentility," says Sir Walter Scott, " the poverty of the country of Scotland, the national disposition to wandering and adventure, all conduced to lead the Scots abroad into the military service of countries which were at war with each other." [1] To France, however, for two centuries and a half the ambitious Scot turned, not only during war but during the unquiet intervals of peace. During

[1] Introd. to *A Legend of Montrose*.

the days of the Auld Alliance, indeed, the Scot, though he crossed the seas, could hardly be described as going abroad : and in the Archer Guard of the French Kings there was a permanent institution that held out to the Quentin Durwards of the age the prospect of a career of distinction.

A picturesque legend ascribes the foundation of the Guard to St. Louis, who is said to have enrolled, as a permanent bodyguard, a number of Scots Crusaders, whose vigilance had protected him against Moslem assassins. History, however, points to Charles VII. as the founder of the Guard, and to the survivors of those Scots auxiliaries who fought so stoutly for France on the deadly field of Verneuil as its first members. It had an establishment of 100 gens d'armes and 200 archers. At the French court it held a position of special honour and privilege. It was responsible for the guarding of the royal dwelling by night. At mass and at vespers two of its members were in close attendance on the King. While he was at table one stood at each side of his chair. At every important court function a detachment of the Guard was on duty. The boat which bore the King across a river carried two of his trusted Scots. When the sovereign entered a town, six of them were beside him ; the keys of the town, handed to the King in accordance with feudal practice, were delivered to the custody of the Captain of the Scots Guard. The defence of Louis XI. by his Scots Guard, on the occasion of the desperate night sortie by the inhabitants of Liège, is but one proof that its duties involved more than court service of unshaken fidelity in an age of treachery and intrigue.

For a century and a quarter the Guard enjoyed without interruption the favour of successive sovereigns : for a century and a quarter it typified the esteem which the Scot enjoyed in France. The year 1560 is mentioned in a " Factum " or statement of their grievances, drawn up in 1611 by some of the Guard, as the date when clouds began to gather on the horizon. The year 1560 marked, indeed, the end of the Auld Alliance : in that year the Scots who had rebelled against the Queen-Regent, Mary of Lorraine, made common cause with England against the French forces in Scotland. But the first symptom of the impending change of fortune might have been observed a considerable time before, when Francis I. decided that a Frenchman should henceforth be appointed to the Captaincy of the Guard, a post of great dignity held hitherto by a Scottish noble. The innovation, however, was made with gentleness and tact. The first commander under the new régime was Jacques de Lorges, Comte de Montgomerie, who claimed descent from the Scottish family of Eglinton. The Comte de Montgomerie was succeeded in the captaincy by his son Gabriel, who, in the course of a tournament held in 1559, had the misfortune to inflict a mortal wound on Henry II. Gabriel de Lorges, whose captaincy was abruptly terminated by this mishap, was regarded by the Scots of a later generation as the last of their native captains.

The innovation in the captaincy was soon followed by changes in the method of recruiting the ranks. But in the sixteenth and in the seventeenth century it generally happened that, when on the Continent one avenue to employment and distinction was closed to the Scottish soldier of fortune, another was opened to him; and thus the traditional tendency to seek a career in continental campaigning was continued and strengthened. Little more than a decade after the severance of the bonds of amity that had linked together France and Scotland since the days of the Scottish War of Independence, the capture of Brill by the Beggars of the Sea inaugurated the revolt of the Netherlands against the dominion of Spain; and both during that fierce struggle and down almost to the end of the eighteenth century Scottish troops distinguished themselves in the service of the United Netherlands. "Being royal troops, they claimed, they demanded, and would not be refused the post of honour and the precedence of all the troops in the service of the States. Even the English regiments yielded it to the seniority of the Scots Brigade. This station they occupied on every occasion for two hundred years, and in no instance did they appear unworthy of it."[1] To this encomium of the Brigade by their chaplain, Dr. Porteous may well be added his remarks concerning their traditional spirit: "The officers entered into the service very

[1] Quoted, *The Scots Brigade in Holland*, vol. i. p. xix.

early; they were trained up under their fathers and grandfathers who had grown old in the service; they expected a slow, certain, and unpurchased promotion, but almost always in the same corps, and before they attained to command they were qualified for it. Though they served a foreign state, yet not in a distant country, they were still under the eye of their own, and considered themselves as the depositaries of her military fame. Hence their remarkable attachment to one another, and to the country whose name they bore and from whence they came; hence that high degree of ambition for supporting the renown of Scotland and the glory of the Scots Brigade." [1]

The Twelve Years' Truce of 1609 brought to a close the first period of the campaigns of the Scots Brigade in the Netherlands. The outbreak of the Thirty Years' War ushered in the Golden Age of the Scottish soldier of fortune. It is not necessary to recapitulate the general characteristics of the Scottish service in the armies of Gustavus and of Wallenstein, but it is not inapposite to contrast the difficulty experienced by Sir William Alexander in 1622 in coaxing a small band of Galwegian peasants to join his Nova Scotian expedition with the ease with which Sir Donald Mackay, first Lord Reay, in 1626 raised his 3600 men within the brief space of nine weeks —a recruiting feat commemorated in an old Gaelic couplet:

> Na h-uile fear a theid a dhollaidh
> Gheibh e dolar bho Mhac Aoidh.[2]
>
> (Every man who's down in his luck
> Will get a dollar from Mackay.)

From Sir James Turner's *Memoirs* one gets a vivid glimpse of the fascination exercised by continental campaigning on the eager, active mind of a young Scot. "I was not seventeen yeares old," writes Turner, "when I left the schooles, where haveing lightlie passed thorough that course of philosophie which is ordinarlie taught in the Universities of Scotland, I was commanded by my father and my grandfather to

---

[1] Quoted, *Scots Brigade in Holland*, vol. i. p. xxiv.

[2] Fischer, *The Scots in Germany*, p. 74; Dunbar, *Social Life in Former Days*, pp. 58 and 179-183.

commence Master of Arts at Glasgow, much against my will, as never intending to make use of that title which undeservedlie was bestowed upon me, as it was on many others before me, and hath been on too many since. I stayed a yeare after with my father at Dalkeith, applying myself to the study of humane letters and historie, in bothe which I always tooke delight. I did reade also the controversies of religion betweene us and the Roman Catholickes (for the Presbyterians at that time made little or no noyse) whereby I might be enabled to discern the truth of the Protestant persuasion and the fallacies of the Popish one or any other, that so I might not, in traversing the world, be carried away with everie wind of doctrine. But before I attained to the eighteenth yeare of my age, a restles desire entered my mind to be, if not an actor, at least a spectator of these warrs which at that time made so much noyse over all the world, and were managed against the Roman Emperor and the Catholicke League in Germanie, under the auspitious conduct of the thrice famous Gustavus Adolphus, King of Sweden. Sir James Lumsdaine was then levieing a regiment for that service; with him (my neerest freinds consenting to it) I engaged to go over ensigney to his brother Robert Lumsdaine, eldest Capitaine." [1]

To the persistence of the tradition of a continental career among the Scots interesting testimony is afforded by the passage in the *Diary* of Patrick Gordon of Auchleuchries, which records the motives that induced him to set out on his travels. Gordon was a Buchan man who rose to a position of the highest honour in the service of Peter the Great. After a brief account of his Aberdeenshire school days, Gordon proceeds, under date 1651: "Haveing thus, by the most loveing care of my dear parents, atteined to as much learning as the ordinary country schools affoard, and being unwilling, because of my dissenting in religion, to go to the University in Scotland, I resolved, partly to dissolve the bonds of a youthfull affection, wherein I was entangled, by banishing myself from the object; partly to obtain my liberty, which I fondly conceited to be restrained by the carefull inspection

[1] Turner, *Memoirs of his own Life and Times*, pp. 1-2.

of my loveing parents; but, most of all, my patrimony being but small, as being the younger sone of a younger brother of a younger house, I resolved, I say, to go to some foreigne country, not careing much on what pretence, or to which country I should go, seeing I had no knowne ffriend in any foreign place." [1]

On the military tradition that mainly inspired Gordon of Auchleuchries interesting light is thrown by a passage in the *Description of Aberdeen* by his kinsman Robert Gordon of Straloch: Negotiatio urbanis relinquitur: meliores (magno suo malo) id vitae genus, ut natalibus suis impar dedignantur; unde inopia multis; cui levandae, ad tractanda arma se accingunt, quae multis locis apud exteros, Belgas praesertim, Germanos et Gallos, semper amicam et illis adamatam gentem, a multis annis, cum laude, exercuerunt; ingeniis, enim, acribus et fervidis, sive Musis sive Marti se mancipent, non leviter proficiunt. [2]

The influence of this military tradition and its deterrent effect on Scottish colonial schemes were clearly recognised by those who were interested in these efforts. "Bee we so farre inferiour to other nations," asked Sir Robert Gordon of Lochinvar indignantly in his *Encouragements for New Galloway*, "or our Spirits so farre dejected froun our ancient predecessours, or our minds so upon spoyle, pyracie, or other villanie, as to serve the Portugal, Spaniard, French or Turk (as to the great hurte of Europe too many do) rather than our God, our King, our Countrie, and ourselves, excusing our idleness, and our base complaynts by want of employment? When heere is such choyse of all sorts, and for all degrees in this plantation?" But the eloquence of Lochinvar was drowned amid the clatter of accoutrements as the levies crowded the East Coast ports on their way to the plains of Germanie. [3]

Even at the very end of the seventeenth century, at the time of the Darien expeditions, the Scottish tradition of military

---

[1] *Diary of Gen. Patrick Gordon*, Spalding Club, p. 5.

[2] Quoted *Gordon's Diary*, p. xx n.

[3] Dunbar, *Social Life in Former Days*, Second Series, pp. 58 and 179-183; *Records of Burgh of Aberdeen*, 1625-1642 (Burgh Record Socy.), p. 8.

adventure was not without influence on the progress of colonial schemes, though that influence was exerted along unusual lines. The first Darien expedition sailed from Leith in July of 1698. In the previous autumn the Peace of Ryswick, which brought to an end the long-drawn-out war of the League of Augsburg, caused a sweeping reduction in the number of Scots required both in the Scots Brigade in Holland and in the Scottish regiments of the British army : during the winter of 1697-1698 nine Scots-Dutch companies were disbanded ;[1] the Records of the Scots Privy Council for this period reveal continued zeal and activity in the reduction of the strength of the Scottish regiments. To the Scottish soldiers thus thrown out of employment the adventurous possibilities of the Darien expedition and its semi-military organization offered just such prospects of a career as would appeal strongly to the soldier who had sheathed his sword but who did not altogether relish that return to civil life which, in the course of an arduous campaign, might have appeared to him so alluring. But the very qualities which won distinction for the Scot in the sieges and battles of the Low Countries were found to be those for which the Darien enterprise gave but little scope ; letters, from Darien, especially those of the Rev. Alex. Shields, reveal only too clearly that Scottish " planters " and " volunteers " in ceasing to be soldiers had acquired but little proficiency as colonists.[2]

II.

To the persistency of the Scottish tradition of military adventure the conservative ways of the Scottish merchants and seamen offer an interesting parallel. It is true that in the closing years of the sixteenth century the good folks who directed the affairs of the Burgh of Aberdeen had their minds stirred by the contemplation of the achievements of the Age of Discovery. On the 25th January, 1597 " the provost, baillies and counsell ordaint the dean of gyld to pay Robert

---

[1] *Scots Bgde. in Holland*, vol. i. p. 575.

[2] Letter from Rev. Alex. Shields to Colonel Erskine, Feb. 2, 1700. (Printed *Erskine of Carnock's Journal*, Appendix iii.)

Lyndsey, pylot, the sowme of fourtie merkis for ane gratitude for the sey kart presentet this day be him to the provest, baillies and counsell, conteining money guid profitable vreitis, instructione and devyses necessar for sic as treddis on sey, to ony forane countreis, viz. : the haill universall see kart of Europe, Affrica, and Asaia and new found landes of America, with the townes armes theiron affixit, quhilk the provest, bailleis and counsell ressavit presentlie fra the said Robert, and ordainit the same to remaine in the handes and custodie of Mr. Thomas [Mollisoun], common clerk, quhill they appoint ane commoun place to affix the samen quhilk sowme of fourtie merkis sall be allowed to the dean of guild in his comptes." [1] But it was probably long after the acquisition of this 'sey kart' before any Aberdeen shipmaster steered his course north about and braved the storms of the Atlantic.

The essential difference between the instincts of Scot and Englishman is revealed broadly but significantly in the popular literature of Scotland and England. The interests and activities of the Elizabethan age are reflected in the sea songs, the narratives of the voyages, and the plays of the time. Thoroughly versed in the mystery of his calling, his skill tested in long and hazardous voyages, the English seaman could celebrate his dangerous existence in bluff and hearty rhyme, carrying the very tang of the sea, as in the following ditty (as old at least as 1576), with the rollicking chorus :

> Lustely, lustely, lustely, let us sayle forth,
> The winde trim doth serve us, it blowes at the north.
>
> All thinges wee have ready and nothing wee want,
>   To furnish our ship that rideth hereby :
> Victals and weapons they be nothing skant,
>   Like worthy mariners our selves wee will try.
>
> Her flags be new trimmed set flanting aloft.
>   Our ship for swift swimming oh shee doth excell,
> Wee feare no enemies, we have escaped them oft,
>   Of all ships that swimmeth shee bareth the bell.

[1] *Aberdeen Records*, Spalding Club, vol. ii. p. 158.

And here is a master excelleth in skill,
  And our master's mate hee is not to seeke :
And here is a boteswaine will do his good will,
  And here is a ship boy we never had his leeke.

If fortune then faile not, and our next viadge prove,
  Wee will returne merely and make good cheere :
And hauld all together as freends linkt in love,
  The cannes shall be filled with wine, aile and beere.

Of the narratives of the voyages there stand out pre-eminent the " three severall volumes " of Hakluyt, the outcome of that burning interest in navigation and discovery that urged their author to the completion of his task in despite of " great charges and infinite cares, many watchings, toiles, and travils, and wearying out of his weake body." Of Elizabethan plays reflecting the sea-faring interest, *The Tempest* is of course the chief ; but a less familiar drama, John Lyly's *Gallathea*, " playde before the Queen's Majestie at Greenwiche on New Yeeres Day at Night," furnishes a passage that yields an even more significant commentary on the Elizabethan attitude to nautical life than does *The Tempest*. *Gallathea*, which preceded *The Tempest* by about forty years, is a romantic play having its setting on the Lincolnshire coast of the Humber estuary. In the first act Lyly brings on to the stage, for comic relief, a Mariner and Raffe, Robin, and Dicke, three sons of a miller.

Robin. Now, Mariner, what callest thou this sport on the Sea ?
Mar. It is called a wracke.
Raffe. I take no pleasure in it. Of all deaths I wold not be drownd ; one's clothes will be so wet when hee is taken up.
Dicke. What calst thou the thing wee were bounde to ?
Mar. A raughter.
Raffe. I wyll rather hang my selfe on a raughter in the house, then be so haled in the Sea : there one may have a leape for his lyfe : but I marvaille how our Master speedes.
Dicke. Ile warrant by this time he is wetshod. Did you ever see water buble as the Sea did ? But what shall we doe ?

Mar. You are now in Lyncolnshire, where you can want no foule, if you can devise means to catch them: there be woods hard by and at every myles end houses: so that if you seeke on the lande, you shall speed better than on the Sea.

Robin. Sea? nay I will never saile more, I brooke not their diet: their bread is so hard, that one must carry a whetstone in his mouth to grinde his teeth: the meate so salt, that one would think after dinner his tongue had been powdered ten daies.

Raffe. O thou hast a sweet life, Mariner, to be pinde in a few boardes, and to be within an inch of a thing bottomlesse. I pray thee how often hast thou been drowned?

Mar. Foole, thou seest I am yet alive.

Robin. Why be they dead that be drowned? I had thought they had been with the fish, and so by chance been caught upwith them in a nette againe. It were a shame a little cold water should kill a man of reason, when you shall see a poor mynow lie in it that hath no understanding.

Mar. Thou art wise from the crowne of thy heade upwards: seeke you new fortune nowe, I will follow mine olde. I can shift the moone and the sunne, and know by one Carde, what all you cannot do by a whole payre. The lode-stone that alwaies holdeth his nose to the North, the two and thirty poynts for the winde, the wonders I see woulde make all you blinde: you be but boyes, I fear the Sea no more than a dish of water. Why fooles, it is but a liquid element. Farewell. *(Going)* ...

Now the jesting in this passage is conceived in the very spirit of the British soldier in France, and across the centuries Bairnsfather might hail the author as a brother. But at present we are concerned less with the persistence of literary traditions than with the revelation the dialogue just quoted affords of the Elizabethan attitude towards seafaring. That attitude is one of familiarity which breeds, not contempt, but humorous tolerance of hardship and danger.

When we turn to the few Scottish poems of early date that deal with sea-faring we are conscious at once of a change of mood. The sea is no longer a rough but hearty antagonist: it is a fierce implacable spirit: and sea-faring is a tragic contest between antagonists unequally matched. There is no drawing back from the contest when duty demands it: but the struggle is envisaged with grim and desperate resolution:

> Our King has written a braid letter,
>   And seald it with his hand,
> And sent it to Sir Patrick Spens
>   Was walking on the strand.
>
> " To Noroway, to Noroway,
>   To Noroway o'er the faem;
> The King's daughter of Noroway
>   'Tis thou maun bring her hame! "
>
> The first word that Sir Patrick read,
>   Sae loud, loud laughed he;
> The neist word that Sir Patrick read,
>   The tear blinded his e'e.
>
> " O wha is this has done this deed,
>   And tauld the king o' me,
> To send me out at this time of the year
>   To sail upon the sea?
>
> Be it wind, be it weet, be it hail, be it sleet,
>   Our ship must sail the faem;
> The King's daughter of Noroway,
>   'Tis we must fetch her hame. "

From stern and desperate strife the note now changes to plaintive keening:

> My love has built a bonny ship, and set her on the sea,
> With seven score good mariners to bear her company;
> There's three score is sunk, and three score dead at sea,
> And the Lowlands of Holland have twind my loved and me.
>
> My love he built another ship, and set her on the main,
> And none but twenty mariners for to bring her hame;
> But the weary wind began to rise, and the seas began to rout,
> My love then and his bonny ship turned withershins about.

The Scot, if a wanderer both by instinct and by tradition, was neither by instinct nor by tradition a seafarer. The French and Spanish voyages of the sixteenth century, and those wonderful English voyages of the same age when English seamen crept down the coast of Africa in search of the ivory and gold and slaves of Guinea, crossed the Indian Ocean in quest of the spices and silks of the Orient, threaded the ice-lanes of the Arctic in search of that wondrous passage which was to lead to Kathai, and slipped from the narrow cliff-fringed passage of the Straits of Magellan into the vastness and solitude of the South Sea—to none of these activities does Scottish maritime history yield any parallel. Apart from the traditional poverty of the country—which in view of the history of the Netherlands may be regarded rather as an effect than as a cause of the lack of maritime enterprise—we may trace this lack of maritime enterprise on the part of Scotland to two main causes : these were the undeveloped nature of the fishing industry, and the rigid and conservative system of trading with the Low Countries.

"Among the more romantic and spectacular happenings of the sixteenth century," says Professor Farrand, "the humble industry of fishing has been too little regarded, but it was of enough importance then to have special measures taken to encourage it. Protestant England, for example, found it desirable to re-establish Catholic fast-days with their abstinence from meat, and to that end issued a whole series of ordinances and proclamations. That there should be no misunderstanding, the very first of these, an ordinance of Edward VI. in 1548 averred ' that one daye or one kynde of Meate is of it selfe not more holie more pure or more cleane than an other ' ; but ' that due and godlye astynence ys a meane to vertue and to subdue mens Bodies to their Soule and Spirite, and consideringe also speciallye that Fysshers and men usinge the trade of lyvinge by fysshinge in the Sea, may there by the rather be sett on worke.' Abstinence from meat in Lent and on other specified days was duly ordered and heavy penalties imposed for disregard of the injunction. Apparently this proved to be worth while, as the number of these days was gradually extended, and a century later, it is said, over one hundred and forty days of each year were set aside on which the eating of flesh was forbidden." [1]

[1] Farrand, *The Development of the United States*, pp. 2 and 3.

INTRODUCTION 17

Not only did fishing provide a livelihood, but it also furnished a splendid training in seamanship. On the demand for fish in England and on the Continent followed incessant efforts of enterprising fishers to meet it. During the fourteenth century English fishermen worked the Iceland waters.[1] The discovery of Newfoundland by Cabot in 1497 was soon followed by the development of the fisheries on the banks, and within a very short time considerable fleets from the West of England and from the Breton and Basque coasts were using St. John's as a base for cod-fishing. And from the West of England came a goodly number of the great English sailors and explorers of the sixteenth century; from St. Malo and La Rochelle sailed the expeditions that laid the foundation of New France.

In the prosecution of the " trade of lyvinge by fysshinge in the Sea " Scotland was decidedly backward. "The only fish exported in Halyburton's time (1492-1503) were salmon with the varieties of grilse and trout, the produce of the rivers. No sea fish was yet taken and cured in sufficient quantity for export."[2] The improvement of the sea fisheries was, however, a problem that at sundry times in the second half of the fifteenth century engaged the attention of the Scottish Kings and their parliament. The parliament of James III. that met on 6th May, 1471, considered it " expedient for the comone gud of the realme and the gret encrese of riches to be brocht within the realme of uther countries that certain Lordes spirituale and temporale and burrowis ger mak or get schippis buschis and uther gret pynk botis witht nettis and al abilymentis gaining tharfor for fisching."[3] In October, 1487, the parliament dealt with " the fisching and making of hering at the West Sey " ;[4] three months later this same phase of the fishing industry was again under consideration.[5]

The most determined effort made by the government of Scotland to grapple with the problem of the sea fisheries

---

[1] K. H. Vickers, *England in the Later Middle Ages* (Second Edition), p. 374.

[2] C. Innes, *Introd. to Halyburton's Ledger*, p. lxx.

[3] *A.P.S.*, vol. ii. p. 100, c. 10. [4] *A.P.S.*, vol. ii. p. 179, c. 18.

[5] *A.P.S.*, vol. ii. p. 183, c. 15.

found expression in the celebrated act passed by the parliament of James IV. that met in the summer of 1493. The preamble gives a succinct account of the evils for which a remedy was sought : " anent ye greit innumerable ryches yat is tint in fault of Schippis and buschis to be disponit for fischeing siclyke as utheris realmes hes yat are marchand wt ye sey and for ye policy and conquest there may be had heirintill and to cause idill men to laubor for their leuving for the eschewing of vices and idilness and for ye commoun proffeit and universall weil of ye Realme." The statute then seeks to inaugurate a reform which, if effectively carried out, would inevitably have exerted a far-reaching influence both on the economic and on the political history of Scotland : " It is . . . statute and ordaint . . . yat thair be Schippes and buschis maid in all Burrowis and Towns within ye realme. And yat ye leist of ye said Schippis and buschis be of xx tun." These fishing smacks were to be properly equipped and to be provided with " marynares, nettes, and ye graith convenient for ye taking of greit fische and small." The fishing fleet was to be ready for the ensuing spring. Stringent regulations were laid down to ensure that energetic efforts should be made to recruit the crews by the inclusion of " all stark idill men." [1]

This insistent legislation seems, however, to have had but little effect on the Scottish sea fisheries. The only area where the industry appears to have flourished before this time was the Firth of Clyde; and after this time the Firth of Clyde and the adjoining sea lochs continued to be the principal district for sea-fishing.[2] And if one contrasts even to-day the small half-decked Loch Fyne skiff with the stout seaworthy drifter or " liner " that puts out from Wick or Peterhead one realises that the sheltered waters of the West Coast can hardly have provided at any time a training ground for venturous explorers.

The Scottish government did not entirely abandon its efforts to improve the fisheries. In 1535 " Oure Sourane lord Ordains ye acte and statute maid of before for making of buschis for fisching to be observit and kepit and to be putt to

[1] *A.P.S.*, vol. ii. p. 235, c. 20.
[2] Cochran Patrick, *Mediaeval Scotland*, p. 71.

Executioun in all punctis."[1] This, however, is but a feeble echo of the bold trumpet-blast of 1493. Early in the seventeenth century there is found some curious testimony regarding the persistent neglect of the North Sea fisheries. In 1601 there was published John Keymor's "Observation made upon the Dutch Fishing ... Demonstrating that there is more Wealth raised out of Herrings and other Fish in his Majesty's Seas, by the Neighbouring Nations, in one Year than the King of Spain hath from the Indies in Four."[2] Perhaps even more significant testimony to the extent to which the Dutch fishermen monopolised the traffic in the northern seas is afforded by the experience of Captain John Mason, who later played an important part in colonial history as the founder of New Hampshire. A native of King's Lynn and a whilom student of Oxford[3] Captain Mason first sails into the unquiet waters of Scottish history in command of "Two Shipps of War and Two Pynasses," with which he had been engaged by King James to escort Bishop Andrew Knox to the completion of his task of pacifying the Hebrides— "the Redshankes Islandes," Mason terms them.[4] The personnel of Mason's little Armada consisted of four score mariners and some gentlemen volunteers, and, owing to the death of the Earl of Dunbar, Lord Chancellor and Treasurer of Scotland, the expenses of an expedition lasting fourteen months had, in the first place, to be borne by Mason himself. To recompense him for this outlay Mason was in May, 1622, granted the Assize of herring in the Northern seas.[5] But it was easier for the Scots Privy Council to make the grant than for Mason to collect the assize herring. The Dutch fishers succeeded in evading the impost entirely: both the methods by which this evasion was accomplished and the effects of it are of interest : the Dutch envoys who attended the marriage of the Princess Elizabeth, "after congratulations of the said marriage and presents delivered, made suit to the King for a Remission of the Payments of the said assize Herring due by

[1] *A.P.S.*, vol. ii. p. 345, c. 18.
[2] Davidson and Gray, *Scottish Staple at Veere*, p. 73 *n*.
[3] *D.N.B.* [4] *Nova Scotia Papers*, Bannatyne Club, p. 4.
[5] *Register P.C.S.*, vol. ix. p. 18.

their nation : which was granted to the disannulling of the said Captain John Mason his whole interest therein." [1]

But if the development of the Scottish sea fisheries was retarded by persistent neglect, that of the Scottish mercantile marine was hindered by a too officious supervision. The exclusive spirit of the burghs and the eventual limitation of trade with the Netherlands—by far the most important branch of Scottish overseas commerce—to the staple town of Veere were in themselves repressive influences of no little effect; but when to these general influences are added definite restrictions on seafaring, it becomes apparent that little could be expected from the Scottish seaman in the way of initiative and enterprise. In January, 1466, "it is statute and ordaint that in tyme to cum no schip be frauchtit furth of our Realme with any staple gudis fra the fest of symonds day and Jude (28th October) on to the fest of the purification of oure lady callit candilmes (2nd February) under the pane of five pundis of usuale monie of our Realme to be raisit til oure Souranes Lordes use of ilk persoun frachting any schip in contrary hereof." [2] Even if this regulation were merely a precautionary measure, like the winter close season of the Hanse ships, the need for such extreme caution can hardly have existed three quarters of a century later when the statute was re-enacted, the penalty for breach of it being then increased fourfold. That the restriction was designed rather in consonance with government policy than out of regard for the safety of the mariners is shown by the proviso in the Act of 1535, that "it salbe lefull to send any kynde of merchandise furt of the Realme in the tyme forsaid in ony schippis that bringes in salt or wyne." [3] That the re-enactment of the statute of 1466 formed part of a definite policy of restricting seafaring is shown by the very next measure on the Parliamentary record—"that na man sale in flandres bot twiss in the zeir." "It is Statute and ordainit for the honeste of the realme wele and proffett of all our sourane Lordis liegis specialie his burrowes and merchandis of his Realme that na schip be frauchtit nor merchands sale therein

[1] *Nova Scotia Papers*, p. 6.   [2] *A.P.S.*, vol. ii. p. 87, c. 5.
[3] *A.P.S.*, vol. ii. p. 348, c. 33.

with thare gudis and merchandise furth of the Realme in flandres bot twiss in the zeir. That is to say to the pasche (Easter) mercate and Rude (September) mercate under the pane of Ilk persoun cuming in the contrar hirof of xx li to be Rasit and Inbrot to the Kingis grace use."[1] It is only too evident that the royal regard for the "burrowis and merchandis" can hardly have been attended by consequences favourable to the "wele and proffett" of Scottish mariners.

To this persistent lack of appreciation of the importance of a large, vigorous and enterprising mercantile marine can be traced the comparative obscurity that, except at one dazzling epoch, surrounds the history of the old Scottish navy. Rarely indeed in Scottish history do the sails of Scottish warships come clearly into view. The galleys of Alexander III., their scanty canvas trimmed to catch a favouring breeze, their oar-thresh urging the prows against the Hebridean tide-race : the stately carvels of the days of James IV. with their tall forecastles bristling with moyennes, falcons, and other antique ordinance, and their towering poops, from which Sir Andrew Wood and other " captains courageous " scanned the North Seas for the sails of English privateers—these fleets, indeed, sail bravely into our ken. But the little squadrons of warships fitted out from time to time by the Scottish Government during the seventeenth century, and the armed merchantmen bearing letters of marque that sailed from the Forth or the Clyde, loom dimly through the mists of time to vanish like phantom ships.

III.

Important as Scottish military and economic traditions undoubtedly were in influencing the trend of Scottish emigration and in determining the objectives of Scottish maritime enterprise, their importance in this respect is rivalled by that of the political and religious history of Scotland during the period of a century and a quarter that intervened between the Reformation and the Revolution of 1688. It is a fundamental axiom of colonial history that no state can engage

[1] *A.P.S.*, vol. ii. p. 349, c. 34.

effectively in colonising activities until it has developed harmony and security within its own borders. The voyages of Columbus, and the conquests of Cortes and Pizarro, were the efflorescence of the vigorous national life enjoyed by Spain, in virtue of the union of Castile and Aragon and the conquest of the Moorish Kingdom of Granada. The voyages of Cartier to the St. Lawrence were succeeded by half a century during which the French monarchy, engaged in deadly strife against foes both without and within its borders, had no energies for traffics and discoveries : the year 1598, the year of the Treaty of Vervins and the Edict of Nantes, marks the beginning of the second and greater epoch of French exploration of Acadie and New France, the period of the activities of De Monts and Champlain. In English history the Elizabethan church settlement prepared the way for the Elizabethan voyagers ; and in the history of English colonial enterprise of the seventeenth century there is a well marked gap between the years 1639 and 1655—between the Scottish campaign that prepared the way for the Civil War and the expedition sent to the West Indies by Cromwell. From the Reformation to the Revolution Scotland was a country that "knew rest and peace only by snatches." The influence of these unquiet years is seen not only in the small part that Scotland took in the colonial enterprise of the early and middle seventeenth century, but in the widespread enthusiasm for the Darien scheme manifested in Scotland at a period when acute religious dissension was a thing of the past : long pent up, the torrent broke forth with irresistible force : and it was of a piece with the tragic traditions of Scottish history that the work wrought by this new power should have been one of destruction.

In one way, indeed, the religious controversies that are such a marked feature of Scottish seventeenth-century history might have been expected to influence the Scottish attitude towards colonisation. The persecution of the Covenanters might conceivably have been followed by an exodus to America, and by the foundation of colonies of refuge beyond the Atlantic. The part played in English colonial history by the exodus of the Puritans during the third and fourth decades of the seventeenth centuries at once occurs to the mind. The Pilgrim colony of New Plymouth; the plantation at Salem, established by the Massachusetts Bay Company, and the settlement at Boston where the leading men of the Company took up their abode when, in 1630, they carried their charter across the Atlantic; Connecticut and Rhode Island; the station of Saybrook at the mouth of the Connecticut river; the Island of Santa Katalina, or Providence, off the coast of Central America, romantically held against the might of Spain for over a decade,—all these represent colonies formed by the English Puritans as permanent homes beyond the sea. In contrast to this imposing list of settlements, the historian of Scottish colonial enterprise can point only to the small Presbyterian colony of Stuart's Town, in South Carolina, founded late in the seventeenth century and swept away by a Spanish raid after a brief and troubled existence.

In the main this difference between the Scottish Covenanter and the English Puritan is to be ascribed to a difference in national temperament. The English Puritan, recognising the might of the forces against which he struggled—the strength of the church, the Court party and the landed aristocracy—sought like a prudent man to betake himself to a land where these powers exerted comparatively little influence. The Scottish Covenanter, with a grim resolution inherited from centuries of warfare with a more powerful neighbouring state, would not admit to himself the possibility of the final downfall of his cause. This note of impassioned confidence throbs alike in the letters of Samuel Rutherford and in the homilies of Alexander Peden. "Our Clergie is upon a Reconciliation with the Lutherans," wrote Rutherford from Aberdeen, on 7th February, 1637,[1] "and the Doctors are writing books, and drawing up a Common Confession at the Counsel's command: Our Service book is proclaimed with sound of trumpet: The night is fallen upon the Prophets: Scotland's day of visitation is come: . . . But our skie will clear again: The dry branch of cut-down Lebanon will bud again, and be glorious, and they shall yet plant vines upon our Mountains." And almost half a century later the

[1] *Rutherford's Letters*, edit. 1675, epistle 198.

venerable Alexander Peden, in the closing years of his trying life, could thus exhort his old congregation of Glenluce: "Once Scotland sent out her glory into all the lands about her. Now she sits as a widow and few to take her by the hand. But yet her husband will not forsake her. He will yet return to Scotland, and send òut her glory unto all the lands around, and that more gloriously than it formerly was."[1]

In 1648 Rutherford refused an invitation from the Dutch University of Harderwyck to become Professor of Hebrew and Divinity; three years later he refused a call to the chair of Divinity at Utrecht, and, though the invitation was repeated, he remained firm in his refusal to leave his native land. "Sed cum interea Oliverus Cromwellus Regem, eodem anno in Scotia coronatum, profligato ejus exercitu, regno ejecisset, omnia jam mala patriae metuens, negavit se, salva conscientia, in tantis periculis, eam posse deserere; sed teneri patriae ecclesiae, jam animam agenti, adesse et saltem funeris deductioni et sepulturae adesse."[2]

"Dear and much honoured in the Lord," wrote Rutherford[3] from Edinburgh on 18th May, 1651, to Colonel Gilbert Ker, one of the officers of the West County Army, "let me entreat you to be far from the thoughts of leaving this land. I see it and find it, that the Lord hath covered the whole land with a cloud in His anger. But though I have been tempted to the like, I had rather be in Scotland beside angry Jesus Christ, knowing that he mindeth no evil to us, than in Eden or any garden in the earth. ..."

Yet there were times when circumstances seemed too powerful for even the iron resolution of the Covenanter. "... there were many things that might engage people to leave Scotland," wrote John Erskine of Carnock in his *Journal*, under date 7th January, 1685,[4] "and I knew few there who had any sense of its condition, who were not desiring to be away, tho they did linger very much, few having

---

[1] Quoted Dr. Carslaw, *Exiles of the Covenant*, p. 3.

[2] Nethenus, *Prefatio to Rutherford's Examin*. Quoted Murray's *Life*, p. 261.

[3] *Letters*, edited Bonar, p. 662.

[4] *Journal*, Scottish History Socy., p. 103.

determined what to do themselves or able to advise others. ... Many of the most serious and godly of the land were now taken away by violent deaths on scaffolds (which it seems is not at an end) or otherways, or then leaving the land, and many in prisons. There was little now that the rulers set themselves for, but what was effectuated."

When, in the day of tribulation, the Covenanter thought of seeking refuge abroad, it was not to the American plantations but to Rotterdam or Utrecht that he instinctively looked for an asylum. The Scottish trade routes led naturally across the North Sea, and there was at no time any great difficulty in obtaining a passage on some smack bound for Holland. The Scots Brigade formed a renowned detachment of the Dutch army. The law classes of Leyden or Utrecht were the natural pathways to the Scottish bar. The Scottish exile found himself, on landing, in the midst of friends. Let us note the experience of Erskine of Carnock during the opening week of his sojourn in Holland :

(March 4th, 1685.) This forenoon I landed at Rotterdam, and went to James Bruce's coffee-house, where I met first with my brother Charles.

5th. I was dining in Mr. Robert Fleming's, and did see the Laird of Westshields.

6th. I met with Mr. Robert Langlands, my old master, whom I longed much to see. I was with William Sythrum and several other friends.

7th. I dined with Mr. Forrester, and was afternoon in Mr. Russell's, and with Mr. P—— and Doctor Blackader, in the Scots coffee house. . . .

8th. I was at the Scots church, and did hear Mr. Robert Fleming, Acts 14, 22, and Mr. John Hogg, Psalm 11, 1, both ministers of the Scots congregation at Rotterdam. I heard also Mr. Patrick Verner in the Kirk.

9th. I took a chamber this day in Robert Gibb's, sometime merchant in Stirling, having staid until now with my brother Charles.

I was afternoon with Mr. Thomas Forrester, and with Andrew Turnbull a while.

10th. I did see Waterside, William Cleland, and was much

with Mr. Robert Langlands, and hearing Mr. Kirktown's evening exercise.¹

To the Scot obliged to quit his native land the Netherlands offered a kindly welcome. And not the least commendable feature of this asylum was the convenience with which events in Scotland could be followed, and the ease with which the return to Scotland could be accomplished. Mr. Robert M'Ward, the well-known Covenanting minister of the Outer High Church of Glasgow, from his place of exile in Rotterdam, " kept up a close correspondence with his friends in Scotland, sending them frequent letters and pamphlets suited to the times." ² When in 1675 the Scots Consistory at Rotterdam decided to appoint an additional minister to the Scots Church there, their choice fell upon Mr. M'Ward. Mr. M'Ward accepted the call, " on a mutual understanding, that, as soon as public affairs in Scotland allowed his return, he should be at liberty to proceed thither." ³ When the Revolution brought happier days for Scotland the quays of Rotterdam were thronged with returning exiles.⁴

¹ *Journal*, pp. 108, 109.
² Dr. Carslaw, *Exiles of the Covenant*, p. 113.
³ Steven, *The Scottish Church at Rotterdam*, p. 26.
⁴ *Ibid.* p. 102.

CHAPTER I

NEWFOUNDLAND

SCOTTISH traditions, military, economic and religious—traditions deep-rooted and powerful—united, we have seen, to direct to the Continent of Europe, Scotsmen who quitted their native shores to live by the sword, to find a competence in trade, or to seek a temporary shelter from the rigour of political-ecclesiastical persecution. When, indeed, the question of transatlantic enterprise was first brought to the notice of the Scots Privy Council, the emotions which it excited were those of distrust and repugnance.

It must, however, be admitted that the suggested exodus from Scotland against which the Lords of the Privy Council made a diplomatic but firm protest to King James, Sixth and First, had been designed by that monarch not wholly in the interests of the prospective emigrants. Towards the close of the year 1617, the Star Chamber, in pursuance of the royal policy of establishing a lasting peace throughout the Debatable Land, had evolved a code of stringent regulations for the suppression of disorder there. This code was, of course, applicable only to those districts of the Middle Shires that belonged to England, but the King had sent a copy of it to the Scots Privy Council with instructions to consider how far the measures designed to impart docility to the English Borderers might be made to apply North of the Tweed.[1] This question was dealt with by the Scots Privy Council on the 8th January, 1618. To the line of policy suggested by the thirteenth section of the code, the Council took decided exception. This section provided for " a survey and information

[1] *Register Scots Privy Council*, vol. xi. p. 288.

to be taken of the most notorious and leude persones and of their faultes within Northumberland, Cumberland, etc.," and declared that the royal purpose was " to send the most notorious leiveris of thame into Virginia or to sum remote parts, to serve in the wearris or in collonies." On the course of action implied in this section the comment of the Council was discreet but unequivocal : " Sieing be the lawes of this Kingdome and General Band everie landislord in the Middle Schyres is bunded to be answerabil for all theis that dwell on his land, the Counsell sees no necessitie that the course prescryveit in the xiij article be followed out here." On this judicious remonstrance the editors of the *Privy Council Records* make the apposite remark, that " Virginia and all the other available colonies of that time being English, the Council probably disliked the idea of trusting even Scottish criminals to the tender mercies of English taskmasters."

Three months after the despatch of this diplomatic non-placet, the sage of Whitehall informed the Scottish Council that their judgment seemed " strange and unadvysed " and insisted on their acceptance of the principle in dispute. Dutifully they deferred to the royal mandate. Yet the Conciliar conscience was not altogether easy concerning the possible fate of kindly Scots from the Borders :- at the beginning of 1619, the Council instructed the Commissioners of the Middle Shires to intimate to the Transportation Sub-Committee " that in the execution of that peece of servise concredit unto thame they use the advyse and opinoun of the Lords of his Majestie's Previe Counsall." [1]

It is perhaps more than a coincidence that almost at the very time when the King's desire to employ Virginia as a convenient penitentiary for unruly Scots was engaging the attention of the Scots Privy Council, the Lord Mayor of London and Sir Thomas Smyth, the Treasurer of the Virginia Company, should be not a little puzzled by a problem that had arisen from King James' determination to send some of his English subjects to Virginia. It was on 8th January, 1618, that the Scots Privy Council discussed the King's plan for dealing with turbulent Borderers. On 13th January, 1618,

[1] *Register P.C.*, vol. xi. p. 506.

King James wrote thus from his " Court att Newmarkitt " to Sir Thomas Smyth :

"Trustie and well beloved wee greet you well; whereas our Court hath of late been troubled with divers idle yonge people, who although they have been twise Punished still continue to followe the same havvinge noe ymployment; wee havvinge noe other course to cleer our court from them have thought fitt to send them unto you desiringe you att the next oportunitie to send them away to Virginia and to take sure order that they may be sett to worke there, wherein you shall not only doe us good service but also doe a deed of Charitie by employinge them who otherwise will never be reclaymed from the idle life of vagabonds. . . ."[1]

This letter Sir Thomas Smyth received on the evening of the 18th of January : some of the prospective deportees had already reached London. The perturbation of the worthy Treasurer reveals itself clearly in the letter which he addressed to the Lord Mayor immediately on the receipt of the royal mandate :

"Right honoble : I have this eveninge receaved a lre from his Matie att Newmarkitt requiring me to send to Virginia diverse younge people who wanting imployment doe live idle and followe the Courte, notwithstanding they have been punished as by his highnes Lres (which I send you Lp. herewith to yo to see) more at large appeareth. Now for as much as some of thies by his Mats royall comand are brought from Newmarkitt to London alreadie and others more are consigned after, and for that the companie of Virginia hath not anie shipp att present readie to goe thither neither any means to imploy them or secure place to detain them in untill the next oportunitie to transport them (which I hope wilbee very shortlie) I have therefore thought fitt for the better accomplishing his highness pleasure therein to intreat yor L'ps favour and assistance that by yr. L'ps favour these persons may be detained in Bridewill and there sett to worke untill our next

[1] City of London Archives—Guildhall, *Remembrancia*, vol. v. fol. 8 (A Ltre from the King's Matie to Sir Tho. Smyth touching idle persones for transportation to Virginia).

shipp shall depte for Virginia, wherein yor Lp. shall doe an acceptable Service to his Maty and myself bee enabled to pforme that which is required of me. Soe I comend you to God and rest.

Yr Lps. assured Louvinge friend
Tho: Smith.

This Mundaie eveninge
  18 Januar 1618."[1]

Of the subsequent experiences of the young rufflers for whom the Treasurer in his perturbation besought the temporary hospitality of the Bridewill the London Records give no account.

. . . . . .

The Deloraines of the Debatable Land were not the only Scottish subjects of King James for whom the New World seemed to offer itself obligingly as a spacious and convenient penitentiary. In the spring of 1619, while the religious controversy aroused by the issue of the Five Articles of Perth was still raging bitterly, one of the arguments by means of which Archbishop Spotswood sought to influence the recalcitrant ministers of Midlothian was a threat of banishment to America[2]—an ominous foreshadowing of the practice that was to become all too common in Covenanting days.

I.

At the very time when both King and Archbishop were concerning themselves with the repressive efficacy of exile to Virginia, an obscure group of Scottish adventurers had found in the oldest of England's transatlantic possessions an attractive, if somewhat exciting sphere of enterprise; and the claims of Newfoundland as a place of settlement suitable for Scottish emigrants were soon to be urged with some degree of ostentation. It is, indeed, but a brief glimpse that we

---

[1] *Remembrancia*, vol. v. ff. 8 and 9 (A Lre from Sr. Tho: Smyth to ye Lo: Maior wherein his Mats. Lre above inserted is sent inclosed).

[2] *Reg. P.C.*, vol. xi. p. 562 n.

obtain from colonial records of the activities of these Scottish pioneers. In March, 1620, there was received by King James a petition from "the Treasurer and the Companie with the Scottish undertakers of the plantations in Newfoundland." After references to the growing prosperity of the country and to the magnitude of the fishing industry, the petitioners complain of the losses caused by the raids of pirates and by the turbulence of the fishermen. Steps, however, have been taken to combat these evils: "And theirfor since your Maties subjects of England and Scotland are now joyned togither in hopes of a happy time to make a more settled plantation in the Newfoundland. Their humble petition is for establishing of good orders and preventing enormities among the fishers and for securing the sd. Plantations and fishers from Pyrates. That your Matie would be pleased to grant a power to John Mason the present governor of our collonies (a man approved by us and fitting for that service) to be Lieftenant for your matie in the sd. parts." This petition is endorsed: "The Scottish undertakers of the plantation in the new found land."[1]

Brief as is this glimpse of the activities of the early Scottish planters in Newfoundland, and tantalising as is its lack of detail, the meagre information it yields is of no little interest to the historian of colonial enterprise, for it is the first evidence that has come down to us of Scottish colonising activity in the New World. Moreover, it affords an eminently reasonable explanation of why Captain John Mason should seek to stimulate Scottish interest in Newfoundland by the compilation of his "Brief Discourse of the New-found-land . . . inciting our natione to go forward in the hopefulle plantation begunne." Fortunately we can gather from the general course of colonial development in Newfoundland a tolerably complete idea of the plantation in which the Scots were undertakers: and it is possible to trace with some fulness both in Scottish and in Colonial history the romantic career of Captain John Mason.

[1] Public Record Office, *C.O.*, 1/1, No. 54; *Col. Cal.*, vol. i. p. 25.

II.

By the time of Sir Humphrey Gilbert's visit to Newfoundland in 1583, the island—or at least its southern shore—was well known both to the fishermen and to the merchant seamen of the Western Counties of England. Indeed, the visit of Sir Humphrey was made primarily in order to revictual after the Atlantic voyage : St. John's was the last outpost of civilisation, the last glimpse of the familiar world, ere the voyagers should steer forth into those strange and baffling waters that lured them northward and westward towards the fabled treasures of the east. On the hillside above St. John's Harbour, Sir Humphrey, in full view of an assembled fishing fleet, carried out, with impressive symbolism, the formal annexation of the island to the crown of England. But for a quarter of a century after this annexation, Newfoundland remained merely a depot for the fishing-vessels operating on the Banks, in the Gulf of St. Lawrence, and along the shores of the Bay of Fundy.

This slow progress in the development of Newfoundland was due less to lack of effort on the part of Englishmen interested in colonisation than to misdirection of effort. Soon after the annexation there was published " A True Report of the Late Discoveries," by Sir George Peckham—the first of a series of commendatory pamphlets that are useful guides to the early history of Newfoundland. In the retrospective light shed by the later history of the English plantations, it is instructive to consider the nature of the inducements held out, in the year of grace 1583, to prospective pioneers. Much is naturally made of the claims of the fishing industry ; but the importance of Newfoundland as a base for a voyage to India by the North-West Passage is also urged ; and any feudal instincts that may have survived the ungenial régime of the early Tudors are appealed to by the promise to £100 subscribers of a grant of 16,000 acres of land with authority to hold Court Leet and Court Baron.

It lies, of course, primarily within the province of the feudal lawyer to determine how these franchises were to be exercised when there were no vassals to assemble in Court Baron, and when such inhabitants of Newfoundland as might, by the potency of seal and parchment, find themselves transformed into customary tenants of a manor were by no means likely to accept with docility such a change of status. For the "winter crews," whose scattered settlements fringed the southern and south-eastern shores of the island, belonged to a class of men long noted for turbulence and independence of spirit.

The first effective plantation of Newfoundland was carried out early in the seventeenth century by a company imbued with a spirit differing widely from the feudal and romantic tendencies of Peckham. The "Company of adventurers and planters of the cittie of London and Bristol for the colony or plantation in Newfoundland," which received its charter in 1611, had as one of its leading members Sir Francis Bacon, and it was probably through his influence that it obtained, despite the royal impecuniosity, a considerable subsidy from King James. Of the merchants identified with the company, the most prominent was Alderman John Guy of Bristol, who in 1611 conducted the first colonists from the Severn sea-port to Cupid's Cove, a land-locked anchorage at the head of Harbour Grace. The prosperity that attended this settlement from its earliest days may be ascribed almost with certainty to the guidance it received from the practical counsel of Bacon and the commercial acumen of Alderman Guy. It was with the activities of this settlement at Cupid's Cove that the Scottish planters had identified themselves.[1]

III.

The only dangers that in any way threatened the success of the colony were the hostility shown towards the planters by the fishermen and the devastation caused by the raids of pirates, and when, in 1615, Guy was succeeded in the governorship by Captain John Mason, the colonists might with reason feel confident that their destinies had been entrusted to a man well fitted, both by character and by experience, to protect them from their foes. In his personality the new governor

[1] D. W. Prowse, *History of Newfoundland*, chs. iv. v.

combined not a little of the fascinating daring of the Elizabethan adventurer with the stern resolution and sound commonsense that marked the pioneer of early colonial days.

Of the circumstances under which Mason entered the service of King James we have no information. But the fact that Mason sailed out of King's Lynn, added to the fact that the royal commission for Mason's voyage to Scottish waters was dated from Thetford,[1] leads one to infer that King James learned of Mason in much the same way as his royal ancestor learned of the reputation of Sir Patrick Spens. The royal commission was "for furnishing and setting forth of Two Shipps of Warr and Two Pynnasses to attend his Maty service conioyntly with Mr. Andrew Knox, then Bishopp of the Isles, for subduing of the then rebellious Redshankes in the Hebrides Islandes."[2] Some of the difficulties Mason experienced in seeking recompense for his outlays we have already seen.[3] But the loss of his assize herring through the astute diplomacy of the Dutch envoys did not complete his tale of woe. The Scottish fishermen were less diplomatic in their resistance to the assize grant than their Dutch fellows, and Mason found himself thrown into prison by the magistrates of the Fifeshire burgh of Anstruther. He was released by order of the Privy Council,[4] who thereafter received from the burghs of Fife a strongly-worded petition against the obstruction to the work of the fishermen, caused by the activities of Mason, who was described as "an Englishman pretending to have a commission for lifting the assize herring of the Northern Isles."[5]

For three years Captain Mason apparently vanished—and with good reason—from the Scottish seas: when he did reappear he was, on his arrival in the Pentland Firth, regarded by the good folks of Caithness as a pirate. Off Thurso he was pursued and captured.[6] Along with his mate and his crew he was taken to Edinburgh and lodged in the Tolbooth. There is not lacking a hint that the arrest of Mason had in it either some element of irregularity, or at least some possibility of

[1] *Nova Scotia Papers*, p. 4
[2] *Ibid.*
[3] *Vide supra*, p. 19.
[4] *P.C. Reg.*, vol. ix. p. 377.
[5] *P.C. Reg.*, vol. ix. p. 531.
[6] *Ibid.* vol. x. p. 348.

offence to the Court at Whitehall, for the Scots Privy Council assured his captor that they exonerated him " of all payne and cryme that might be impute to him thairthrow for ever," and they were also careful to treat Mason and his crew not as pirates, but as prisoners of war.[1] The significance of the subsequent proceedings in Mason's case is baffling in the extreme. Mason reached Edinburgh at the end of June, 1615. We get no hint of any trial by the Court of Admiralty, yet towards the end of August we find Mason making surrender to the Deputy Treasurer of his ship " callit the Neptune of King's Lynn of the burdyne of forty tuns or thairby, togidder with his ankeirs, cabillis, towis, munitioun and apparelling pertaining thereunto." On the day on which it was surrendered, the *Neptune* was disposed of for 800 Merks.[2] Might it be that Mason had by this time received from King James notice of his appointment as governor of Newfoundland, and that, in order to save delay in disposing of his property, he had taken an unconventional method of effecting a speedy sale of his ship?

It has been conjectured [3] that Mason's appointment as Governor of the Plantation at Cupid's Cove was in some degree a recompense for his outlay in the Hebridean expeditions. It does not appear that Mason himself was inclined to this view: fourteen years later he was urging his original claim on the notice of Charles I.[4] It is more probable that the choice of Mason was due partly to the desire of King James and Bacon (now Attorney General) to appoint a man thoroughly suitable for the strenuous task that lay before the governor of the settlement in which they were deeply interested, and partly as a solatium for the indignity of his capture and incarceration. By his activity and enterprise Captain Mason in every way justified his selection, and, as the petition of 1620 shows, had gained the confidence and the esteem of his planters over whom he was placed. It is no slight tribute to his magnanimity that, despite his experiences in Scotland, he harboured no rancour against the Scots.

[1] *Reg. P.C.*, vol. x. p. 350.
[2] *Ibid.* vol. x. p. 389.
[3] *D.N.B.*
[4] *Nova Scotia Papers*, pp. 4 and 5.

IV.

In carrying out the duties of governor of the little plantation of Couper's Cove—now Mosquito Cove, in Conception Bay—Captain Mason displayed both zeal and enterprise. Of some of the activities pertaining to the government of such a colony we get a glimpse in a letter penned by Mason " from the plantacioun of Cuper's Cove in Terra Nova ult. Augusti 1617 and addressed 'To the right worshipfull Mr. John Scot of Scottisterbat in Scotland, Director of His Majestie's Court of Chancery there, in his house on the Cawsey of Edinburgh.' " After a reference to a hope of being able to furnish his correspondent with " A Mapp thereof, with a particular relacioun of the severall parts, natures, and qualities," Mason proceeds, " I am now asetting my foote into that path where I ended last, to discover to the westward of this land; and for two months absence I have fitted myselfe with a small new galley of 15 tonnes, and to rowe with fourteen oars (having lost our former). We shall visit the naturalls of the country, with whom I propose to trade, and thereafter give you a tast of the event, hoping that withall Terra Nova will produce Dona Nova, to manifest our gratificacioun. Untill which tyme I rest and shall remayne tuus dum suus, John Mason." [1]

The interest which linked together Sir John Scott of Scotstarvet and Captain Mason gives rise to some interesting speculation. Was it due mainly to Sir John's public-spirited zeal for the welfare of his country—so different from his private animadversions on the statesmen of his time—and to a desire to direct westward the unceasing stream of Scottish emigration? Can Sir John, in his capacity of Director of the Scottish Chancery, have been in some way instrumental in delivering Mason from his captivity in the Tolbooth of Edinburgh? The question of the connection between Scott and Captain Mason is highly enigmatical, but as regards his " particular relacioun " we know exactly where we are. It took definite and practical shape in Mason's " Brief Discourse," a tract of seven pages dedicated to Sir John Scott and printed at Edinburgh by Andro Hart in the year 1620.[2]

[1] *Nova Scotia Papers*, p. 5. [2] Reprinted *Nova Scotia Papers*.

In its moderation of tone and its precision of detail, this account of the possibilities of Newfoundland as a home for Scottish emigrants reveals Mason as eminently clear-headed and practical—the very man to guide, with energy and discrimination, the development of a young and struggling colony. Admitting that, in fertility of soil and " temperature of the climate," Newfoundland cannot compare favourably with Virginia, he yet advances " foure maine Reasons " for which " it is to be paralleled to it, if not preferred before it." These reasons are : firstly, " the nearness to our own home " ; secondly, " the great intercourse of trade by our Nation these threescore years and upward " ; thirdly, " the conveniency of transporting planters thither at the old rate, ten shillings the man and twentie shillings to find him victuals thither, likewise other commodities by shippes that goe sackes [1] at ten shillings per time out, and thirtie shillings home, whereas Virginia and Bermuda fraights are five pound the mann and three pound the tunne " ; fourthly and lastly, " Securetie from foraine and domestick enemies, there being but few Salvages in the north, and none in the south parts of the countrie. . . . Also, if any warres should happen betwist us and other Nations, we should not fear rooting out. For the sea is a bulwark all Aprill commonlie, and after that, during the whole summer, we have a garrison of 9 or 10 thousand our owne Nation, with many good and warlike shippes, who of necessitie must defend the fishing season for their living's sake, as they always formerlie have done in the warres with Spain. And afterwards, in the monthes of Harvest and Winter, the winds are our friends and will hardlie suffer any to approach us, the which if they should, the cold opposite to the nature of the Spaniards will give him but cold entertainment ; neither will the planters be altogether puffed up with careless securitie, but fortifie in some measure, knowing that Non sunt securi qui dant sua Colla securi."

On the soundness of Mason's reasoning the whole course of English colonial history supplies a poignant commentary. But the governor's interests and activities were soon to be directed into other channels, and though his influence can

[1] Freight ships.

certainly be traced in the history of the Scottish attempt to colonise Nova Scotia, those who undertook the direction of that scheme were unable, unfortunately, to obtain his counsel and co-operation. The esteem in which Mason was held by the Newfoundland planters found expression in their petition to the King for the grant of " a power to John Mason the present governor (a man approved by us and fitting for that service) to be Lieftenant for your matie in the sd. parts." To uphold Mason's authority the petitions request " that he may have 2 shippes or more as shall be found requisite," and that the upkeep of these ships be met by a levy on each boat of " the som of five nobles in money or five hundred dry fishes, which is but the ffifteieth part of a boat's ordinary fishing voyadge in the somer time in Newfoundland."[1] The petition bears the following endorsement: " At the Court of Wokinge 16° Martii 1620. His Maties pleasure is that the Lo: Steward, Lo: Chamberlain, Earl of Arundell, the Lo: Viscount ffaulkland and Sir George Calvert, one of his Matie's principall secretaries or any ffoure of theme Doe consider of this petition and of the reasons thereto annexed." The commission issued to Mason by the Lord High Admiral would appear to be the result of this petition.[2] By the grant of this commission the home government greatly enhanced the status of Mason: " Thitherto he had been governor of an unimportant company: this made him Lieutenant of the King with large powers and the jurisdiction of the whole island."[3]

The return of Mason to England, in the spring or early summer of 1621, brought to an end his connection with the Newfoundland plantation, but not his influence on Scottish colonial schemes. Through his official position Mason was inevitably brought into contact with Sir Ferdinando Gorges, " The Father of English Colonisation in North America "— Gorges was one of the English commissioners for the regulation of the Newfoundland fisheries—and thenceforth in colonial history it is with the schemes of Gorges for the development of New England that the name of Mason is associated. In

[1] *C.O.* 1/1, No. 54.   [2] Tuttle, *Memoir of Captain John Mason*, p. 13.
[3] *Ibid.*

1629 Mason and Gorges took the leading part in the formation of the Laconia Company—a company formed with the design of making a settlement in the territory adjacent to the Iroquois Lakes. It is chiefly, however, in connection with the foundation of New Hampshire—the outcome of a grant to Mason and Gorges in 1631 of territory in the Piscataqua River—that Mason occupies an important position in English Colonial history.

On his return to England in 1621 Mason had met Sir William Alexander,[1] who had turned his versatile fancy towards a scheme of Scottish colonisation. It would seem that the counsel of the Governor of Newfoundland played no slight part in inducing Alexander to undertake the plantation of the land lying between New England and Newfoundland.[2] For more than a decade Scottish colonial history was to be dominated by the romantic and visionary zeal of the Laird of Menstrie.

[1] Tuttle, *Memoir of Captain John Mason*, p. 14.
[2] Letter of King James to Scots Privy Council, 5th Aug., 1621; Rogers, *Memorials of the Earl of Stirling*, vol. i. p. 61.

CHAPTER II

NOVA SCOTIA

From Stirling with its clustering memories of so much that is grim and fierce and crucial in the history of Old Scotland, it is but a short pilgrimage to the birthplace of the founder of New Scotland. After circling round the wooded slopes of the Abbey Craig, the highway that strings together the villages nestling at the base of the Ochils strikes due eastward. To one's right the Carse of Stirling stretches away to a dim horizon; on one's left the dark-green, far-stretching rampart of the Ochils rears itself abruptly from the plain. Soon one passes a single row of cottages flanking the highway, and crosses a little bridge, beneath which the Menstrie Burn trickles along its stone-strewn channel. And now before one, raising its time-worn red-brown roof above a cluster of weaving sheds, is the goal of the pilgrimage, the House of Menstrie—that old mansion which gave to British History two men so diverse in personality and in destiny as Sir William Alexander and Sir Ralph Abercrombie.

The weather-beaten old building seems to feel, and to resent dumbly, the desolation that has fallen upon it. Its roof of weather-stained tiles sags despondently. Along the greater part of its grey stone facade three tiers of boarded-up windows stare blankly down at a forlorn yard, where weeds and rough grass flourish rankly. A rudely built, unrailed flight of steps leads up to a mean wooden doorway fastened with a leathern hasp. But at the southern end a part of the building is still inhabited; one climbs up a railed stairway to a trim lobby; small neatly curtained windows peep out from the midst of the thick growth of ivy that has cast its sheltering mantle over the ancient wall.

A low-browed Norman gateway leads to the inner court, from which one looks across a small orchard to the little parish church of Menstrie and the cluster of tiled or slated roofs of the village cottages. Behind the village a clump of woodland leads the eye upward to where, by turfed slope and dark rocky scarp, Dunmyat heaves up its huge shoulder and prints its blunt summit on the northern sky. In its strange mingling of pervading desolation and sporadic vitality, the old House of Menstrie stands to-day as a not unfitting memorial of the history of Sir William Alexander's efforts to colonise Nova Scotia; while its background of clustering woodland and steep mountain side may not inappropriately suggest memories of the romantic age of French colonial enterprise that furnished the historical setting of the Scottish scheme.

I.

From the homely courtyard of Menstrie it is a far cry to the Court of Whitehall. And the story of the Laird of Menstrie's progress in the royal favour has in it some hint of the career of the old Scots adventurer, but of an adventurer who, instead of trailing pike or wielding broadsword, relied on the potency of his pen. It is a strange, romantic record, this life-story of Sir William Alexander; a tale that touches the history of both Scotland and England at many important points; a tale that furnishes the best clue to the understanding of what manner of man this was who sought to plant a New Scotland beyond the Atlantic.

Born, it is presumed in 1567 [1]—the fateful year that witnessed the assassination of Darnley, the surrender of Mary at Carberry Hill, and the accession to the throne of Scotland of that infant prince who was to be his friend and patron—William Alexander passed his boyhood close to the picturesque glens and hillsides of the Ochils. It is a district the scenery of which has been the theme of some of the most tender and charming lyrics inspired by the Scottish Muse. But on the

[1] Rogers, *Memorials of the Earl of Stirling*, vol. i. p. 33.

verse of Alexander the influence of this scenery is slight and faint—almost, indeed, non-existent. The impressions of his boyhood were elbowed aside by his interest in the classical studies begun, it is conjectured, in the Grammar School of Stirling under the nephew of George Buchanan.[1] There is a tradition that Alexander's later studies were carried on in the Universities of Glasgow and Leyden.

Proficiency in literary studies gave Alexander his passport to advancement. It was his achievements in the lore of the schools that led to his selection as a companion to Archibald, seventh earl of Argyle, on a tour through France, Spain, and Italy.[2] The Earl of Argyle brought Alexander to Court, and there his learning and his poetical skill commended him to King James, who appointed him tutor to Prince Henry. When King James passed southward to his new realm, the Bard of Menstrie was moved to let the English people know how highly they had been favoured by fortune:

> But this age great with glorie hath brought forth
>   A matchless monarke whom peace highly raises,
> Who as th' untainted ocean of all worth
>   As due to him hath swallowed all our praises;
> Whose cleere excellencie long knowne for such,
>   All men must praise and none can praise too much.
>
> For that which others hardly could acquire
>   With losse of thousand lives and endless pain
> Is heapt on him, even by their owne desire
>   That thirst t'enjoy the fruits of his blest raigne,
> And never conqueror gained so great a thing
>   As those wise subjects gaining such a King.[3]

Nor did the bard, while dwelling on the good fortune of the Southron, forget the consequences to Scotland of the migration of her king:

> We must our breasts to baser thoughts inure
>   Since we want all that did advance our name,
> For in a corner of the world obscure
>   We rest ungraced without the boundes of fame.

---

[1] Rogers, *Memorials of the Earl of Stirling*, vol. i. p. 33.
[2] *Ibid.* p. 32.
[3] *Poetical Works of Sir Wm. Alexander*, vol. ii. p. 328.

> This hath discouraged my high-bended minde,
>   And still in doute my drouping muse arrayes,
> Which if my Phœbus once upon me shin'd,
>   Might raise her flight to build amidst his rayes.[1]

Of the sincerity of the sentiments expressed in these stanzas we have no reason to doubt : they are touched by that spirit of devoted personal loyalty to which must be attributed much both of the romance and of the tragedy of Scottish history.

When in 1604 Alexander journeyed to London he entered upon a career which seemed at first merely a continuation of the scholastic pursuits in which he had distinguished himself in Scotland. Ere quitting his native land he had published at Edinburgh his *Tragedie of Darius*. Having been appointed to the suite of Prince Henry, he published in 1604 *A Paraenesis to the Prince*—a poetical homily inspired by a manly common-sense conception of the duties of princes. The year 1604 saw the publication of a considerable amount of Alexander's more purely literary work. In this year appeared his *Aurora*—a sonnet series—and his *Monarchicke Tragedies*, containing his "Croesus" and the second version of his "Darius." Next year he published a third tragedy—*The Alexandræan*. In 1607 there was issued a quarto volume, containing "The Monarchicke Tragedies—Croesus, Darius, The Alexandræan, Julius Caesar ; newly enlarged, by William Alexander, Gentleman of the Prince's Privie Chamber." One interesting feature of Alexander's revision of his poems is that many Scottish turns of phrase that appeared in the earlier editions are eliminated from the later versions.

The lamented death of Prince Henry in 1612 called forth from Alexander his *Elegie*. Next year Alexander turned his attention to prose, and wrote an addition to Sidney's *Arcadia* ; and the curious reader can detect some traces of the influence of the *Arcadia* in the brocaded prose of Alexander's *Encouragement to Colonies*. A correspondence begun in this year with Drummond of Hawthornden [2] was followed in the autumn of 1614 by the visit of Drummond to the House of Menstrie.

---

[1] *Poetical Works of Sir Wm. Alexander*, vol. ii. p. 330.
[2] *Archæologica Scotica Col.*, iv. p. 84.

The account of the meeting of the two poets is thus described by Drummond in a letter to a friend :

" As to my long stay in these parts, ye sal rather impute it to so sociable a companie from whom I am even loth to depart, then to a wilful neglect of promiset coming to yow. Fortune this last day was so favourable, as be plaine blindnesse to acquent me with that most excellent spirit and rarest gem of or North S.V.A. (Sir William Alexander) ; for coming neare his house, I had almost beene a Christiane father to one of his childring. He accepted me so kindlie, and made me so good entertainement (which, whatsomever, with him I culd not have thocht but good) that I can not well schow. Tables removed, efter Homer's fassion well satiat, he honord me so much as to schow me his bookes and papers. This much will I say, and perchance not with out raison dar say, if the heavens prolong his dayes to end his Day,[1] he hath done more in One Day, then Tasso did al his lyff ; and Bartas in his Two Weekes ; thocht both the ane and the other be most praise worthie. I estimed of him before I was acquent with him, because of his Workes ; but I protest henceforth, I will estime of his Workes, because of his owne good courtes meeke disposition. He entreatit me to have made longer stay ; and beleave me, I was as sorrie to depart as anew enamouret lover wold be from his mistress."[2]

" Talk of the first meeting of Goethe and Schiller," says Drummond's biographer, " or of this other modern poet with that ! Have we moderns alone the deliciousness of such first meetings ? Could not two people meet for the first time before the eighteenth century ? Why here, two hundred and sixty years ago (three hundred years now), in the House of Menstrie near Alloa, in Clackmannanshire, which anyone may see to this day, there was a model first meeting of two poets, with a pleasant dinner between them to begin with, and,

[1] " The Day " referred to is Alexander's longest and most ambitious poem, " Doomes-day ; or, The Great Day of the Lords Ivdgement, by Sr. William Alexander, Knight." A sonnet by Drummond preceded the first part of it, which was published in 1614. In 1637 there was published a longer version, in which the four books or hours of the earlier edition were increased to twelve.

[2] Quoted Rogers, *Memorials*, vol. i. p. 47.

after the cloth was removed, an infinity of literary chat, and as much inspection as you like of papers and proof-sheets. . . . Alexander, though rather verbose in his printed remains, for our modern tastes, may have been a most agreeable man personally, and full of interesting talk. At all events, he was 'the rarest gem of our North' for young Drummond, and Drummond looked up to him admiringly. . . ."[1]

About this time, however, there were some of Alexander's fellow-countrymen who regarded him with sentiments widely different from those he inspired in Drummond. "Right honorable and most loving Brother," wrote Andro Murray of Balvaird on 31st January, 1615, to John Murray, afterwards Earl of Annandale, "their hes been much mervelling heir how it cumes that the goodman of Menstrie doeth now send and resaue the Bischopes packets, since your wer heirtofore imployed be them in all their business; and thoght it be a matter of smal or no moment yet hes it been the subiect of much speeche, and sum their bie who wold faine builde therupon ane argument to persuad others that your credit with his maiestie was in the decaye. I could not abstein from laughing, whan I hard such idle tales, and yet I thoght it was my dewtie, sa far as I could, to search their grund and to advertise you. For any thinge, I can learne, the change proceids only from the Bischope of Saintandrous levitie and inconstancie, to the which humour, they say, that he is so naturallie inclyned, that nothinge can please him longe. All the rest of the Bischopes ar so angrie with him for imploying Menstrie and leving you, as they can bie, and ye will not believe how hardlie they have censured him for it. He can not tell how to sett a goode face upon it, yet for his excuse, he alledges, (as I hier say) that he was commandit, and least willed so to do, both be his Maiestie and by my Lord Summerseat, and he sayes that his sone the archdean broght him home this commandement when he returned from Court last. Their is no man that ever hard this tale, bot they think it a meir fictioun. The only dout is whidder it be of the father or the sones invention. The archdean, indeed, since his last returne from Court, hes given out many great speaches, both of the

[1] Masson, *Drummond of Hawthornden*, p. 42.

credit he had when he was their, and of his purpose to returne in hope to have more ; bot he most find cautioun or he be belived in all. It is supposed that he has also said more to his father nor he had in commission, and his father belives him because he loves him. It could be no worse for them both to be somewhat more circumspict nor they are. ...."[1]

The career of Alexander as a man of affairs had, however, begun some years before the date when his "Sending and resauing of the Bischopes packets" caused "much mervelling." The first of those forlorn hopes that constitute his record of political experiment belongs to the year 1608. In that year William Alexander and a kinsman Walter Alexander approached the King with an ingenious financial scheme. No modern summary of the proposal can vie in effectiveness with the recital of the high hopes that gleam through the official prose of the royal patent: "Whereas we have been informed by our wellbeloved subjects William Alexander, one of the gent. of the Privy Chamber to our Right Wellbeloved sonne Henry, and Walter Alexander, one of the gent. Ushers to our said Sonne, that divers debts of divers kinds and of great value did grow due to the Crown of England in the thirteenth year of the raigne of our late Sister, the late Queene Elizabeth, and at divers times before upward to the first year of the raigne of King Edward the Sixt inclusively, which by the neglect of Sheriffs and other officers have not been levied nor paid, but are yet due to us—manie of which debts (at the first good and sperate) be now in process of time become either verie doubtfull and more desperate, and almost all of them, by reason that the debtors bee dead or deceased, and the estates hertofore subject and lyable to the payment of the same be now either consumed, or disposed, or aliened into so manie hands that it shall be verie difficult or chargeable at this daie to levage the same." Undaunted by the difficulty of the task, the two Alexanders were willing to attempt the recovery of these debts—amounting, it was estimated, to £12,000 sterling—and were to be rewarded by a grant of one half of any money that should accrue to the Crown, "by the

[1] Reprinted *Analecta Scotica*, vol. ii., from the Balfour MSS., Advocates' Library.

labour, meanes, industry, or endeavours of them, the said William Alexander and Walter Alexander." [1]

In this sanguine scheme, alas, desire did vastly outrun performance, and there is not the slightest reason to question the cautious averment of Alexander's biographer that " it is extremely improbable that any substantial emolument accrued." Alexander's next financial experiment was both more romantic and, to all appearance, more promising. In 1613 Alexander, in company with an Edinburgh goldsmith and a Portuguese prospector, received from the King the grant of a silver mine at Hilderston, near Linlithgow. Silver ore was actually brought to the surface. To a mind depressed by fruitless quest of occult Edwardian and Elizabethan debts this must have proved reassuring. But the outlay involved in the digging and refining of the ore was too great to make the working of the mine remunerative, and the scheme was soon abandoned.[2]

In the year following the futile Linlithgow prospecting, Alexander received from King James an appointment designed to benefit both him that gave and him that took—the office of Master of Requests.[3] The principal duty of this post was to protect the king from the importunities of needy Scots. This opened to Alexander an almost unlimited field of endeavour. His policy may be traced in a royal edict of April, 1615, wherein King James " discharges all maner of persones from resorting out of Scotland to this our Kingdome, unlesse it be gentlemen of good qualitie, merchands for traffique, or such as shall have a speciall license from our Counsell of that Kingdome, with expresse prohibition to all masters of shippes that they transport no such persones." [4] Prevention was all very well in its way, but some more stringent measures were felt to be necessary, and the same edict let it be known that " Sir William Alexander, Master of Requests, has received a commission to apprehend, and send home, or to punish, all vagrant persones who come to England to cause trouble or to bring discredit to their country."

[1] Rogers, *Memorials*, vol. i. pp. 40-43.
[2] *Ibid.* p. 45.   [3] *Ibid.* p. 49.
[4] Earl of Stirling's *Register of Royal Letters*, vol. i. p. 3.

But though the work done by the Master of Requests doubtlessly contributed to the amenity of court life at Whitehall, there were other court interests that appealed more strongly than the duties of court-constable to the sanguine and imaginative temperament of Sir William. Almost from the time of his arrival in England there had been displayed a keen interest on the part of the king and various prominent courtiers in the progress of the efforts made to colonise the territory claimed by England on the Atlantic seaboard of America. As the years went on that interest grew wider and more active. By 1619 Virginia had safely weathered the storms of the early years of its existence. The grant in November, 1620, of the fresh charter to the Plymouth Company, remodelled as "The Council established at Plymouth in the County of Devon, for the planting, ruling, ordering, and governing of New England in America," seemed to promise a more successful issue to the efforts to colonise the more northern part of the territory. The leading part in the reorganisation of the Plymouth company was taken by Sir Ferdinando Gorges—"The Father of English Colonisation in North America." With Gorges Sir William was on terms of friendship. The colonising zeal of Gorges proved contagious.[1] Alexander's mind was fired by the possibilities of colonial enterprise. His resolution to engage in such enterprise seems to have been strengthened by arguments adduced by Captain John Mason on his return to England in 1621.[2] Alexander no longer hesitated : he, too, would play his part in colonial enterprise. "Having sundry times exactly weighed that which I have already delivered, and being soe exceedingly enflamed to doe some goode in that kind," he declares in his *Encouragement to Colonies*, "that I would rather bewray the weaknesse of my power than conceale the greatnesse of my desire, being much encouraged hereunto by Sir Ferdinando Gorge and some others of the undertakers of New England, I shew them that my countriemen would never adventure in such an Enterprise, unlesse it were as there was

[1] Letter of King James to Scots Privy Council, 5th Aug., 1621. Rogers, vol. i. p. 61.
[2] *Ibid.*

a New France, a New Spaine, and a New England, that they might likewise have a New Scotland, and for that effect they might have bounds with a correspondencie in proportion (as others had) with the Country thereof it should beare the name, which they might hold of their owne Crowne, and where they might be governed by their owne Lawes." [1]

Sir William's patriotic desires were respected. On August 5th, 1621, King James intimated to the Scots Privy Council that Sir William Alexander had " a purpose to procure a forraine Plantation, haveing made choice of landes lying betweene our Colonies of New England and Newfoundland, both the Governors whereof have encouraged him thereunto " and signified the royal desire that the Council would " graunt unto the sayd Sir William . . . a Signatour under our Great Seale of the sayd lands lying between New England and Newfoundland, as he shall designe them particularly unto you. To be holden of us from our Kingdome of Scotland as a part thereof. . . ." [2] A charter under the Great Seal was duly granted at Edinburgh on 29th September, 1621.[3] For Alexander's New Scotland—the Nova Scotia in America of his Latin charter—the New England council had surrendered a territory comprising the modern Nova Scotia, New Brunswick and the land lying between New Brunswick and the St. Lawrence.

Over the province thus assigned to him Sir William Alexander was invested with wide and autocratic power. Some of the sweeping benefactions of the charter seem to contemplate the transference of Scottish home conditions across the Atlantic with almost too pedantic completeness. Along with many other strange and wonderful things Sir William was to hold and to possess " free towns, free ports, towns, baronial villages, seaports, roadsteads, machines, mills, offices, and jurisdiction; . . . bogs, plains, and moors; marshes, roads, paths, waters, swamps, rivers, meadows, and pastures; mines, malt-houses and their refuse; hawking, hunting, fisheries, peat-mosses, turf bogs, coal, coal-pits, coneys, warrens, doves, dove-cotes, workshops, malt-kilns,

[1] *Encouragement*, pp. 31 and 32.   [2] Rogers, vol. i. pp. 60-62.
[3] Rogers, vol. i. p. 62.

breweries and broom; woods, groves, and thickets; wood, timber, quarries of stone and lime, with courts, fines, pleas, heriots, outlaws, . . . and with fork, foss, sac, theme, infangtheiff, outfangtheiff, wrak, wair, veth, vert, venison, pit and gallows. . . .[1]

II.

The colony which was to enjoy the quaint and multitudinous benefits of Scots feudalism as it then existed—and was to exist for another century and a quarter—occupied a definite place in the scheme of English colonial expansion, and the effort to found and to hold it was a definite strategic move in the triangular contest of Spain, France and Britain for the dominion of the continent of North America.

The Spanish conquest of Mexico and the establishment of the outpost of St. Augustine on the Florida coast had provided Spain not only with a valuable strategic base in America, but with a claim to the coast lying to the north of Florida. The voyages of Cartier to the St. Lawrence had given France pre-eminence in the North. The seaboard stretching from the St. Lawrence to the peninsula of Florida was claimed by England in virtue of Cabot's discoveries. The foundation of the Virginia Company in 1606 was a definite effort to make good the English claim.

The Virginia Company had two branches. To the London Company, or southern colony, was given authority to settle the territory between the thirty-fourth and forty-first degrees of north latitude. The founding of the settlement of Jamestown in 1607 by the expedition sent out by the London Company was regarded by the Spanish authorities as a challenge, but the Spanish disfavour did not find expression in open hostilities. A more serious menace than Spanish enmity was found in the life of hardship of the earliest colonists —the struggle for subsistence, the hostility of the Indians, the harsh régime of Dale and Argall. But the recognition of the value of the tobacco crop soon brought economic security to the young colony, and the grant in 1619 of a certain measure

[1] *Nova Scotia Papers*, pp. 2-15; Rogers, vol. ii. p. 179-195; *Reg. P.C.*, vol. xii. pp. 570 and 775.

of self-government to the colony by the establishment of the House of Burgesses, marked the beginning of a happier state of political affairs.

In the Plymouth, or Northern Company, to which was given the right to plant lands between the thirty-eighth and forty-fifth degrees of north latitude the most influential man was Sir William Alexander's friend, Sir Ferdinando Gorges, one of the most interesting characters in early colonial history. Gorges belonged to an old Somerset family. He held the post of governor of the forts and islands of Plymouth, but varied his garrison duty with spells of service abroad. In 1591, when about twenty-five years of age, he was knighted by the Earl of Essex for valiant service at the siege of Rouen. When Essex rose in revolt against Elizabeth, Gorges played a vacillating and not too creditable part towards his old commander.[1]

The active interest of Gorges in colonial affairs began in 1605 when Captain George Weymouth sailed into Plymouth Sound in the *Archangell*, a vessel that had been fitted out for trade and discovery by the Earl of Southampton and Lord Arundell of Wardour. From America Weymouth had brought home with him five Indians. Of these, three were quartered in Gorges' house. As they became more proficient in the English tongue they had long talks with the Governor, who learned from them much concerning the climate, soil and harbours of their native land. And to the knowledge thus romantically acquired was due the desire on the part of Gorges to take some part in the colonising of these regions beyond the Atlantic.

As a colonising agent the Plymouth Company, in which Gorges was interested, was less successful than the London Company. The expedition sent out in 1607 by the Plymouth Colony did indeed effect a settlement—the Popham Colony—on the coast of Maine, but the rigours of the first winter spent on that bleak sea-board proved too much for the colonists. After the survivors of these settlers returned to England, the activities of the company were connected solely with trading voyages until, in 1620, it was remodelled as the Council for

[1] D.N.B.

New England. To the Council was assigned the territory lying between the fortieth and forty-eighth degree of north latitude. Within those limits, too, fishing could be carried on only by permission of the Council for New England, who thus acquired what amounted to a monopoly of the lucrative American fisheries. Both from the rival company of London and from those who, on political grounds, were opposed to monopolies, the Council for New England met with determined opposition. During the meetings held prior to the autumn of 1621 the chief subjects under discussion were the settlement of the company's territories and the prevention of the infringement of the company's rights by interlopers trading within its territories or fishing the adjoining seas.

It soon became evident that, for the time being, the company was more concerned with exploiting its privileges than with settling its territories, and soon a scheme was evolved for passing on to others the burden of colonisation. In September, 1621, Gorges himself laid before the Mayor of Bristol the "Articles and Orders Concluded on by the President and Counsell for the affaires of New England for the better Government of the Trade and for the Advancement of the Plantation in those parts."[1] The salient features of this scheme are contained in Articles 1, 2, 3, and 9:

"1. First that, in the City of Bristol and Exon, and in the Townes of Plymouth, Dartmouth, Waymouth, and Barnstable, there shalbe a Treasauror in either of them, together wth certayne Commission chosen by the Adventurers. To all whome the Treasure, Government, and pollicye of Trade for New England shall bee Comitted; as alsoe such other officers as shall bee founde convenient for that Service shalbe designed to their particular charge.

"2. And for the better Government of the said affaires: It is further ordered that there shalbee chosen xviij Commissioners out of the Adventurers of the Citty of Bristol and the parts thereunto adjoyning and xviij out of the citty of Exon and the parts thereunto adjoining, and xij out of the Towne of Plimouth and the parts thereunto adioyning, and xij out of the Towne of Dartmouth and the parts thereunto

[1] *American Historical Review*, vol. iv. No. 4, p. 686 *et seq.*

adioyning, and xij out of the Towne of Barnstable and the parts thereunto adioyning; out of wch nomber they ar to choose their Treasouror for evry of the said places : And they soe chosen to nominate their Register, Auditors, Clarke, and other officers.

"3. And it is further ordered that the Treasourors and Commissioners (being so chosen by the Company of Adventures of the Seu^rall cities and Townes Corporate or the greater parte of thim that shalbee present) shall receyve their commission for the Manadging of their affaires from us, the President and Counsell, according to his Mats authoritie in that behalfe granted unto us.

.   .   .   .   .   .

"9. That ev^ry yeere about Michaelmas and Easter, there shall be a Generall Meeting at Teuerton, in the County of Devon, of the said sev^rall Citties and Townes, whither they are to send three out of either Cittie and twoe out of either Towne, to resolve uppon their Mutuall proceeding; as, namely, to what Porte or portes of those Territories they will send any shipp or shipps and what marketts are fittest to vent their commodities in, and what shipps are meetest to go into those marketts, as, alsoe, whether the whole shall proceed uppon a jointe stocke or that ev^ry Cittie and Towne doe proceed upon their sevrall adventures, wch by all meanes is conceyved to bee the worst, both for the publique and private good."

With this grandiose scheme the cautious Merchant Venturers of Bristol would have nothing to do. But the scheme brings out clearly the circumstances in which the Scottish venture had its origin, and reveals the exact significance, from the English standpoint, of the Nova Scotia scheme. By the reorganisation of 1620 the northern boundary of the Plymouth Company had been advanced two hundred miles farther north. This northern frontier had now reached the sphere of French influence on the lower St. Lawrence. Already in 1613 an attempt on the part of the French to extend their sphere of influence southward had evoked reprisals on the part of the Virginian colonists, and the French Jesuit settlement at Desert Island on the coast of Maine had been broken up by an expedition under Captain Argall; in the following year Argall sailed north again and sacked the French settlement at Port Royal in the Bay of Fundy. But the French settlers had not been wholly driven from these northern latitudes, and the hope that the occupation of the northern territory by the Scots would prove a barrier against French aggression was responsible for the cordiality with which the Nova Scotia scheme was urged on Alexander by Gorges and the others interested in English colonial projects.

III.

But if the Scottish scheme has an intimate connection with English colonial history, it has an even more intimate connection with French colonial history. Though claimed by England in virtue of Cabot's discoveries,[1] the district allotted to Sir William Alexander was definitely regarded by the French as their territory: it was, indeed, the old French province of Arcadie, the Debatable Land of the northern latitudes of America. When a decade later the restoration of this territory to France was under discussion, English diplomatists could not understand the reasons of the vehemence and pertinacity with which the French urged their claim. The region was sparsely settled: economically it had proved of little value. But the romantic history of Acadie had already become part of the colonial history of France.

It was in Acadie that the French had established in these regions the first settlement that held out any promise of permanence. Their tentative pioneering expeditions of the sixteenth century to the St. Lawrence had been succeeded, after the accession of Henry IV., by a systematic attempt to explore and colonise the northern coasts of America. Appointed in 1603 Lieutenant-General of Acadie, a Huguenot noble, the Sieur de Monts had, in the following year, set sail for his transatlantic province. With him went Samuel Champlain. To Champlain the commodious and picturesque harbour of Port Royal (now Annapolis Basin), opening off

[1] *S.P. Col.*, vol. i. p. 119.

the Bay of Fundy, owed the name which it bore all through the stormy and romantic days of the old French régime. The beauty of Port Royal Harbour—its calm waters mirroring its wooded islands, its sheltering rampart of forest-clad hills—made a strong appeal also to the Sieur de Poutrincourt, who had accompanied the expedition as a volunteer, and to him de Monts willingly made a grant of this fair seignory. Hither the French colonists, after the disastrous winter, 1604-1605, spent on the bleak shores of the island of Ste. Croix, on the western coast of the Bay of Fundy, transferred their settlement. On the western side of Port Royal—at the very spot where a quarter of a century later the Master of Stirling was to plant his short-lived Scottish colony—there soon rose the " habitation," a small cluster of timber buildings—workshops, stores, dwelling quarters—built round a rectangular courtyard : on the left projected a square gun platform that mounted four small cannon : on the right was a small bastion constructed of palisades.[1]

De Poutrincourt had returned to France in the autumn of 1604, but eighteen months later he sailed again for Port Royal. With him went on this occasion his friend Marc. Lescarbot, advocate, orator and poet, who acted both as the Laureate and as the special correspondent of the colony. Left in charge of the settlement when de Poutrincourt and Champlain set off on a voyage of exploration across the Bay of Fundy and down the New England coast, Lescarbot supervised the labour of the workmen. Lescarbot himself toiled hard and happily in his garden, and when night had fallen on the little settlement he retired to his study to read and write.

It was the middle of November ere de Poutrincourt returned. To greet him there issued from the fort a merry procession of Neptune and his tritons, who welcomed him in neatly turned verse. In the course of the winter, too, ceremonial gilded the routine of daily life. The ingenious mind of Champlain suggested the institution of the Order of Good Cheer. The duties of Steward of this Order were undertaken in turn by each man of de Poutrincourt's table. The Steward held office for one day : his duty was to provide, by his own

[1] Lescarbot, bk. iv., chaps. 2 and 3; *C.O.*, 1/1, p. 4.

hunting or fishing, some special delicacy for the table. When the hour for the mid-day meal arrived the Steward marshalled the Companions of the Order: each of the latter picked up some dish destined for the table: then the Steward, wearing the Collar of the Order, raised his wand of office, and, with a napkin flapping gallantly from his shoulder, headed the procession to the dining-hall. Nor were spectators lacking: a band of Indians, whose material wants were amply provided for, gazed daily with solemn admiration at this cheerful ritual.

Spring came; in the fields and gardens work was resumed; on the banks of a small river near the head of the Basin, de Poutrincourt constructed a water-mill. Now the settlers began to look eagerly for news from France. But when the long expected relief ship arrived it bore the unwelcome tidings that the colony must be abandoned: the fur trade, on which depended the prosperity of de Mont's venture, had proved unprofitable: to crown all, his monopoly of that trade had been revoked. De Poutrincourt lingered until the grain he had sown had ripened, and he could carry some of it home with him. Then, amid the lamentations of his Indian friends, he steered slowly for the harbour mouth.

Indomitable in his efforts to perpetuate the existence of the settlement, de Poutrincourt returned to Acadie in 1610. But the next few years were marked by many vicissitudes. The attempt made in 1613 by the French to extend their influence southward led to the destruction of their settlement on the coast of Maine by Argall: next year Argall, in command of a fleet of three vessels, destroyed Port Royal. The French, however, still clung to their settlement. Port Royal was rebuilt; in the south of Acadie, in the neighbourhood of Cape Sable, another small fort provided an additional rallying point for the French pioneers.

• • • • • • • •

But not alone did the romantic history of Acadie endear it to France. Its position—it lay between the seaboard territories of England and the inland settlements of France—gave it a supreme strategical importance in connection with the

control of the St. Lawrence, the only route into New France.
If to her Newfoundland colony England could add a strong
naval base on the northern coast of Nova Scotia, she would
hold the gateway of the St. Lawrence. To France, therefore,
the retention of Acadie was of vital importance for the development—nay, for the very existence—of her struggling settlements on the St. Lawrence. In taking upon himself the
responsibility of carrying out the settlement of Nova Scotia,
Alexander was unwittingly making the first move in what was
destined to be a prolonged and embittered colonial struggle.
Of the French claims to Acadie he was not unaware ; but he
does not seem to have realised fully the significance of the
issues involved in his attempt to supplant the French pioneers.

IV.

Years were to pass, however, before in the New World the
Old Allies were to come into conflict. When, however, at the
opening of the third decade of the seventeenth century, Sir
William Alexander essayed the task of diverting to the New
World the unceasing flow of Scottish emigration, the time
seemed not unpropitious for such an enterprise. Both
merchant and soldier were now lamenting the loss of the old
friendship with France. The emigration to Ulster had
dwindled, not because there were no more planters anxious
to cross the North Channel, but rather because there was
little more land available. King James had endeavoured,
with some degree of sternness, to repress the tendency of his
Scottish subjects to seek for El Dorado on the banks of the
Thames. The Northern War between Sweden and Poland
and the earlier campaigns of the Thirty Years' War offered,
indeed, a martial career to young and adventurous Scots ;
but the king, with his innate kindliness and humanity, resented
the drain of the levies continually made for foreign wars in
which Scotland's interest was mainly a mercenary one. By
his patent of 1621, for the plantation by the Scots of the lands
lying between New England and Newfoundland, he sought
expressly to provide a career for Scottish gentlemen : " The
same being ane fitt warrandable and convenient means to

disburding this his Majestie's said ancient kingdome of all such younge brether and meane gentlemen, who otherwayes most be troublesome to the houses and friends from whence they are descendit (the common ruynes of most of the ancient families), or betak themselves to forren worke or baisser chifts."[1]

But, in spite of apparently favourable circumstances, the Nova Scotia scheme was long in obtaining even a small measure of success. The first expedition sent out by Sir William Alexander did not even reach the shores of his new domain. Its record is one long tale of disappointment and delay. The ship which in March, 1622, he procured at London he sent round to Kirkcudbright in order that some interest in his project might be aroused among his fellow-countrymen and that "the businesse might beginne from that kingdome which it did concerne."[2] It was the end of May when the emigrant ship steered up the estuary of the Dee, and prudence might well have suggested to those responsible for the expedition the advisability of proceeding upon the Atlantic voyage with as little delay as possible. But various obstacles to a speedy setting forth were encountered, and Alexander's personality was never seen to advantage in dealing with problems of practical life. In choosing Kirkcudbright as his port of call, Sir William had been guided by the prospect of taking advantage of the local influence of some of his friends, such as Sir Robert Gordon of Lochinvar. But at the very time when their aid would have been invaluable, these gentlemen happened to be away from the neighbourhood. Provisions, too, had of late grown very scarce and very dear, as the season had been marked by great dearth:[3] but to abandon the enterprise at this point meant for Alexander not only loss of prestige among his fellow-courtiers, but also the loss of all money already expended on the charter and employment of the vessel: so Sir William did his utmost to procure stores. His main difficulty, however, was to induce any of the Gallovidians to bid even a temporary farewell to the shores of Scotland: some were reluctant to embark on so long a voyage;

[1] Rogers, vol. i. p. 72.   [2] *Encouragement*, p. 32.
[3] *Reg. P.C.S.*, vol. xiii. p. 257.

others were sceptical about the very existence of Sir William's transatlantic province; artisans, in particular, the very class whose services he most desired to enlist, were most reluctant to venture forth.

June was already drawing to a close ere the little emigrant ship with its small band of pioneers, consisting of a minister, a smith and a company of farm labourers, at length dropped down the quiet reaches of the Dee with the ebb-tide and the hills of Galloway faded from view. Even now there was little continuity in their voyage. At the Isle of Man they remained for more than a month—probably wind-bound. Hindered in their Atlantic passage by baffling headwinds, they did not make the coast of Newfoundland till mid-September, and as they struggled on towards the shores of Cape Breton Island a fierce westerly gale swooped down on them and thrust them far back. They decided to winter in St. John's Harbour—in all probability they imitated the procedure of the winter crews—and they sent their ship back to London for fresh supplies.

A ship laden with the stores requisitioned by the advance-guard was despatched from London in March, 1623. Delayed at Plymouth, " first upon some necessaire occasion and later by contrary winds," this ship, the *St. Luke*, did not get clear of the English Channel till the end of April. When on the 5th June it dropped anchor in St. John's Harbour, its passengers found things had not gone too well with the advance-party. The minister and the smith, "both for Spiritual and Temporal respects the two most necessary members," had died during the winter. Some of the company, not relying too absolutely on the coming of the relief ship, had, during the month of May, taken service with the fishing fleet. In these circumstances an effective attempt at planting a colony seemed out of the question, and it was resolved to limit the activities of the expedition to an exploration of the coast of Nova Scotia and to the selection of a site where a settlement might be made the following year.

Accordingly on the 23rd June the *St. Luke*, having added to its personnel a contingent of ten of the leading members of the first party, cleared from St. John's. For a fortnight the voyagers groped blindly amid the fogs of the Gulf or wrestled with unfavourable winds. Making at length the west coast of Cape Breton Island, they crept down the rugged shores of Acadie, exploring various harbours : if they brought back to Sir William little in the way of solid gain, they were able to furnish him with the compensatory benefit of abundance of picturesque detail. On the 20th July the *St. Luke* turned its bow towards Newfoundland, there to receive a cargo of fish.

These two expeditions had involved Sir William in heavy expense : they had effected nothing. It was not without reason that when a year later fresh efforts were being made to carry the plantation of New Scotland to an effective issue, the Scots Privy Council suggested to King James that affairs might go more prosperously if the assistance could be obtained " of some of the English who are best acquainted with such forrayn enterprises." [1]

Despite the losses caused by the Nova Scotia voyages, however, Sir William was by no means inclined to abandon his enterprise. Ever sanguine and ever ingenious, he resolved to employ the learned pen which had attracted to him the royal favour, in an appeal to a wider circle of readers. In 1624 he published his *Encouragement to Colonies*, a treatise which is at once a tribute to the scholarly and magnanimous aspects of his personality and a convincing revelation of his inability to grasp the nature of the difficulties against which his scheme had to struggle. It is highly instructive to compare with the *Encouragement* Captain Mason's *Brief Discourse*. Mason's pamphlet opens with a clear, precise account of the geographical position and the climate conditions of Newfoundland : the first six pages of the *Encouragement* contain a sketch of the history of colonisation from the days of the Patriarchs down to those of the Roman Empire ; the next twenty-five pages are devoted to a masterly résumé of American history from the time of Columbus down to the settlement of New England. It will be remembered how definitely Mason set out the particular advantages Newfoundland offered to prospective settlers : Alexander's appeal,

[1] Letter of P.C.S., 23 Nov., 1624 (quoted Rogers).

if addressed to higher instincts, was correspondingly vaguer:
" Where was ever Ambition baited with greater hopes than
here, or where ever had Virtue so large a field to reape the
fruits of Glory, since any man, who doth goe thither of good
qualitie, able at first to transport a hundred persons with him
furnished with things necessary, shall have as much Bounds
as may serve for a great man, whereupon he may build a
Towne of his owne, giving it what forme or name he will, and
being the first Founder of a new Estate, which a pleasing
industry may quickly bring to a perfection, may leave a faire
inheritance to his posteritie, who shall claime unto him as
the author of their Nobilitie there. . . . "[1] It is with little
surprise that we learn that the only person who seems to have
been encouraged by the publication of this treatise was
Alexander himself.

To the text of the *Encouragement* there was added a map
of New Scotland. With the object of either satisfying an
academic craving for patriotic consistency or of dispelling that
dread of an unknown land which had proved such a deterrent
to the peasants of Galloway, Alexander besprinkled his map
with familiar names. And what Scot could persist in regarding
as altogether alien, that land which was drained by a Forthe
and a Clyde, and which was separated from New England by
a Twede?

If the *Encouragement* did little to stimulate colonial enterprise in Scotland, it has an intrinsic interest as a literary
production. To a modern reader Alexander's verse, despite
its great reputation in his own day, seems to be strangely
lacking in vital interest. It may be that the themes of his
Monarchicke Tragedies, and of his long poem on *Doomesday*,
appealed to his intellect and not to his heart. But when he
wrote of colonial enterprise, he was treating a theme that had
fired his imagination, and his prose is vigorous and impressive.
Now it is vivid with Elizabethan brightness and colour: his
explorers " discovered three very pleasant Harbours and went
ashore in one of them which after the ship's name they called
St. Luke's Bay, where they found a great way up a very
pleasant river, being three fathoms deep at low water at the

[1] *Encouragement*, p. 42.

entry, and on every side they did see very delicate Medowes having roses red and white growing thereon with a kind of wild Lilly having a very daintie Smel."[1] Again, it strikes a note of solemn grandeur that anticipates the stately cadences of Sir Thomas Browne: "I am loth," says Alexander, in referring to Roman military colonisation, "by disputable opinioun to dig up the Tombes of them that, more extenuated than the dust, are buried in oblivion, and will leave these disregarded relicts of greatnesse to continue as they are, the scorne of pride, witnessing the power of Time."[2]

V.

But if Sir William Alexander's appeal was made essentially to the higher emotions and interests of his countrymen, his friend the king was ready with a practical scheme designed to impart to either indifferent or reluctant Scots the necessary incentive to take part in colonial enterprsie. There is, indeed, in the closing lines of the *Encouragement*, a hint of the prospect of royal aid: "And as no one man could accomplish such a Worke by his own private fortune, so it shall please his Majestie . . . to give his help accustomed for matters of less moment hereunto, making it appear to be a work of his own, that others of his subjects may be induced to concur in a common cause. . . . I must trust to be supplied by some publike helps, such as hath been had in other parts for the like cause."

For the "publike helps" the ingenious king, well exercised in all the arts of conjuring money from the coffers of unwilling subjects, had decided to have recourse to a device of proved efficiency—the creation of an Order of Baronets. It is true that his first essay in this direction had not been altogether fortunate. Soon after his accession he had sought to finance a project for searching for precious metals in Britain by instituting an Order of Golden Knights: two Knights of the Order had actually been created when, through Cecil's dissuasion, the fantastic scheme was abandoned.[3] But experience

---
[1] *Encouragement*, p. 35.   [2] *Ibid.* p. 4.
[3] Rogers, *Memorials*, vol. i. p. 45 *n*.

brought wisdom, and the next effort was eminently successful. To the Plantation of Ulster welcome assistance had been furnished through the creation of the Order of Knights Baronets: the 205 English landowners who were advanced to the dignity of Baronets had contributed to the royal exchequer the total sum of £225,000.

The Ulster creation formed the precedent that guided King James in his efforts to help Sir William Alexander. In October, 1624, the king intimated to the Scots Privy Council that he proposed to make the colonisation of Nova Scotia " a work of his own," and to assist the scheme by the creation of an Order of Baronets. Both in their reply to the king and in their proclamation of 30th November, 1624, the Council emphasised the necessity of sending out colonists to Nova Scotia. The terms on which Baronets were to be created were set forth with absolute precision in the proclamation. Only those were to be advanced to the dignity who would undertake " To set furth sex sufficient men, artificers or labourers sufficientlie armeit, apparrelit, and victuallit for twa years ... under the pane of twa thousand merkis usual money of this realme." [1] In addition, each Baronet so created was expected to pay Sir William Alexander " ane thousand merkis Scottis money only towards his past charges and endeavouris." [2]

But the Scottish gentry seemed as reluctant to become Nova Scotia Baronets as the Galloway peasants had been to embark on Sir William's first expedition. When the first Baronets were created six months after the Proclamation of the Council, the conditions of the grant were modified in certain very essential respects. The terms on which, for example, the dignity was conferred on Sir Robert Gordon of Gordonston, the first of the Nova Scotia Baronets, make it clear that the main condition of the grant was now the payment to Sir William Alexander of three thousand merks, usual money of the Kingdom of Scotland, and that the interests of the colony were safeguarded only by an undertaking on the part of Sir William Alexander to devote two thousand

---

[1] Proclam. P.C.S. (quoted Rogers, pp. 72-74).
[2] Letter of Privy Council (quoted Rogers, p. 71).

merks of the purchase money " towards the setting forth of a colonie of men furnished with necessaire provision, to be planted within the said countrie be the advice of the said Sir Robert Gordon and the remanent Barronets of Scotland, adventurers in the plantation of the same."[1]

To render attractive the new dignity various devices were employed. To enter upon possession of the broad acres of his Nova Scotia territory, the baronet did not require to cross the Atlantic: he could take seisin of it on the Castlehill of Edinburgh. The king urged the Privy Council to use their influence to induce the gentry to come forward. When the precedency accorded to the baronets evoked a complaint from the lesser Scottish barons and the cause of the complainers was espoused by the Earl of Melrose, principal Secretary of Scotland, Melrose was removed from his office and replaced by Sir William Alexander. Certain recalcitrant lairds were commanded by royal letter to offer themselves as candidates for baronetcies. Yet the number of baronets grew but slowly, and the growth of the funds available for fresh colonial efforts was correspondingly slow.

That during these months of disappointment Sir William abated no whit of his zeal for his colonial scheme is convincingly attested by an account of a conversation between him and Sir William Vaughan, published by the latter in *The Golden Fleece*. Vaughan, a scholar and a poet, had been identified with a Welsh settlement planted in the south-east of Newfoundland. Early in 1626, while on a visit to London, he met Sir William Alexander:

"This learned Knight, with a joyful countenance and alacrity of mind, taking me by the hand thus began: ' I have oftentimes wished to confer with you, but until this present I could not find the opportunity. It is necessary, and this necessity jumps with the sympathy of our constellations (for I think we were both born under the same Horoscope), that we advise and devise some Project for the proceeding and successful managing of our plantations.' "

The remainder of Sir William's conversation—or soliloquy—is made up of eloquently expressed commiseration for the

[1] *Hist. MSS. Com. Report*, 6, p. 684.

small measure of success that has attended the efforts both of
Vaughan and of himself ; of some doubt as to the adequacy
of the revenues derived from the creation of knights baronets ;
and of much rhetorical insistence on the necessity of finding
a suitable outlet for the surplus population of Scotland.
" I would," he concludes, " we could invent and hit upon
some profitable means for the settling of these glorious works,
whereto it seems the divine Providence hath elected us as
instruments under our Earthly Soveraigne."

VI.

By the summer of 1626, Sir William appeared to have hit
upon the desired means, for preparations were being made
for the despatch of a colonising expedition in the following
spring. The exact nature of these means is clearly revealed
in a letter of Sir Robert Gordon, the premier Nova Scotia
baronet, dated from London, the 25th May, 1626. At a
meeting held at Wanstead some time previously certain of
the baronets had covenanted to provide two thousand merks
Scots apiece " for buying and rigging furth of a shipp for the
furtherance of the plantatione of New Scotland, and for
carreing our men thither." [1] In pursuance of this resolution
Gordon wrote on 25th May to the Earl Marischal of Scotland :
" My Lord,—According to the conference wee hade togidder,
at our last meeting, touching the plantation of New Scotland,
and setting furth of a shipp by some of that worthie societie,
to advance the said enterpryse, I, being loth to be posteriour
to any of our number in furthering that noble work, do heirby
intreet your Lordship to answer for my part in buying and
setting furth of the said shipp ; and whatsoever soume your
Lordship will advance for me in this particular (not exceiding
two thousand merks, Scots money), be the advyse of Baronet
Strachan, Baronet Clunie, and Baronet Lesmoir, I do obliss
myself to repay the same to your Lordship again providing I
have my equal portion (*pro rata*) of the gain and comoditie
that (God willing) shall aryse from the traffick of the said
shipp or otherways, from tyme to tyme, and that such men

[1] Dunbar, *Social Life in Former Days*, Second Series, p. 17.

as I shall send over into New Scotland be freelie transported in the said shipp into that Kingdome, and be landed either at the chief colonie or at my owne portion of land by Port du Mutton, at my option. . . ." [1] At Wanstead on the 11th July, 1626, in presence of Sir William Alexander, Knight, Secretarie to His Majestie for Scotland, Gordon, Strachan, and the Earl Marischal concluded an agreement regarding the equal division of " anie prise or prises that shall happen to be taken by the said shipp, commander, souldiers, and marineris therein." [2]

Early in 1627 Alexander, probably in order to dispel an uncharitable assumption that the share of the baronets' money destined for colonial purpose was being diverted to his own use, let it be known publicly that he had fulfilled his share of the compact, " having . . . prepared a schip, with ordinance, munition, and all other furnitour necessar for her, as lykwyse another schip of great burden which lyeth at Dumbartoune." [3] At the same time he made a requisition to the Master of the English Ordnance for sixteen minner, four saker and six falcor, which were to be forwarded to Dumbarton.[4] Strenuous efforts, too, were made by King Charles to further Sir William's plans. The Scottish Treasurer of Marine was instructed [5] to pay Sir William the £6,000 which represented the losses incurred in the former Nova Scotia expeditions, and which, despite a royal warrant, the English Exchequer either could not or would not pay him : it does not appear, however, that in this matter the Scottish authorities proved in any way more complaisant than the English officials. A week after the issue of these instructions the Earl Marischal was directed to make a selection of persons " fitt to be barronetts " both among " the ancient gentrie," and also among " these persones who had succeeded to good estates or acquyred them by their own industrie, and a^r generouslie disposed to concurre with our said servand (Alexander) in this enterprise." [6] A month later the Privy Council were urged to use their influence " both in private and publict " to stimulate the demand for baronetcies.[7]

[1] Dunbar, *Social Life in Former Days*, Second Series, pp. 17-18.
[2] *Ibid.* pp. 18-19. [3] *Nova Scotia Papers*, p. 36. [4] *Ibid.* p. 38.
[5] *Ibid.* [6] *Ibid.* p. 39. [7] *Ibid.* p. 40.

Early in March, 1627, "the good shipp called the *Eagle*, of the burthen of one hundred and 20 tunnes," lay in the Thames, "laden with powder, ordanance, and other provisions, for the use of a plantation, ordained to be made in New Scotland, ... and for the use of ane other shippe of the burthen of 300 tunnes, now lying at Dumbartane, in Scotland, which is likewise to go for the said plantation of New Scotland." Along with the *Eagle* there was to go from the Thames a consort, the *Morning Star*, belonging to Andrew Baxter, a Scot. However, the *Morning Star* was arrested in Dover Roads by creditors of Baxter, and the *Eagle* continued her voyage to Dumbarton alone. She arrived in the Clyde early in June,[1] only to find that Sir William Alexander's other and larger ship was away on a cruise. Towards the end of June the *Eagle* was in the hands of the painter. At this time the bailies of Dumbarton were looking after the renovation of the burghal property: a broken window in the Tolbooth was down for repair; the old burgh ensign was replaced by a new one; instructions were issued for the painting of the Market Cross and the roof of the Tolbooth. It was resolved to take advantage of the presence in the burgh of the painter who was exercising his craft on Sir William's ship: "They think meit to cause him renew the paynting and cullering of the orloge, if the baillies can agree w^t him chaiplie on the toun's chairges."[2]

The activities of those who were connected with Sir William's expedition did not always so commend themselves to the douce burgher of Dumbarton. The placid life of the little community was at times disturbed by the boisterous frolics of nautical roisterers, and feet that had been wont to scramble briskly up the rigging of the *Eagle* were condemned to a reluctant rest in the burghal stocks.[3]

This ebullition of feeling was nothing new among the personnel of expeditions awaiting orders to sail. Lescarbot had experienced the same sort of thing at La Rochelle in 1606. The workmen bound for New France, who were lodged in the Quartier St. Nicolas near the harbour, and who were not stinted in the matter of living expenses, behaved with a lack of

[1] *Dumbarton Burgh Records*, 13 June, 1627.
[2] *Ibid.* 22 June, 1627.   [3] *Ibid.* 23 Aug., 1627.

decorum ("Faisoient de merveilleux tintamarres," says Lescarbot) that brought upon them inevitably the censure of the stern Calvinistic community. Some of the more obstreperous spirits found themselves shut up in the Hôtel de Ville, and escaped more serious punishment only because the hearts of the magistrates were softened by the premonitions of the hardships that lay before the erring ones. Nor were Scottish magistrates of burghs other than Dumbarton unfamiliar with the problem. In the autumn of 1626, when some of the levies for the German Wars were at Aberdeen awaiting embarkation the authorities of the northern seaport were much exercised " anent the tumultis maid be Macky his souldeours."[1]

* * * * * *

While the *Eagle* lay with folded pinions in the shadow of Dumbarton Rock, and while the vagaries of her personnel vexed the minds of the Dumbarton bailies, what of Sir William Alexander's other ship? During the very month—June, 1627 —when the *Eagle* was working her way up the Firth of Clyde, Sir William's eldest son, William Alexander, later Master of Stirling, steered the larger ship into the Firth of Forth: with him, to Leith Roads, he brought a prize, the *St. Lawrence* of Lübeck, laden with a cargo of salt.[2] To Sir William Alexander had been granted in May, 1627, Admiralty jurisdiction over his American territories with power to seize vessels belonging to the King of Spain, the Infanta Isabella, or others, His

---

[1] On 29th August, 1626, " the provist, baillies, and counsell, considdering the many dissordouris, tumultis, and commotiounes maid within this burght be the souldeouris now present within the samen, levied be Colonell Macky and his capitaines for his Majesties service in the pairtes of Germanie, and how that some of the nichtbouris of the toune hes bein in great dainger for not haveing armes reddie upoun thame the tyme of the saids tumultis. Thairfoir and to the effect the nichtbouris may be upon thair gaird whan any sic tumultis shall fall out heirefter, and for the better repressing thairoff: Ordaines the haill inhabitantes of this burght fensible persones, to wear thair swordis about thame at all occasiounes whan thay walk on the streattes, so long as the saids souldioures remaines within the toune: As lykways ordaines both merchandis and craftsmen to have long wapins in thair boothes to the effect they may be moir reddie to assist the magistrates for repressing such insolencies in tyme cumming...." *Extracts from Records of Burgh of Aberdeen*, 1625-1642 (Burgh Rec. Socy.), p. 8.

[2] *Reg. P.C.*, Second Series, vol. lv. p. 375.

Majesties enemies.[1] The *St. Lawrence* was charged with carrying contraband of war, and was adjudged a lawful prize by the Scottish Court of Admiralty. It is not an unwarrantable assumption that the cargo of salt which Alexander's skipper offered some months later for sale at Dumbarton [2] had at one time been stowed beneath the hatches of the Lübeck trader. After the lapse of several years the owner of the *St. Lawrence* complained, through the magistrates of Lübeck, ruefully but vainly to the Scots Privy Council, that his ship had carried no contraband, and that those members of the ship's company who could have effectively refuted the charge had been landed by William Alexander on a remote part of the French coast.[3]

VII.

Leaving for the present Alexander's little fleet at its northern base under the shadow of Dumbarton Rock, let us consider what was in reality the vital question of the Nova Scotia scheme—the significance of his designs on Acadie from the standpoint of those who were interested in French colonial expansion. The validity of the English claim to the region the French did not admit, and despite the destruction of the "habitation" at Port Royal by Argall, the French pioneers did not abandon Acadie.[4] One section of these pioneers, under Claude de St. Etienne, Sieur de la Tour, and his son Charles, did indeed cross the Bay of Fundy and set up a fortified post at the mouth of the Penobscot River. But de Poutrincourt's son, Biencourt, with the rest of his company, clung to the district round Port Royal, wandering at first amid the Acadian forest, and later succeeding in rendering habitable once more the buildings that had housed the Order of Good Cheer. The death of de Poutrincourt in France in 1615, during civil commotion, left his son in possession of the Acadian seignory. There was at this time a brisk trade between France and the St. Lawrence region, and Biencourt was by no means inclined

---

[1] *Nova Scotia Papers*, p. 41.   [2] *D.B.R.*, 7 Jan., 1628.
[3] *Reg. P.C.*, Second Series, vol. iv. pp. 401-402.
[4] Parkman, *Pioneers of New France*, p. 322.

to take a gloomy view of the prospects of his inheritance. Writing in September, 1618, from Port Royal, " aux Autorités de la Ville de Paris," he suggested the advisability of erecting in Acadie fortified posts which would not only defend the province from incursions of the English, but would also be of service to the fur trade in which the city of Paris was directly interested.[1] Not only was the district around Port Royal in effective French occupation, but on the Atlantic coast, especially in the district around Canseau, there had sprung up a number of sporadic settlements, the homes principally of French and Dutch adventurers. In the presence of these adventurers one writer on Canadian history finds a convincing explanation of why Alexander's second expedition did not attempt to form a settlement.[2]

The expeditions of 1622 and 1623 did not pass without comment on the part of the French Government. In the spring of 1624, the Comte de Tillières, the French ambassador in England, addressed to the British Government a strong remonstrance concerning the English hostilities in Canada, particularly those directed against the Sieur de Poutrincourt (Biencourt), pointing out that such activities might well prove a menace to the friendly relations then existing between France and Britain.[3] The English possessions in America were described, in this memorial, as extending from Virginia to the Gulf of Mexico, and the King of Britain was requested to prohibit his subjects from disturbing the French in their settlements, and especially the Sieur de Poutrincourt in his possessions in those parts. To this remonstrance the British official reply was a complete repudiation of de Poutrincourt's claims to the region in dispute, but a diplomatic desire was expressed to arrive at an amicable understanding with the French in Acadie.[4]

But though the French government thus unequivocally asserted its claim to Acadie, the real centre of French colonial

---

[1] Parkman, *Pioneers of New France*, p. 322, *note* 3.

[2] Kirke, *First Eng. Cong. of Canada*, pp. 58 and 67.

[3] *C.O.* 1/3, No. 13; *Cal. Col.*, i. p. 60. See Appendix A for text of Memorial.

[4] *C.O.* 1/3, No. 14; *Cal.*, vol. i. p. 60.

enterprise by this time was the valley of the St. Lawrence, where had been set up the three trading posts of Tadoussac, Montreal and Three Rivers, and the rock-perched citadel of Quebec. Hither Champlain had been sent by de Monts after the failure of the Acadian venture, and in 1608 the first buildings of Quebec rose on the cliffs above the St. Lawrence. Despite, however, the romantic interest of Champlain's explorations and Indian warfare, the life of the infant colony was by no means either a vigorous or a happy one. The conflicting interests of two powerful commercial companies proved a serious impediment to the progress of the colony. Even when those two companies were amalgamated matters were little better, for the leading men of the United Company proved more intent on the accumulation of profits from the fur trade than on sustaining and strengthening the strategic centre of the colony, the little fort at Quebec, and showed but a faint interest in colonial enterprise in general. In spite of the stipulations concerning the despatch of colonists which were laid down in the charter by which the United Company enjoyed the monopoly of Canadian trade, no serious effort was made to send out settlers.[1]

Such was the state of affairs in New France when Richelieu made good his position as supreme adviser of Louis XIII. Securely entrenched behind their carefully guaranteed privileges, the members of the United Company might well suppose that for a decade at least they could view with little apprehension whatever attitude might be adopted towards them by the new Minister. Little did they realise the character of the man who in 1626 took over the duties of Grand Master, Chief and General Superintendent of the Navigation and Commerce of France. Like some frail fishing craft overwhelmed by a winter gale, the carefully guarded privileges of the United Company went down before the imperious will of the great Cardinal.[2]

In the history of Richelieu's colonial policy one finds a curious parallel to the history of the military fortunes of France in the campaigns of the years immediately succeeding

[1] Biggar, *Early Trading Companies of New France*, chapter vii.
[2] Biggar, p. 132.

her entry into the Thirty Years' War. In each there is the same resolute, clearly defined general policy : in each defeat and disappointment in the early stages due to insufficient expert attention to matters of detail. Among the duties of the Superintendent of Navigation and Commerce was " the consideration of all proposals, articles or treaties in regard to foreign trade or to the formation of companies for home or foreign commence." It was not long after Richelieu had, in the early months of 1627, diverted part of his attention from the many pressing problems of home and foreign politics to questions of commercial policy till it was realised that in trade as in state-craft the Cardinal favoured a policy of centralisation and absolutism. But the proposal to establish at Morbihan in Brittany one great company that should number among its members the leading merchants of France, and to the control of which every department of French trade should be entrusted, failed to win the assent of the Parlement de Paris. Nor did a more prosperous career attend La Compagnie de la Nacelle de St. Pierre Fleurdelisée—a French-Dutch Company planned on a similar grandiose scale. In view of the small success of those all-embracing projects, it was determined to concentrate upon improvement in particular departments of trade and colonisation, and one of the most important results of this more mature policy was the evolution of the Company of New France.[1]

The Company of New France, the formation of which was suggested to Richelieu by the Chevalier de Razilly, who brought to the study of colonial questions knowledge gained from long and varied experience, was the outcome of a policy which had for its leading purpose the strengthening of the French hold on North America.[2] This purpose was to be carried into effect in two ways : Quebec was to be transformed from a frontier outpost to a fortress that could hold the St. Lawrence Valley against any aggression ; the French occupation of the St. Lawrence region and Acadie was to be rendered more effective by the introduction of large numbers of settlers. Thus by a strange juxtaposition of fate the projects of the sanguine visionary who had dreamed of a New Scotland

[1] Biggar, p. 132.   [2] *Ibid.* p. 133.

were brought into conflict with the schemes of the most astute, clear-sighted, and resolute politician of the age. And the interest of this political drama is heightened by the fact that, for not a short season it looked as if the victory lay, not with Richelieu, but with the Laird of Menstrie.

The Company of New France, through which the Cardinal's policy was to be worked out, had a capital of 300,000 livres, subdivided into 100 shares. The grant to the company of many privileges—including twelve titles of nobility—ensured the speedy taking up of these shares. While the earlier traders to New France had been connected mainly with the ports of the Channel or the Bay of Biscay, the Company of New France had its offices in Paris, to which city, indeed, the majority of the shareholders belonged.[1]

Finding that the initial labours of forming a company on such a large scale had been very considerable, the Directors of the Company of New France were inclined to delay the despatch of their first expedition till 1629; moreover, England and France were at war, and though it might be safely assumed that the main English naval activity would be directed in the spring of 1628 to the relief of La Rochelle, the English Channel could not be regarded as altogether free from danger. Such a policy of caution, however, did not commend itself to the eager and resolute spirit of Richelieu, and the work of fitting out a fleet of transports went steadily on throughout the winter of 1627-1628. By April, 1628, the transports, crowded with colonists and laden with stores and ordinance for Quebec and Port Royal, were ready to sail from Dieppe, and a squadron of four warships had been detailed to convoy them across the Atlantic.[2] And during the year that saw the vigorous preparations of the Company of New France, Alexander's two ships had been either lying idle at Dumbarton or engaging in a privateering cruise in home waters. . . .

At the very time, however, when the prospects of the Nova Scotia scheme looked least promising, when Sir William Alexander found his designs seriously menaced by French colonial enterprise, inspired and directed by the indefatigable and undissuadable Richelieu, the Scottish cause received

[1] Biggar, p. 137. [2] *Ibid.*

assistance from a new and altogether unexpected direction. The year 1627, which saw the inception of the Company of New France, witnessed also the outbreak of war between France and Great Britain. The energies of the British navy were, of course, monopolised by the expedition dispatched to act in concert with the Huguenots of La Rochelle. But New France lay open to the attack of any resolute and enterprising privateer. During the winter of 1627-1628, when the royal dockyard at Portsmouth was busy with the preparation of the fleet that was to make the futile attack on the mole at La Rochelle, when Dieppe formed the rendezvous for the transports that were to be convoyed across the Atlantic by de Roquemont's squadron, there was being fitted out in England a fleet of three small privateers that was to shake to its very foundations the French power in Canada.[1]

The guiding spirits of this privateering expedition were an Anglo-French merchant, named Gervase Kirke, and his three sons, David, Lewis and Thomas. Descended from an old Derbyshire family, Gervase Kirke had in his younger days, as a merchant adventurer in London, gained a considerable knowledge of English colonial trade.[2] When later in life he settled down in Dieppe, where he married a Huguenot lady, he must from his residence in the seaport that was the chief starting point for Canadian expeditions, have been well aware of the main trend of the activities of such pioneers as de Monts and Champlain. Bred to the sea, and early noted for their daring and their enterprise, his sons were the very men to

---

[1] *C.O.* 1/6, No. 15; *Cal.*, vol. i. p. 130; Kirke, p. 64. Though the Kirkes were later to find in the Earl of Stirling a powerful opponent, it is clear that Lord Stirling, or at any rate his son Sir William Alexander, had an interest in the expedition fitted out by the Kirkes. *S.P. Col.*, 1574-1660, p. 96; *Crown Office Doquet Bks.*, No. 4, p. 399; Egerton MSS. 2395, f. 25. " Remembraunce concerning the patent granted to Sir William Alexander, George Kirk Esq., Captain Kirke, William Barclay, and Company, for the sole trade unto the Gulfe and River of Canada and for a plantation there, wch is opposed by my Lord Stirling and his sonne the said Sir William Alexander. Imprimis, they alleadge . . . To which wee answer . . . (6) That in this Graunt now made to us Sir William Alexander hath a part with us, so that wee seek not to debarre him, but to strengthen that interest hie hath in it . . . "—*Egerton MSS.* 2395, f. 25.

[2] Kirke, pp. 33-36.

whom colonial adventure with its abundant dangers, but not
less abundant possibilities of renown and reward, was certain
to appeal. It may be surmised that in the Channel seaports
the activities of the Company of New France, which had
ousted from the lucrative Canadian fur-trade the companies
whose shareholders belonged mainly to Rouen and Dieppe,
would be followed with unremitting interest born of impotent
jealousy. In 1627 too, Captain David Kirke, the eldest son
of Gervase, had, it seems, been voyaging in Canadian waters,[1]
and appears to have brought home not only a clear conception
of the commercial possibilities of New France, but also an
intelligent appreciation of the slender hold that had so far
been established by the French on the Valley of the St.
Lawrence. Consequently the outbreak of war between
Britain and France suggested to the enterprising minds of
Gervase Kirke and his sons the possibility of driving the French
from Canada. For this purpose a small company of London
merchants was formed. Three ships were fitted out. The
largest, the *Abigail*, a vessel of some 300 tons, was under the
command of Captain David Kirke; the other two were
commanded by his brothers Lewis and Thomas. Letters of
Marque were obtained empowering the capture and destruction of French ships and of French settlements in Nova
Scotia and in Canada. Ere de Roquemont's convoy had
begun to tail out of the Harbour of Dieppe, the *Abigail* and her
consorts were driving steadily across the Atlantic. The
Elizabethan spirit of adventurous enterprise had again
flared up.

Kirke first resolved to await at Newfoundland the arrival
of the French fleet, but as no enemy appeared the English
squadron passed into the Gulf of St. Lawrence and began to
ascend the river. At Quebec Champlain, after a harassing
winter, was eagerly awaiting the arrival of relief ships from
France. In their stead arrived, to his dismay, two canoes,
one of which bore a wounded refugee from the trading station
at Cape Tourmente, who brought the news of the capture and
destruction of the post by a landing party from the English
fleet. On the following day there arrived a party of Basque

---

[1] *C.O.* 1/5, No. 49; *Cal. Col.*, i. p. 106.

fishermen, captured at Tadoussac by Kirke, and despatched to Champlain with a courteous demand for the surrender of Quebec.

Though the fortress was ill prepared to endure a siege, and though the garrison were on the verge of starvation, Champlain manned his ramparts, and in reply to Kirke's demand returned a courteous but firm refusal. From Quebec Kirke's attention was turned to the lower reaches of the St. Lawrence by news of the approach of de Roquemont's squadron. Setting sail from Tadoussac, he briskly attacked the French warships, overcame them, and captured the transports laden with emigrants, stores and ordnance, for the strengthening of Quebec and Port Royal. He then returned to England. Among the prisoners he took with him were the French Admiral, de Roquemont, and the elder La Tour, who had been captured as he returned from a mission to France, the object of which had been to acquaint the French Government with the plight of the colonists in Acadie.[1]

In France the news of the defeat and total destruction of de Roquemont's fleet caused the utmost consternation. At one blow were dashed to the ground the hopes of the nation that had centred round the efforts of the Company of New France. In Paris the widespread detestation of the Kirkes found significant if somewhat melodramatic expression. The King and his Council condemned the brothers Kirke as public enemies, and gave orders that they should be burned in effigy. The bells of the churches of Paris were set a-tolling: a solemn procession bore through the streets three stout bundles that were supposed to represent the visitors of Gaspé: and in the Place de la Grève, while the leaping flames reduced these effigies to ashes, the popular indignation found an outlet in clamorous vituperation.[2]

In London, as may well be imagined, the tidings of Kirke's success produced a somewhat different effect. Immediately on receipt of the news the merchants of Gervase Kirke's company delegated one of their directors, the Earl of Newburgh, to carry the report to the king and to make a request for " a patent for the sole trade and plantation of these countries."

---

[1] Kirke, pp. 72-78. [2] *Ibid.* p. 79.

This the king at once promised, and declared that when Kirke should arrive with his prizes and with full details of what he had accomplished, the formal grant of the patent would be carried through.[1]

But at this point Gervase Kirke's project found its progress menaced by an antagonism more subtle but more serious than that which his privateers had encountered on the St. Lawrence. In opposition to the request of the London merchants for a patent, Sir William Alexander claimed " a sole right to the trade and plantation òf these countries upon a grant from His Majesty under the great seal of the Kingdom of Scotland."[2] Alexander's province as defined by his charter of 1621, and its various ratifications, did not, as a matter of fact, include any part of the St. Lawrence region beyond Gaspé. Of the precise limits of the Alexandrian domains, and of the scope of Alexander's trading rights, the London merchants were not ignorant.[3] They knew, however, that Alexander stood high in the king's favour.. The Scottish Privy Council, too, petitioned the king not to be neglectful of Alexander's interests.[4] It was therefore deemed expedient by Gervase Kirke and his partners to come to an understanding with Sir William. They offered him " that in the right and interest of the Crown of Scotland he should possess for a sole plantation of his nation all La Cadia and all the country and coasts within the Gulf of Canada on both sides of the river till they arrive within two leagues of Tadoussac; which is much more than half of that which is already planted by the French, and a great part of it adjoining to New Scotland, reserving upon all those coasts free trade and harbours to the mixed company and colony of English and Scotch who should undertake the rest."[5] In addition to this ample concession it was proposed to allow Sir William an interest in the revenues derived from the remainder of the St. Lawrence territory, and a suggestion was also put forward for the plantation of an Anglo-Scotch colony above Tadoussac.

[1] *Couper MSS., Hist. MSS. Com.*, 12th Rep., App. i. p. 376.
[2] *Ibid.*   [3] *Egerton MSS.* 2395, f. 25.
[4] *Nova Scotia Papers*, p. 46.
[5] *Hist. MSS. Com.*, 12th Report, App. i. p. 376.

It was substantially upon the lines of this proposed accommodation that matters were finally adjusted.[1] The Anglo-Scotch Company was formed in the winter of 1628-1629, and energetic preparations were at once set on foot for carrying to its conclusion the work of conquest begun during the preceding summer by Captain David Kirke. Under him there sailed from Gravesend on March 25th, 1629, a fleet of six small warships and three privateers.[2] Using Tadoussac as a base, the British commander sent two ships, commanded by his brothers Lewis and Thomas, on to Quebec. Cut off from communication with France, hemmed in by the hostile Iroquois, with his small garrison sadly wasted by famine and disease, Champlain had now no alternative but to surrender. On 20th August, 1629, Captain Lewis Kirke took possession of the fortress, and to the roll of drums and a salute of musketry and gunfire from the ramparts and the warships, the flag of England was hoisted on the citadel of New France.[3]

. . . .

In the summer of 1629 Sir William Alexander's eldest son, Sir William the younger, had in vessels belonging to the Anglo-Scotch Company carried a company of colonists to Acadie. On the 1st July, 1629, sixty colonists under Lord Ochiltree were landed on the eastern coast of Cape Breton Island: thereafter Alexander sailed for the Bay of Fundy and landed the remainder of the company of colonists at Port Royal. The first Scottish settlement of Nova Scotia was thus carried out in the summer of 1629.[4]

VIII.

The history of the Scots settlement at Port Royal during the few years of its existence (1629-1632) is exceedingly obscure. Of the ingenious and persistent efforts made by Sir William Alexander and his royal master to foster the colonisation of Nova Scotia many traces have come down to us; of the political cross-currents that ultimately wrecked

---

[1] *Hist. MSS. Cam.*, 12th Report, App. i. p. 377.   [2] Kirke, p. 81.
[3] Kingsford, *Hist. of Canada*, vol. i. p. 96.
[4] For discussion of evidence regarding date, see Appendix B.

the enterprise we are also fully cognisant. But the incidents of the Atlantic voyage, the daily life and labours of the Scottish settlers as they tilled the soil or built their dwellings and their fortalice, are known to us only in the dim light of surmise. To turn from the story of the Scots occupation of Port Royal to that of the earlier French settlements in the same region is like viewing in the full light of day a landscape that one has seen before only in the grey mirk of early morning. Now and then, however, when the mist clears away for a brief interval, in one direction or another, a glimpse of some feature of the landscape is obtained. A succession of such glimpses constitutes the history of Port Royal during the years that it formed a Scottish colony.

There is no reason to doubt that the ships in which Sir William Alexander the Younger brought his colonists to Port Royal formed part of the fleet of six privateers and three pinnaces that sailed from Gravesend on 25th March, 1629, under Captain David Kirke. On the arrival of this fleet in Canadian waters, part of it was detached with orders to proceed to Nova Scotia.[1] Of the incidents connected with the visit to the shores of Nova Scotia we have what is practically an official account in the Egerton Manuscript, entitled "William Alexander's Information touching his Plantation at Cape Breton and Port Royal."

"... The said Sir William resolving to plant in that place sent out his son Sir William Alexander this spring with a colonie to inhabite the same who arriving first at Cap-britton did finde three shipps there, whereof one being a Barque of 60 Tunnes it was found that the owner belonged to St. Sebastian in Portugall, and that they had traded there contrary to the power graunted by his Majestie for wch and other reasons according to the process which was formallie led, he the said Sir William having chosen the Lord Oghiltrie and Monsieur de la Tour to be his assistants adjudged the barque to be lawfull prize and gave a Shallop and other necessaries to transport her Companie to other shipps upon that Coast, according to their owne desire, as for the other two which he found to be french shipps he did no wise trouble them.

[1] Kingsford, vol. i. p. 95.

"Thereafter having left the Lo. Oghiltree with some 60 or so English who went with him to inhabit there, at Cap-britton, the said Sir William went from thence directly to Port Royall wch he found (as it had been a long time before) abandoned and without signe that ever people had been there, where he hath seated himself and his Companie according to the warrant granted unto him by his Matie of purpose to people that part." [1]

No opposition was encountered from the French. Claude de la Tour (son of Monsieur de la Tour, Alexander's "assistant"), to whom the seignory of Port Royal had passed on the death of Biencourt, had, after having been driven in 1626 from his fort at the mouth of the Penobscot River, concentrated the remainder of the Port Royal colony at a new station which he had established at the south-eastern extremity of Acadie, in the neighbourhood of Cape Sable.

The Indians of Acadie entered into friendly relations with the new settlers, and during the summer Port Royal became the depot for a thriving trade in furs. When at the close of the season the company's vessels sailed for home, Sir William Alexander remained at Port Royal to share with his colonists whatever trials the coming winter might have in store. To the hardships endured in the course of his colonial experiences has been attributed his death in the prime of manhood.

With the fleet that sailed from Port Royal in the autumn of 1629 there travelled to Britain an Indian chief, the Sagamore Segipt, his wife, and his sons. The ostensible object of the chief's journey was to do homage to the King of Britain and invoke his protection against the French. Landing at Plymouth, the Indian party broke their journey to the capital by a short stay in Somersetshire. There they were hospitably entertained. "The savages took all in good part, but for thanks or acknowledgment made no sign or expression at all." [2]

Another emissary from Port Royal to Britain found himself subjected to attention that might well have disturbed even the taciturn dignity of the Indian chief. Sir George Home

[1] Egerton, 2395, f. 23.
[2] Birch, *Court and Times of Charles I.*, vol. ii. p. 60 (quoted Rogers).

of Eckills, who had sought to save himself from a pertinacious creditor by joining Sir William Alexander's expeditions—he appears to have sailed with Alexander both in 1628 and 1629—had been despatched by the Master of Stirling to Scotland to obtain stores and enlist recruits for the Nova Scotia colony. The indefatigable creditor, however, threatened Sir George with horning, and, it was alleged, did so interfere with his activities on behalf of the colony, that the sorely tried agent besought the protection of the Scots Privy Council. He was granted a license permitting him to go about his business till the last day of April, 1630.[1] On 26th May, 1630, his creditor complained to the Privy Council that " lately the said Sir George, pretending his want of liberty to repair openly to the Burgh of Edinburgh ... obtained a protection from their Lordships, under cover of which he conveyed himself and wife and children to Nova Scotia *animo remanendi*." [2]

The year 1629, which saw the settlement of the Scots at Port Royal, witnessed also considerable activity in Scotland on behalf of the colony. Eager and optimistic as ever, Alexander saw in the aid to be derived from his association with the English merchant adventurers the means whereby his long deferred hopes might be realised, and his imagination showed him the sails of the ships bearing him wealth from his distant domains. His care now was to establish a commercial haven for ships engaged in transatlantic traffic. Like William Paterson, almost seventy years later, Alexander clearly saw the importance of the Clyde Estuary in any scheme of American trade. On 11th April, 1629, King Charles made a grant to Alexander of land at Largs to enable him to establish a port for colonial traffic.[3]

[1] *Reg. P.C.S.*, New Series, vol. iii. p. 488.   [2] *Ibid.* p. 543.

[3] Rex, pro se et tanquam princeps et senescallus Scotiae—pro magnis servitiis sibi et patri suo prestitis per D. Gulielmum Alexander de Menstrie militem principalem suum secretariun Scotiae et ejus laboribus in fundanda colonia in Nova Scotia et Canada et quia terrē infrascriptē idoneē fuerunt ubi fieret emporium *lie staple* pro commercio cum dicta regione—cum consensu ... concessit et quitteclamavit dicto D. Guil. hereditibus ejus masc. et assignatis partem terrarum nuncapat. the Largis and Largismure, una cum villa et oppido de Largis, terris, morris, carbonibus, montibus et communiis eidem spectantibus in balliatu de Cunynghame,

The spot chosen by Alexander for his projected port was one invested with historic interest. It was on the shore at Largs that Hakon's galleys, swept landwards by an autumn gale, had shattered their prows; and it was on the narrow strip of level ground, between the Largs hills and the sea, that the Norse warriors had been decisively beaten by the levies of King Alexander III. But as the site of a seaport Largs had little to recommend it. It had comparatively slight depth of water. It was open to the full sweep of the south-west gales from the Atlantic. It was shut off by the steep escarpment of the Kilbarchan Hills, both from the plains of Ayrshire and from the lower portion of Strathclyde.

The interest shown by King Charles in Sir William Alexander's colonial schemes naturally did not abate after the actual settlement of the Scots at Port Royal. In the letters sent by the king to the Scots Privy Council during the year 1629 appear many traces of the keen desire on the part of Charles to second the efforts of Sir William. On 7th June the Earl of Menteith, the President of the Council, was instructed to negotiate with those who had no heritable office but were desirous of a title of honour, and to find out the number of men that could be provided for the plantation of New Scotland by each of these aspirants for distinction. At this time, too, the President was invited to offer suggestions regarding any other expedients that might be employed to increase the number of baronets.[1] There is no evidence, however, to connect the Earl of Menteith in any way with the decision conveyed to the Council in the course of a royal despatch dated 17th November, 1629: "We have been pleased to authorise and allow . . . the said Leivetennant and Baronettes, and everie one of them, and thare heires, male, to weare and carry about their neckis, in all time coming, ane orange tauney silk ribbone, whairon shalt hing pendant in a

---

vic de Air—quam erexit in liberam baroniam de Largis: cum libertate burgum infra aliquam partem dictarum bondarum condendi, portum et navium stationem *lie hewin* aedificandi: quem erexit in liberum burgum baroniae, Burgum de Largis nuncupand.—*Reg. Mag. Sig. Scot.*, vol. 1620-1633, p. 476, No. 1404.

[1] Menteith Letter, *Hist. MSS. Cam.*, 3rd Report, Appendix, p. 401.

scutchion argent a saltoirë azeur, thairon ane inscutcheone of the armes of Scotland, with ane imperiall crown above the scutchone, and encircled with this motto—' Fax mentis honestae gloria.' "[1] The hand is the hand of King Charles, but the voice is the voice of the author of the *Encouragement to Colonies*.

Of the royal correspondence of this year dealing with Nova Scotia, the most interesting item, both from the standpoint of Scottish and of colonial history, is the despatch of 17th October : "... Whereas our trustie and well beloved Sir William Alexander, our Secretarie hath agreet with some of the heads of the Chief Clannes of the Highlands of that our Kingdome and with some other persones, for transporting themselves and thare followers, to setle themselves into New Scotland, as we doe very much approve of that course for advancing the said plantatione, and for deburdening that our kingdome of that race of people which in former times hade bred soe many troubles ther ; soe since that purpose may very much import the publick good and quiet thereof, Wee are most willing that you assist the same by all fair and lawfull ways...." The despatch then proceeds to direct the Privy Council to arrange for "a voluntarie contributione" in connection with this scheme.[2]

In the summer of 1630 the settlers at Port Royal received a useful reinforcement in the form of a party of colonists under the elder La Tour. Captured by Kirke in 1628, La Tour had been carried to England, and it may well have been his knowledge of Acadie combined with a complaisant disposition that soon advanced him to high favour at Court. He had sailed with Sir William Alexander the Younger to Nova Scotia in 1629.[3] His experiences during this expedition seem to have made him decide to throw in his lot with the Scots, for soon after his return to England there were drawn up, in rough outline, on 16th October, 1629, " Articles d'accord entre le Chevalier Guillaume Alexandre, siegn^r de Menstrie Lieu^t de la Nouvelle Ecosse en Amerique par sa Majeste de

---

[1] *Nova Scotia Papers*, pp. 49-50.
[2] Menteith Letters, *Hist. MSS. Cam.*, 3rd Report, Appendix, p. 401.
[3] Egerton, 2395, f. 23.

la Grande Bretagne, et le Chevalier Claude de St. Etienne, sieg^{nr} de la Tour et Claude de St. Etienne son filz et le Chevalier Guillaume Alexandre filz dud^t seig^{nr} Alexandre cy dessus nomé . . . tant pour le merite de leur persones que pour leur assistance à la meilleure recognaissance du pays." [1]

It was not, however, till 30th April, 1630, that the agreement between Alexander and La Tour was definitely signed. "The s^d Sir Claud of Estienne being present accepting and stipulating by these presents for his s^d son Charles now absent, so much for the merit of their persons as for their assistance in discovering better the said country." La Tour obtained two baronies, the barony of St. Etienne and the barony of La Tour, "which may be limited between the said K^t of La Tour and his son, if they find it meet, equally." [2]

But neither the dignity conferred on him nor the wide stretch of territory that accompanied it appealed particularly to the "s^d son Charles now absent." When the two ships that carried La Tour and his party to Acadie anchored off Fort St. Louis in the neighbourhood of Cape Sable, La Tour found his son staunch in allegiance to France. The paternal arguments having failed to influence the Commandant of Fort St. Louis, La Tour made an attempt to storm the Fort, but was repulsed. He then sailed on to Port Royal.

In the autumn of 1630 Sir William Alexander sailed for Britain, leaving in command at Port Royal Sir George Home, who in the early summer of that year had "conveyed himself and wife and children to Nova Scotia *animo remanendi*." [3] In the summer of 1631 a fleet despatched by the Anglo-Scottish Company landed a band of colonists and some head of cattle at Port Royal.[4] Nor were continued evidences of royal support lacking : in the spring of 1631 the Scots Privy Council had received an assurance from the king that he was solicitous for the welfare of the Nova Scotia colony; a little later intimation was received that the furnishing of assistance to the colony would be rewarded by the grant of baronetcies.[5]

[1] Egerton, 2395, f. 17.
[2] *Ibid.* 2395, f. 31.
[3] *Reg. P.C.S.*, New Series, vol. iii. p. 543.
[4] Biggar, p. 158.
[5] Earl of Stirling's *Register of Royal Letters*, pp. 516 and 518.

IX.

Yet on the 10th July, 1631, Sir William Alexander, now Viscount Stirling, received from King Charles instructions to arrange for the abandonment of Port Royal: the fort built by his son was to be demolished, and the colonists and their belongings were to be removed, " leaveing the boundis altogidder waist and unpeopled as it was at the tyme when your said sone landed first to plant ther." [1]

Like a later, more ambitious, and more tragic Scottish colonial scheme, the Nova Scotia enterprise was to be sacrificed to the exigencies of English Royal policy. Indeed, the forces which were to bring about the ruin of the Scots settlement at Port Royal had been at work practically from the time of its foundation. Quebec, taken almost three months after the signing of the Treaty of Suza, which in April, 1629, terminated the hostilities between England and France, could not well be withheld from the French, though the Kirkes urged King Charles strongly to hold to his conquest: the place was well provided with arms and ammunition: " soe if it please his Matie to keep it " runs their assertion, " wee doe not care what frenche or any other can doe thoe they have a 100 sayle of ships and 10,000 men." [2] To the Scottish mind, however, the Treaty contained nothing prejudicial to Port Royal: " this business of Port royall cannot be made Lyable to the articles of the peace, seeing there was no act of hostilitie comitted thereby, a Colony only being planted upon his Maties ground." [3] Yet the French ambassador demanded both the restoration of Port Royal and Quebec.

This claim on the part of the French to Port Royal stirred the Scots to remonstrance. " Wee have understood," wrote the Privy Council to King Charles on 9th September, 1630, " by yor Maties Letter of the title pretended by the French to the Land of New Scotland: which being communicated to the states at their last meeting and they considering the benefit arising to this kingdom by the accession of these lands to this Crown and that yor Matie is bound in honor carefully to provide that none of yor Majesties subjects doe suffer in

[1] Rogers, vol. i. p. 131. [2] C.O. 1/6, No. 38. [3] C.O. 1/5, No. 102, i.

that which for yor Ma^{ts} service and to their great charge they have warrantably undertaken and successfully followed out, Wee have thereupon presumed by order from the States to make remonstrance thereof to your Matie, And on their behalf to be humble supplicants, desiring your Matie that yor Matie would be graciously pleased seriously to take to hart the maintenance of yor royall right to these lands, And to protect the undertakers in the peaceable possession of the same, as being a businesse which toucheth yor Ma^{ts} honor; the credit of this yor native kingdome, and the good of yor subjects interested therein, Remitting the particular reasons fit to be used for defence of yor Maties right to the relation of Sir William Alexander yor Ma^{s} Secretarie who is entrusted therewith...." [1]

The "particular relation" of Sir William [2] puts the Scots case clearly and emphatically. After tracing the history of Acadie before the Scottish settlement the "relation" points out how the Scots settlement had been followed by the visit of the Indian chief—Sagamore Segipt—to this country. "So that his Matie is bound in honour to maintain them both in regard of his subjects that have planted there upon his warrant and of the promises that he made to the Commissioners of the natives that came to him from thence.... This business of Port Royall cannot be made Lyable to the articles of the peace, seeing there was no act of hostilities comitted thereby, a Colony being planted upon his Maties owne ground, according to a Patent granted by his Maties late deare father and his Mat^{s} self, having as good right thereunto as to any part of the continent, and both the patent and the possession taken thereupon in the time of his Maties late dear father, as is set downe at length in the voyages written by Purchas. But neither by that possession nor by the subsequent plantation hath any thing beene taken from the frenche whereof they had any right at all, nor yet any possession for the time, and what might have been done either before the warre or since the warre without a breach of peace cannot be justly complained upon for being done at that time."

That these representations were not altogether without

[1] *C.O.* 1/5, No. 102. [2] *C.O.* 1/5, No. 102, i.

effect on the king is evident from the draft of a dispatch " to o^r trusty and well beloved Sr. Isaac Wake, Knight, our Ambassador resident with the French King." This dispatch belongs to a comparatively late period in the negotiations, when the question of the payment of the Queen's portion money was under discussion : " . . . we have formerly consented and still continue our purpose and resolution that the one, that is Quebec, shalbe restorit and from the other such of our subjects as are there planted shall retyre, leaving these parts in the same state as before they appeared : wch wee doe not out of ignorance as if wee did not understand how little wee are thereunto obliged by the last treaty . . . but out of an affection and desyre to complye with our good brother the King of France in all things that may friendly and reasonably, though not rightly and duly be demanded from us." [1]

The story of the negotiations for the restoration of Port Royall to France is long and complicated.[2] The British diplomatists were inclined to leave the question as "a disputed point " to be decided apart from the general post-bellum settlement. To the French this proposal did not commend itself. Their unequivocal demand was for the surrender without delay of Port Royal " as both agreeable to reason and to the treaty itself." To Richelieu, keenly interested in the development of the French navy, Acadie and its proximity to the great fishing grounds of the West assumed importance from its possibilities as a training ground for a race of seamen. Nor could he have been ignorant of its strategic importance. Moreover, French prestige demanded that a territory the French claims to which had always been strongly asserted [3] should not be allowed to remain in the hands of interloping foreigners. The English representatives in Paris were much impressed by the strong attitude adopted by the French. By it, indeed, they were more than a little puzzled : as far as they could gather all that the French had ever received from

[1] Harleian, 1760, f. 11.

[2] Biggar, pp. 151-165 : Parkman, *Pioneers of France*, p. 444 ; Kingsford, vol. i. pp. 105-109 ; C.O. 1/5, 102, 102, i. ; C.O. 1/6, 38, 39 ; Harleian, 1760, ff. 10711 ; Egerton, 2395, ff. 19-25.

[3] *Vide* Appendix A.

Acadie had been a few yearly cargoes of beaver skins and elk skins. Was it worth while to risk a recurrence of hostilities for such an unproductive province?

And so from year to year the negotiations dragged on, interrupted now by the pressure of other questions of Richelieu's intricate and far-reaching foreign policy, now by the difficulties experienced by the plenipotentiaries who had to chase after the French king from chateau to chateau. In the persistence of the French demand for a concession which, it might plausibly be argued, went beyond the terms of the treaty of Suza,[1] King Charles saw an opportunity that might be turned to his advantage. Of the dowry of Queen Henriette Marie one half had been paid at the time of her marriage; the other money amounting to 400,000 crowns, due in 1626, had not yet been paid: the demand of Port Royal might be turned to account to exact a reciprocal advantage in the way of a monetary concession from France: "in balance, if not in contract, against the porcon money is the rendition of Quebec in Canada . . . and the retyring from Port Royal."[2] Finally the question at issue was narrowed down to the "the retyring from Port Royal." King Charles was careful to impress on his agent in France that all vulgar huckstering was to be avoided in regard to the balance of the dowry: De Vic, the English agent, was warned not "to make tender of his Majesties giving contentment in the point of Port Royal by way of bargain, which were a merchandly proceeding and in no way becoming negotiations betwixt Princes":[3] if, however, the French king proved complaisant in the matter of the dowry, "Port Royall should not breed any interruption to a total agreement."[4]

These instructions enjoining delicacy in discussion of the Port Royal business were penned by Secretary Dorchester on 2nd March, 1631. The instructions issued to Viscount Stirling for the abandonment of Port Royal bear the date 10th July, 1631. But the matter was not finally settled until nine months more had passed. Alexander renewed his protest against the surrender of his settlement to France.[5]

[1] C.O. 1, 102, i.; Harleian, 1760, f. 11. [2] Harleian, 1760, f. 11.
[3] Quoted Biggar, p. 156. [4] Ibid. [5] C.O. 1/6, 56.

But the financial needs of the king were pressing; the problem of carrying on the government of the country without supplies from Parliament was one of unending difficulty; the army and the navy were mutinous from lack of pay. The balance of the marriage portion offered a welcome if temporary alleviation of pressing difficulties, and in March, 1632, King Charles agreed to the terms of the Treaty of St. Germain-en-Laye. On the St. Lawrence the British garrison evacuated the rock-perched citadel, from before which, sixty years later, the fleet of Sir William Phips was to retire, baffled and discomfited, and above which the fleur-de-lys was to wave until Wolfe should climb the Heights of Abraham. At Port Royal the Chevalier de Razilly, whose ingenious mind had suggested to Richelieu the formation of the Company of New France, received from the Scottish commandant the surrender of the little colony established three brief years before.

. . . .

Despite the failure of his Nova Scotia scheme, Sir William Alexander did not abandon his interest in colonial problems. In January, 1634-1635, Sir William, now Earl of Stirling, and his son the Master of Stirling, were admitted Councillors and Patentees of the New England Company.[1] On the 22nd April, 1635, the Earl of Stirling received from the " Councell of New England in America beinge assembled in publique Courte " a grant of " All that part of the Maine Land of New England aforesaid, beginninge from a certain place called or known by the name of Saint Croix next adjoininge to New Scotland in America aforesaid, and from thence extendinge alonge the Sea Coast into a certain place called Pemaquid, and soe upp the River thereof to the furthest head of the same as it tendeth northward, and extendinge from thence att the nearest unto the River of Kinebequi, and so upwards alonge by the shortest course which tendeth unto the River of Canada, from henceforth to be called and knowne by the name of the Countie of Canada. And also all that Island or Islands heretofore comonly called by the severall name or names of Matowack or Longe Island, and hereafter

[1] C.O. 1/8, No. 44.

to be called by the name of the Isle of Sterlinge. . . .[1] Sir William sent out no more colonists: he was fully occupied with the stormy politics of Old Scotland. Long Island did not change its name. But the earliest settlers on Long Island bought their lands from James Farrell, who acted as Deputy for the Earl of Stirling.[2]

[1] *C.O.* 1/8, No. 56.   [2] *C.O.* 1/10, Nos. 25 and 34.

CHAPTER III

NEW GALLOWAY

I.

IF Sir William Alexander was essentially a man of contemplation who became by misadventure, as it were, a man of action—one who " was born a Poet, and aimed to be a King; therefore would he have his royal title from King James, who was born a King and aimed to be a Poet " [1]—his coadjutor in his earliest colonising efforts, Sir Robert Gordon of Lochinvar, was from his youth to his latest days a man of action— and of very decided action. Endowed with great physical strength and mental vigour—*excelsi corporis robore, et animi magnitudine in omni aetate conspicuus viguerat* [2]—Lochinvar soon attracted the notice of King James the Sixth for turbulence, in an age that was not remarkable for docility. In the summer of 1601 his father, Sir John Gordon of Lochinvar, was ordered to present the young Laird, his cautioners, and servants before the Privy Council : the servants were to answer " for their accompanying and assisting of Sir Robert Gordoun, Younger, of Lochinvar, in his persute of the Laird of Barnbarro in his hous, for convocatioun of our lieges in weirlyke maner and for beiring and weiring of pistolettis, prohibite to be borne or worne be our lawes." [3]

Lochinvar's physical prowess, if it did lead to official reprobation on the part of King James, appealed strongly to the youthful instincts of Prince Henry : *Unde singularem*

[1] Scot of Scotstarvet.
[2] R. Johnstone, *Historia*, p. 714. (Quoted *Nova Scotia Papers*, p. 109.)
[3] *Register Scots Privy Council*, vol. xiii. p. 391.

gratiam apud magnanimum Principem Henricum promeruerat.[1] During the years that the Laird of Menstrie was advancing himself in the royal favour by devotion to the Muses, Lochinvar was equally conspicuous at Court through his skill in arms : *solenni Armorum exercitatione, in Aula victor evaserat; ac premium meritae palmae tulerat.*[2] From the hands of the Princess Elizabeth he received on Twelfth Night, 1609-10, a prize he had gained at the tilting match—Prince Henry's Barriers.[3]

Despite his prestige at Court, the life of the courtier does not seem to have appealed to Lochinvar. His frank, simple, vigorous mind viewed with contempt the ignoble shifts to which some of the less opulent members of the Court of King James were constrained to descend. Years after, when his days as a courtier were but a memory, indignation at the less worthy aspects of such a life could inspire his ingenuous pen to noble scorn : " Then, who would live at home idle (or think in him selfe any worth to live) onlie to eate, drinke, and sleepe, and so to die ? or by consuming that carelesslie, which their predecessors hath got worthilie ? or, for beeing descended noblie, pyne with the vaine vaunt of kinred in penurie ? or (to maintaine a sillie show of braverie) toyle out the heart, soule, and time baselie, by shiftes, trickes, cardes, or dyce ? or by relating newes of others actions, Sharke here or there for a Dinner or Supper ? deceiving his friends by faire promises and dissimulation, in borrowing where he never intendeth to pay ? offending the Lawes, surfeiting with excesse : burthening his countrie, abusing himselfe, despairing in want, and then cousening his kinred ? although it is seene what honours the world hath yet, and what affluence of all things ; for such as will seeke and worthilie deserve them. Heere were courses for Gentle-men (and such as would be so reputed) more suting their qualities than begging from their Princes generous disposition the labours of his other subjects."[4]

Lochinvar's acquaintance with the decorum of the Court does not seem in any way to have subdued the vehemence of

---

[1] R. Johnstone, *Historia*, p. 714.   [2] *Ibid.*
[3] *Nova Scotia Papers*, p. 107.
[4] Lochinvar's *Encouragements for New Galloway.*

his spirit, for early in 1611 he was " fyned in ane thousand merkis, my Lord Hereis in fyve hundreth merkis." [1] From this point until the time when, a decade later, he began to share the colonising labours of the Laird of Menstrie, the Privy Council had no occasion to concern themselves with the activities of Lochinvar. But both from the tone of his *Encouragements to New Galloway*, and also from his record of public service in the years immediately following 1621, it may be presumed that the ten years preceding his colonising activities were occupied in energetic and devoted attention to the work that fell to the lot of a country gentleman of patriotic spirit and conscientious mind.

In November, 1621, Cape Breton Island—part of the original grant bestowed on the Laird of Menstrie—was allotted to Lochinvar and his second son, Robert, in order to be formed into the Province of New Galloway.[2] At a later period Lochinvar's eldest son John, afterwards first Viscount Kenmure, was closely associated with his father's colonial schemes. For the appearance of Robert's name in the charter of 8th November, 1631, two explanations are possible. In the first place Lochinvar may have intended to emphasise the importance of colonial enterprise in affording a career to younger members of a gentleman's family: the fact that " wee have not such occasions, and uses at home for the Brethren, and second sonnes of our houses to get them preferment as of old," is regarded by Lochinvar in his *Encouragements* as one of the " three things that troubleth our estates that wee cannot live as our Predecessoures did before us." In the second place, it is highly probable that in 1621 John Gordon was not in Britain. Educated abroad, John Gordon, after the completion of his studies, resided for some time at St. Jean d'Angely,[3] in the household of Mr. John Welsh, one of the Presbyterian divines exiled by James for having, in despite of the King's command, taken part in the General Assembly at Aberdeen in 1605. The fact that in the year 1622 Mr. Welsh addressed to King James a petition in which permission to emigrate to Nova Scotia was suggested as an

---

[1] *Reg. Sco. P.C.*, vol. xiii. p. 618.
[2] *Nova Scotia Papers*, Charters, p. 16.   [3] *Dict. N.B.*

alternative to permission to return to Scotland may certainly imply that knowledge of the Nova Scotia projects had penetrated to St. Jean d'Angely through the medium of the correspondence of John Gordon, then a young man of twenty-one.

Having received an ample grant of territory and the usual accumulation of feudal powers and privileges over his distant domains, Lochinvar was not the man to delay his preparations for the effective occupation of New Galloway. "Knowing that the chief commendation of vertue consisteth in action "— he says in his preface of 1625, " to the Adventurers, favourers, and well-willers of the enterprise for the inhabiting, and planting in Cape Briton, now New Galloway in America "—" I have resolved a practice, and to trace the footsteppes of those heroic forerunners, whose honourable actions shall ever live upon Earth." He was equally resolute three years earlier. In the summer of 1622 he had two ships fitting out at Beaumaris in Anglesey,[1] which he had chosen as the base for his expedition. Winter interrupted these preparations. They were resumed next summer, but with no more definite result. In view of the resolution and energy of Lochinvar's character, and of the important part he played at this time in the public life of Scotland, such a discrepancy between intention and attainment certainly calls for comment. The circumstances which crippled the activities of Lochinvar were exactly similar to those by which Sir William Alexander had been hampered. The season 1622-1623 proved to be one of extraordinary dearth,[2] and provisions naturally became very scarce and very expensive. Propagandists of colonial enterprise, again, were met in Galloway by a disappointing lack of enthusiasm on the part of the Scots, and even by expressions of frank incredulity.[3] Finally, the opening campaigns of the

[1] Biggar, pp. 122, 123. [2] *Reg. P.C. Sco.*, vol. xiii. p. 257.
[3] Alexander's *Encouragements*, p. 33.
To arouse interest and to remove this ignorant prejudice were the twin objects of Lochinvar's *Encouragements*: "The chiefe (then) and the farthest point," he declares in his epistle dedicatory, "that my intention shall seek to arrive at; shall be to remove that unbeliefe, which is so grounded in the minds of men, to discredite most noble and profitable endevoures with distrust; and, first, to shake off their colourable pretences

Thirty Years' War, and the renewal of the war between Spain and Holland, held out to adventurous Scots the prospects of congenial employment in Central Europe and the Netherlands: Lochinvar, ever alive to the practical questions of his day, does not neglect the influences of European warfare on his projects: " Bee wee so farre inferiour to other Nations," he asks indignantly, " or our Spirites so farre dejected from our ancient Predecessoures, or our minds so upon spoyle, pyracie, or other villanie, as to serve the Portugale, Spaniard, Dutch, French, or Turk (as to the great hurte of Europe too manie do) rather than our God, our King, our Countrie, and ourselves? excusing our idleness, and our base complaynts by want of employment? when heere is such choyse of all sorts, and for all degrees in this plantation."

An important commentary on Lochinvar's colonising activities is furnished by a consideration of some of the other questions that engaged his attention at this time. In October, 1622, he was summoned by the Privy Council to attend a conference to discuss economic problems connected with the exportation of wool.[1] In the following January he attended, as one of the representatives of Nithsdale and Galloway, the conference " anent the propositioun made by his Majesty for sending of commissionaris to England, to confer, resoun, treate and conclude upon some goode way how the whole woll of Scotland not draped and wrought at home mycht be send to England, and sauld thair and no quhair els," and sat with delegates from other parts of Scotland in the Laich Counselhous of Edinburgh."[2] In April, 1623, King James intimated to the Scots Privy Council his wish that " manufactures of all sortis, and speciallie of woll, sould be maid in that our kingdome:[3] On the 6th June, 1623, Lochinvar was summoned by the Privy Council to attend at Edinburgh a conference " anent the establishment of manufactoris."[4] The conference met on 9th July, and a week later Lochinvar was appointed a member of the standing Commission on

of ignorance, and then, if they will not be persuaded to make their self-willes inexcusable."

[1] *Reg. S.P.S.*, vol. xiii. p. 70.   [2] *Ibid.* p. 141.
[3] *Ibid.* p. 235.   [4] *Ibid.* p. 236.

manufactures—a commission appointed in deference to King James's desire to improve existing manufactures in Scotland and to introduce new industries north of the Tweed.[1]

On other points, too, Lochinvar was appealed to by the Council as an authority. The season 1622-23 had been a time of great dearth. To provide temporary relief it had been proposed that a special eleemosynary tax should be levied in each parish on all who were well able to contribute : on 14th June, 1625, Lochinvar's "opinions wer craved anent the poor."[2] The wide range of his interests and his thorough acquaintance with local conditions are testified to by a query propounded to him by the Council a year later. The Council had been discussing "the transportation of unlauchfull personis and guidis too and fra Ireland," and had been furnished by the Border Commissioners and the Commissioners of Western Burghs with a list of ports employed in this traffic : this list comprised a number of small ports in Renfrewshire and Ayrshire and a few in Galloway : the Council resolved "that the Earle of Galloway and Lochinvar be demandit what otheris portis are in Galloway."[3] In July, 1625, Lochinvar was one of a Committee of ten—noblemen and lairds—summoned to give expert advice regarding the state of affairs disclosed by a petition from the Burghs of the Kingdom representing the widespread misery caused by the exportation of wool, and praying for a revival of the Acts prohibiting its export.[4] Still further testimony is borne to Lochinvar's position by his appointment in November, 1625, as one of the Commissioners of the Middle Shires.[5]

A man with such a record might well be expected to do his utmost for the success of any enterprise with which he identified himself, and Gordon's efforts on behalf of Scottish colonial schemes are marked by zeal, enterprise, and pertinacity. Following the example of Sir William Alexander, who had issued his *Encouragement to Colonies* in 1624, Lochinvar published in 1625 at Edinburgh his *Encouragements / For such as shall have intention / to bee Undertakers in the new*

[1] *Reg. S.P.C.*, vol. xiii. p. 300.   [2] *Ibid.* p. 257.
[3] *Ibid.* p. 553.   [4] *Ibid.* New Series, vol. i. p. 75.
[5] *Ibid.* New Series, vol. i. p. 188.

ENCOVRAGEMENTS,
For such as shall have intention
to bee Vnder-takers in the new plantation
of *CAPE BRITON*, now *New Galloway*
in AMERICA,

BY MEE
LOCHINVAR.

*Non nobis nati sumus; aliquid parentes, aliquid
Patria, aliquid cognati postulant.*

EDINBVRGH,
Printed by Iohn Wreittoun. Anno *Dom.* 1625.

plantation / of Cape Breton, now New Galloway / in America / By mee / Lochinvar." The tract is dedicated, "To the Right Worshipfull / Sir William Alexander of Menstrie Knight,/ Master of Requestes for Scotland, / and Lievetenant Generall to his / Majestie in the kingdome / of New Scotland / and To the remnant the noble / men, and knights Baro / nets in Scotland, Undertakers / in the plantations of New Scotland in America."

If the little work shows traces of the influence of Alexander in its references to classical and scriptural history and to the exploits of the Age of Discovery, it resembles Mason's *Discourse* in the precision with which it sets out the shortness of the Atlantic voyage, the topography and the products of the Island, and the lack of danger from the natives. In other respects, too, Lochinvar favours the precise spirit characteristic of Mason : in the *Encouragements* are set out in detail the inducements offered to intending settlers. To ministers he offered a free passage for themselves, their families, and " theire necessaire household stuffe " ; " their entertainment . . . in their whole passage on the ways thither " : maintenance in New Galloway for three years ; the creation of Parishes as soon as possible ; the support of their authority " by causing the transgressours, and contemners of the same bee severlie punished." For " gentlemen and others undertakers," Lochinvar promised to provide free passage for themselves, their families, their household goods, " their provision of victuals for their intertainment . . . together with as much cornes as they shall be able to sowe upon their lands, the first year " : and that they would " bee established and placed in the land : each man according to his qualitie "— the various grants of land being clearly defined. In return Lochinvar would be " contented to receive from everie one of the said undertakers, the thirteenthe parte of that increase and commoditie, which their lands shall have made worthie unto them in the said plantation " : but " each undertaker of the plantation of New Galloway shall bee free from the payment of any duetie for his landes, for all and whole the space of the first three yeares."

These " Offers " were preceded by an analysis of " The Motives which hath induced mee, and may happilie encourage such as have intention to bee Under-takers with Mee in the plantation of New Galloway in America." These motives are thus summarised by Lochinvar in his simple and direct phraseology : " And since I doe propone to myselfe the same ends, which are first for the glorie of my great and mightie God ; next the service of his M. my dread Soveraigne, and my native Countrie ; and last the particular weale and utilitie of my selfe, and such as shall be generouslie disposed adventurers with me : Why shall it be lawfull for others and not for mee : and not as possible and as commodious for mee as unto others of my qualitie ? "

It is one of the interesting features of Lochinvar's tract that he possesses the power of viewing a problem clearly from his own standpoint. After setting out at length his " Motives " and " Offers," he gives in his " Conclusion " an interesting glimpse of the troubles that afflicted the Scottish country gentleman of his day. "There are three thinges that troubleth our estates that wee cannot live as our Predecessoures did before us : First, the prodigalitie, both in ourselves, our servants, and our houses. Secondlie, wee have not such occasions and uses at home for the Brethren, and second sonnes of our houses to get them preferment as of old. Thirdlie, that universall plague of Cautionarie, throughout the whole kingdome, whereby their is such a generall intercourse of distresse, each one for another, as all are linked into it : which all in following out such honourable and honest indevoures abroad might bee remedied. I speake not of the favoured Courteour, nor of the fortunate States-man, for they have their owne blessinges from God, and favour of their Master in their severall places : but unto such, my noble friends, and Countrie-gentlemen, such as myselfe is, and so distressed as I am : and speaking out of mine owne experience ; protesting that cautionarie hath been unto me ; upon mine honour, and credite, the value of an Hundreth thousand pounds ; which any imployment abroad, either in the service of my king, or my Countrie, might have spared unto me, and bettered the estate of mine House. Neither doe I speake so farre of my self, for want of abilitie to doe mine owne businesse, which I praise God is known to such, as knowe myself ; but to give everie man a sense, and feeling out of mine owne experience, howe I see the estate of the Kingdome."

II.

In his " Offers " Lóchinvar had promised generous assistance to the " Adventurers in the new plantation of Cape Breton." He had, moreover, offered to find substantial security to colonists against any loss that might be sustained : " For their assurance of a securitie and peaceable quietness in the possession of their Landes of New Galloway, whereof they bee undertakers : I shall find sufficient caution, and suretie unto each one of them within the Shyre where hee dwelleth in Scotland, that whatsoever his goods or geare thither transported, and placed upon the ground of the saids Landes, shall bee taken from him by violence of the Natives, or forraine Nations, that the double thereof shall be payed and refounded againe unto him in Scotland or to his heires, executors, or assignayes."

Despite Lochinvar's proffered assistance and his readiness to provide security against loss, nothing came of his New Galloway project. For this negative result two explanations suggest themselves—one general, the other particular. In the first place there was in Scotland at this time a general apathy towards colonial schemes, which even Lochinvar's direct and spirited call to action could not at once dispel : it was not till four years later that Sir William Alexander, even though assisted by the institution of the Knights Baronets of Nova Scotia, was able to settle his first band of colonists in America. In the second place, an unexpected strain came upon Lochinvar's finances from another direction.

This strain was due to Cautionarie—villainous Cautionarie ! It will be remembered that Lochinvar was appointed in 1625 one of the Commissioners of the Middle Shires. He was sworn to the Commission on 18th November. On the very same day the name of Lochinvar came before the Privy Council in connection with a totally different activity : the Council ordained the finding of " caution by John Gordoun, younger of Lochinvar, in 10,000 marks, for Sir Robert

Gourdoun of Lochinvar, his father, and by James Gordoun of Butill, John Fullertoun of Cairleldin, and John Lennos of Caley, for the said John Gordoun, younger, in like amount, that they will keep the peace with John Lord Hereis, and John, Master of Hereis, his son." At the same time a similar demand for caution was made from John Master of Hereis, for John, Lord Hereis, his father.[1]

But though his efforts in connection with the settlement of a plantation in North America were doomed to disappointment, Lochinvar, with characteristic energy and enterprise, soon turned his attention to South America, and on 1st May, 1626, he received from King Charles a grant of " Insula Caroli "—an island occupying rather a vaguely defined position off the coast of Brazil—*ab equinoctiali linea meridiem versus prope latitudinem* $12\frac{1}{2}$ *et* 14 *gradum*." [2] Four days later Lochinvar received a license for a ship " to pass to the southward of the Equinoctiall lyne." [3] Lochinvar's ship, however, was not ready to proceed for some three months. On 20th August, 1626, he applied to the Clerk of the Privy Council for Letters of Marque. After intimation that his messenger has been despatched with a reply to a query addressed to him by the Council, he proceeds : " Lykwyse I have written for a letter of Marc, quhilk I will desyr yow to drawe uppe in als ample manner as ye may, or at least as uthers gets thame, and send it to me with this bearer : for I have a schippe to go out within four dayes. Quhat is requisite to be done on my part I sall do : and shall satisfie yow to your contentment." [4]

The other letter which his messenger bore to Edinburgh was his reply to the charge of the Privy Council to report the names of wearers of fire-arms.[5] " My werie honourable Lords," he writes, " my service most respectivelie remembered —I have receaved your Lordshippe's letter whereby your Lordshippes directis me to give uppe the names of such as weirs hacquebuts and pistolettes in this countrie. It will

---

[1] *Reg. P.C.S.*, Second Series, vol. i. p. 195.
[2] *Reg. Mag. Sig.* (1620-33), p. 344.
[3] *Nova Scotia Papers*, Preface, p. 35.
[4] *Reg. P.C.S.*, New Series, vol. i. p. 678.   [5] *Ibid.*

please your Lordshipis understand that it is so usuall and ordinarie in this countrie that it is a greater difficultie to give uppe their names that weirs nor of those that weirs not, for almost every man caries pistoletts. Yet gife it will please your Lordshipes, albeit I confesses it is a great wrong but that his majesties statutes suld be observed and keepit, alwyse I wold wysche that your Lordshipis wold correct it with lenitie." He then suggests that in order to minimise trouble and expense, " four sufficient men in everie schyre throughout the kingdom " be appointed " to compone with such as hath offendit : wilfull transgressouris to be punished in greater severitie both of bodie and goods." " Your Lordshipis," he continues, "will excuse my boldnesse in wryting of my simple opinioun to your Lordshipis therein." His concluding sentence recalls the spirit of his *Encouragements* : " Whereas your Lordshipes doth promis that it sall not be reveilled, for that I schall not care how publict it be quhat I can do in the service of my God, loyaltie to my King, and dutie to my countrie."

There is every reason to believe that Lochinvar's request for letters of marque was granted at this time—in view of the outbreak of hostilities between Spain and Britain letters of marque had been granted to two Fifeshire skippers as early as April, 1626 [1]—but there is no record of his ship putting the letters of marque to use during the autumn of 1626. Early in the following spring, however, Lochinvar's privateer set sail from Kirkcudbright, in charge of two of his servitors, William Weir and Andro Martine.[2] Urged by somewhat indiscriminating zeal, the said William and Andro, while cruising off Waterford,[3] " in hostile manner boorded and tane a ship of Middleburgh, laidind with merchandise and goods perteaning to his Majestie's friends and confederats in the Netherlands, removed and sett on land the whole companie and equipage of the said shippe, and brought the said shippe with her laidining to the Port of Kirkcudbright, where she with the said Sir Robert his owne shippe now presentlie (25. Apr. 1627) lies." [4]

[1] *Reg. P.C.S.*, New Series, vol. i. pp. 283-4.   [2] *Ibid.* p. 601.
[3] *Ibid.* p. 633.   [4] *Ibid.* p. 582.

On receipt of the intelligence of this seizure the Scots Privy Council took immediate measures for the securing of the Dutch ship pending investigation of the case. The Provost and Baillies of Kirkcudbright were instructed " to remove and take out of the saids two shippes the haill munitioun, ordinance, poulder, leid, and matche, and all kyndes of armour being within thame, together alsua with the haill sailes of the said shippes." To support them in carrying out these orders the Provost and Baillies were authorised to " convene and assemble, if need beis, the haill inhabitants and bodie of the toun." [1] It is evident that the Lords of the Privy Council were well aware of the salient characteristics of the Lochinvar temperament.

While the Scots Privy Council were taking official measures for the security of Lochinvar's prize, one of her owners, a Dutch merchant, Gerard Scorar, had made his way to Kirkcudbright, where the ship lay " under the charge and power of John Gordon, appearand of Lochinvar." [2] The worthy Dutch trader's memories of his trip to Galloway must have been anything but pleasant. " The said Gerard was shifted and putt aff be the said John Gordoun with manie impertinent and ydle excuisses, some tyme pretending his father's hame coming, which he made the poore stranger beleeve was daylie looked for, and when that served not his turn he pretended other excuisses ; and in the meane tyme the said Gerard was keeped in a maner as a prissoner, depryved of freedom to come here and compleane (*i.e.* to the Privy Council).[3]

Being apprised by Thomas Buglair in Diveling, " commissioner and agent for the said Gerard " of the worthy Dutchman's plight, the Privy Council issued a peremptory order for John Gordon, William Weir, Andrew Martine and Gerard to appear before them on the 22nd May.[4] On 14th June Lochinvar himself appeared before the Privy Council, and " being demandid yf he wolde insist again the ship of Middleburgh broght in be him for declaring hir to be a laughful pryse? he answered that he wold not insist." [5] The matter was finally settled by the issue, on 23rd June, by the Council, of

[1] *Reg. P.C.S.*, New Series, vol. i. p. 582.   [2] *Ibid.* p. 601.
[3] *Ibid.* p. 601.   [4] *Ibid.* p. 601.   [5] *Ibid.* p. 630.

instructions to Alexander, Earl of Linlithgow, Lord Admiral of Scotland, " to caus restitution and delyverie be maid of the said shippe and of her whole loading, with the sea brieff, cocquets, and uthers writs tane out of her, to Gerard Shorer and Giles Leanars, indwellers of Middleburgh, who has heir attendit thir diverse weiks biggans upon the recoverie of the same shippe and goods." [1]

The tedious and unsatisfactory interlude of the Middleburg merchants now ended, Lochinvar resumed with his wonted energy his colonial scheme. On 12th July, 1627, " Rex concessit D. Roberto Gordoun de Lochinvar, militi et ejus deputato vel deputatis—commissionem suscipiendi expeditionem pro plantatione insule Caroli, utendi aperta hostilitate contra Hispaniarum regem, archiducissam, et eorum subditos vel contra subditos quorumcunque regis hostium, exercendi autoritatem, apprehendi praedas." [2] On the day on which this commission was issued to him " in presence of the Lords of Secreit Counsell compeirit personallie Sir Robert Gordoun of Lochinvar Knight, and declairit that notwithstanding of the Commissioun grantit and exped unto him this day for his furtherance and advancement in the Kingis Matie service against the enemie, he was content, of his owne consent, that all the pryses that sall be tane be him, or be utheris having warrant and power from him, on this syde of the Equinoctiall Lyne shall be judged in no cuntrie but in this Kingdome be the Admirall of this Kingdome, and that he sall make payment to the King's Matie and the Admirall of the proportion dew to thame out of the prysses." [3]

Lochinvar died in November, 1627. It seemed at first as if his colonial schemes were to be taken up by his son, to whom in January, 1628, the concessions regarding Insula Caroli were transferred—" Quia Jac VI. rex concesserat quondam D. Roberto Gordoun de Lochinvar militi literas patentes pro plantatione Insulae Caroli,[4] et Deo visum fuerat dictum Rob.

[1] *Reg. P.C.S.*, New Series, vol. i. p. 633.
[2] *Reg. Mag. Sig.* (1620-33), p. 387.
[3] *Nova Scotia Papers*, Preface, p. 108.
[4] The official memory is here at fault. The grant made by King James was that of Cape Breton Island (*Nova Scotia Papers*, p. 16). The first grant of Insula Caroli was made on 1st May, 1626.

ex hac vita vocare—concessit Joanni Gordoun filio et heredi dicti D. Rob. et ejus deputato vel deputatis—licentiam dict, plantationem suscipiendi—cum omnibus libertatibus antea dicto Rob. concessis." [1]

But during the remainder of John Gordoun's life—he died in 1634—his interests centred chiefly round the religious controversies of the day; and the colonial projects that had appealed so strongly to the mind of Sir Robert Gordoun apparently offered no attraction to that of his son.[2]

III.

When we turn from the record of Lochinvar's varied and strenuous activities in the cause of Scottish colonisation to follow the narrative of the actual settlement in the summer of 1629, on one of the coves of the Cape Breton Coast, of a party of Scottish colonists, it is impossible to suppress a feeling of disillusionment: the story of the things that were not done is, as so often happens, infinitely more fascinating than the tale of the things that were actually accomplished. Yet the nobleman who led the Scottish colonists to Cape Breton was the son of a man who had played a notable part in a particularly stormy epoch of Scottish history; and the title that he bore had descended to him from a family that has left its mark on the story of our country.

Lord Ochiltree, who founded the Scots settlement at Cape Breton, was the son of Captain James Stewart of Bothwellmuir, Captain of the King's Guard, "whose flaming career as Chancellor and Dictator of Scotland under the usurped title of Earl of Arran, from 1583 to 1585, is one of the most extraordinary romances of Scottish history." It was Captain Stewart of the Guard who thrust Morton to his doom by accusing him, before the Council, of being a party to the assassination of Darnley. It was Captain Stewart, now Earl of Arran—the real Earl was living in retirement—who freed the young King James from serious menace by the capture

[1] *Reg. Mag. Sig.* (1620-33), p. 414.

[2] "... verum morte ejus tam laudabilis conatus evanuit."—Johnstone, *Historia*.

in 1584 of Gowrie at Dundee, and by the defeat of the force with which the Earl of Mar and Angus had advanced into Scotland. It was Captain Stewart, Earl of Arran, who fell from power through the unscrupulous intrigues of the Master of Gray at the Court of Elizabeth.

In 1615 Arran's son, Sir James Stewart of Killeith, became fourth Lord Ochiltree as the result of a family arrangement among the members of the Ochiltree branch of the Stewarts. In the reign of Queen Mary, Andrew, second Lord Ochiltree, father-in-law of John Knox, had been prominent in the party of the more extreme Reformers, and had been one of those who signed the " Bands " for the advancement of Darnley and the despatch of Rizzio. " The good Lord Ochiltree's " grandson, the third Lord Ochiltree, had taken an important part in Scottish politics during the reign of James VI., and had acted as Lieutenant for the King during the Hebridean expedition of 1608 that had effectively curbed the power of the chieftains of the Isles. Thereafter Lord Ochiltree had played a leading part in the colonisation of Ulster, and ultimately he and his son, the Master of Ochiltree, had resolved to devote themselves entirely to the development of their extensive Irish estates. With characteristic care for the family welfare—south of the Border they put the thing more bluntly—Lord Ochiltree arranged for the transference of his hereditary Scottish peerage to his uncle, Sir James Stewart of Killeith, who in 1615 became fourth Lord Ochiltree.[1]

---

[1] " To the Counsell.

" Right etc., Haveing receaved a humble supplication from the Lord Ochiltree and his sonne makeing mention where the said Lord, being to retire himself to live in Ireland, and desireing exceedinglie that his place and estate may continue with the ancient familie for benefit and other regards, hath made choice of Sir James Stewart of Killeith Knight, hee and his sonne being as it were dead within that our Kingdome as next of the race to succeed him, earnestlie entreating our favour thereanent : whereupon considering that no party can justly complaine as any way interested by this course, the said Sir James comeing in by a kind of succession as well as by purchase, out of that affection which wee have ever had, that all such houses as have deserved well of us or of our ancestours should contynue and floorish : Our pleasure is, after the said Lord hath surrendered in his favours, that immediatly you accept the said Sir James in his place, enableing him, by as sufficient a warrant as can be given in such things, that he

Sir James Stewart's enjoyment of the revenues of the Ochiltree estates was no more permanent than his father's tenure of office at the court of King James. Lord Ochiltree "enjoyed the estate a few years, and was forced to sell all for defraying his debts."[1] It has been opined, probably with justice, that it was Ochiltree's impecuniosity that turned his attention to colonial enterprise. He stood well in the favour of King Charles, and it is more likely—as he is not heard of in connection with colonising activities till 1629—that Ochiltree hoped to share in the prosperity that seemed to be dawning for Sir William Alexander after his entry into partnership with the London merchant venturers. To aid Ochiltree's enterprise, King Charles in April, 1629, authorised the borrowing of £500 sterling for him.

Lord Ochiltree sailed with the fleet sent out by the Anglo-Scottish Company in 1629. On the arrival of Sir William Alexander's squadron off the Cape Breton coast three ships were discovered at anchor. The largest of these was a "Barque of 60 Tunnes." According to the Scots account this Barque was a Portuguese interloper, and was confiscated after a "process which was formallie led," Lord Ochiltree acting as one of the two assessors chosen by Sir William Alexander to aid him in the exercise of his admiralty jurisdiction.[2] This Barque appears to have been, in reality, the French ship *Marie* of St. Jean de Luz.[3] On 1st July, 1629, Sir William Alexander landed Lord Ochiltree at a small cove near where later the great citadel of Louisbourg was to be erected. The colonists erected a small fort, and seem to have entered upon fishing and other occupations with energy and enterprise.

Four days, however, before Lord Ochiltree landed with his small band of pioneers on the shores of Cape Breton Island,

may enjoy all the priviledges, honours, and dignities belonging to the Lordship of Ochiltree, in as lardge and ample maner as the said Lord might have done befor his dimission, to contynue with him and his posteritie: Whereanent their presents shall be a sufficient warrant unto you—Greenwich, the 27 of May, 1615" (*Register of Royal Letters*, vol. i. p. 5).

[1] Scot of Scotstarvet.   [2] Egerton, 2395, f. 23.
[3] C.O. 1/5, No. 50.

there had sailed from France a squadron of four vessels and a barque which was to effect the destruction of the Scottish settlement.

On the 22nd of April, 1629, Captain Daniel left Dieppe in command of two ships, the *Grand S. Andre* and the *Marguerite*, " sous le congé de Monseigneur le Cardinal de Richelieu, Grand Maistre Chef et Surintendant Général de la Navigation et Commerce de France." Daniel's instructions from " Messieurs les Intendants et Directeurs de la Nouvelle France," were to join the Chevalier de Razilly either at Brouage or at la Rochelle, and thence proceed, under the escort of Razilly, to relieve Champlain at Quebec. After waiting for de Razilly for almost six weeks, Daniel was forced, by the lateness of the season, to sail without him. To the ships which Daniel had brought from Dieppe were added two ships and a barque. Before Daniel started on the Atlantic voyage peace had been proclaimed between Great Britain and France.

On the 28th of August, Daniel dropped anchor in one of the Cape Breton harbours, *la rivière nomée par les sauvages* " *Grand Cibou.*" Next day he sent a boat with ten men to cruise along the coasts and learn from the natives the state of affairs at Quebec. From the skipper of a Bordeaux vessel which Daniel's boat's crew found at anchor in the Port aux Baleines, a piquant narrative was obtained of international complications much nearer at hand than Quebec.

About two months previously, the worthy Bordelais averred, le Sieur Jacques Stuart, Milor Ecossais, had sailed into these waters with two large ships and a patache. On his arrival he had made prize of a French ship, which he found busy fishing and curing her catch. Soon afterwards le dit Milor had dispatched the two big ships and the French prize to Port Royal, *pour y faire habitation*. At the Port aux Baleines le dit Milor had built a fort, and in it he had mounted three guns commandeered from the Bordeaux ship. These doings of the Milor Ecossais were detailed by the Bordeaux shipman in a document which contained the additional information that no Frenchman might fish in these waters nor trade with the natives unless there was paid to the Milor an octroi of ten per cent. : the Milor, too, had a commission from the King of Great Britain authorising the confiscation of any vessel frequenting these waters without the permission of le Sieur Jacques.

Here obviously was a state of affairs that demanded strong and immediate action. This usurpation of French authority in French territory must cease at once. This exaction of tribute from French subjects must be brought to an end immediately. Captain Daniel, accordingly, prepared to enforce the authority of the king, his master. A landing party of 53 men was selected, and was provided with ladders " et autres choses nécessaires pour assiéger et escalader le dit fort." On the eighteenth of September, the landing party, in six boats, approached the fort. Attacking from several sides and covering their advance with grenades, *pots à feu, et autres artifices*, they soon forced the defenders to display a white flag. Daniel, forcing his way quickly in at the door of the fort made prisoners of Ochiltree and the men he found inside. The English (?) colours were lowered and replaced by those of the French King.

Making a tour of the fort, Daniel came upon a Frenchman, a native of Brest, detained as a prisoner until his captain, who had cast anchor two days before in a bay two leagues distant, should forward to the Milor Ecossais a gun he had in his ship and pay the tenth part of his catch of fish.[1]

Lord Ochiltree's official narrative—"The Barbarous and perfidious carriage off the frenche zowards the Lo. Wohiltrie in the Isle off Cape-Britaine proved in the Court of Admiralty off Dieppe [2]—gives some incidents not mentioned in Daniel's account. Daniel with " three score soiours and one certaine number off Savages in six shallops coming to the coasts off Cape Britaine and surpryzing too shallops and six fishermen in thim who were at fishing for the entertienment off the sayd Lo. wohiltrie his colonie—having surpryzed the shallops, he seased upon the fishermen, inclosed them in one waste Ile

---

[1] " Relation du Voyage fait par le Capitanie Daniel de Dieppe, en la Nouvelle France, la présente année, 1629."—Samuel de Champlain, *Les Voyages de la France Occidentale*, Edition 1632, Part ii. pages 271-275.

[2] *C.O.* 1/5, No. 46; *Col. Cal.*, 1574-1660, p. 105.

without meatt drink fyr houses or any shelter from the rayne or cold.

" Thereafter with his soiours and six shallops enterit the harborye the said Lo. wohiltrie and the greatest part of his men being abroad at bissinize. The said Lo. wohiltrie perseaving them enterit his fortalis with the few that wer ny it esteming the said Captain danyell and his people to have been savages caused discharge sum muskattrie att the schallopes to make them discover who they wer wch did so fall further, for they did immediatly approach the fortlys and the said Lo. wochiltrie finding by thayre apparell that they wer not savage did demand to them who they wer—frenche. He said the french and they were friends because of the peace between the two kings. They replyed that they wer french and that they did know the peace and wer our friends." The new comers were welcomed, entered the fortalice—" and seased on us all and disarmed us."

Ochiltree's subsequent career showed that in formulating an accusation he was no meticulous stickler for a close adherence to facts, but in the tactics of Captain Daniel he seems to have thought he had reasonable ground of complaint against "the barbarous and perfidious carriage off the frenche." His narrative receives corroboration, not, however, from an independent source, in the declaration by Captain Constance Ferrer, one of Ochiltree's companions, that they were " treacherously surprised." [1] It is difficult, however, to see any reason why Daniel should have recourse to " perfidious carriage " : accurate intelligence of the strength of the Scots settlement was easily obtainable, and the French possessed a decided superiority in number.

The Scottish fortalice was demolished. A short distance from its ruins the French commander set up a small fort that ultimately developed into the key-fortress of Louisbourg. The prisoners were transferred to Daniel's warships, which then steered for France. The sufferings of the captives, crowded in the dark and noisome holds of the small warships, were intense. The majority of the displanted Scots were landed at Falmouth ; sixteen of the leading men, among

[1] Col. Cal., 1574-1660, p. 104.

them Lord Ochiltree, were carried on to Dieppe. In France, the achievement of Daniel was hailed as affording, in some measure, a counterpoise to the surrender of Quebec.

Before the Admiralty Court at Dieppe Ochiltree averred that the break up of his settlement had involved him in losses exceeding £20,000. As he had apparently begun his colonial venture on the capital of £500 borrowed for him by King Charles, Ochiltree seems either to have adopted a singularly sanguine estimate of the possibilities of his settlement or to have assessed fairly highly the injury to his self-esteem caused by its destruction. To the British government he complained bitterly of the treatment meted out to him by Daniel. This complaint was brought to the notice of the French authorities. In justification of his actions Daniel alleged " an expres warrant from the Cardinal from whom he had shown a commission to recover for the French all plantations between 40 and 60 degrees." [1]

IV.

With a tenacity thoroughly in harmony with the spirit that had inspired both Sir William Alexander and Gordon of Lochinvar, Lord Ochiltree was soon busy with a new colonial scheme. On 18th April, 1631, Ochiltree's name was added to the list of Nova Scotia baronets : next day the king was considering a point arising out of a novel scheme for providing fresh funds for this enterprising baronet. In the spring of 1631, the king must have found it a task of some difficulty to decide where this new capital was to be obtained, but recourse was had, optimistically, to one of the old feudal revenues of the crown—there was a good deal of antiquarian zeal at this particular epoch—and Ochiltree was granted a lease " for twentie-one yeres of the benefite which may happin to w^s by the year and day wast(e) of all fellones landis and houses rendring 500^{lib} st. per annum." There was, however, an obstacle to the free enjoyment of these feudal revenues— Ochiltree was not *post natus :* ' Bot be reasoun the said Lord Ochiltrie is not a free denizene, he cannot reallie enjoy

[1] *C.O.* 1/5, No. 46; *Col. Cal.*, 1574-1660, p. 105.

the said grant in his owin name which he desyreth." But administrative dexterity could make good this defect : " These are therefor to will and requyre you to repair a bill readie for our signatur whereby to mak the said Lord Ochiltree a free denizen of this our Kingdom of England and dominions thereof." [1]

On the very day—19th April, 1631—of the issue of these instructions designed to clear away the legal difficulties attending the grant to Ochiltree, King Charles wrote also to the Justices of Ireland, intimating that " our right trustie and weillbeloved the Lord Ochiltrie, our Trustie and weilbeloved Counsellour Sir Peirse Corsbie and Sir Archibald Achiesone Kny[ts] and baronets, and our trustie and weilbeloved Sir Walter Corsbie, Kny[t] and baronet " [2] had the intention of planting a colony " near unto the river of Canada." This colony the Judges were directed to assist both by arranging for " transporting thither such persones as shalbe willing to be imployed in that plantation " and by granting facilities for the dispatch of " provisions of Victuall, Ordinance, munition, and all other necessaries whatsoever fitt for their use." [3]

This second venture of Lord Ochiltree was to come to grief from a cause more akin to some of the difficulties that had hampered Gordon of Lochinvar than to the misfortunes experienced by Sir William Alexander. Within six months of the time when King Charles had been taking steps to secure for Ochiltree the uninterrupted enjoyment of the year and waste of the felons' lands, Ochiltree was himself under arrest. His arrest was due to his activities in one of the great family feuds of Scottish history—that of the Stewarts and the House of Douglas—albeit the part played by Ochiltree seemed almost a travesty of the feud as it had been but a generation before.

Ochiltree's father, Captain James Stewart of the Guard, had

[1] *Register Royal Letters*, vol. ii. p. 513.

[2] Sir Archibald Achison had been created a Nova Scotia Baronet on 1st January, 1628 ; Lord Ochiltree on 18th April, 1631 ; " Sir Peirs Corsbie Knight one of the Privy Council in Ireland, and Walter Corsbie of Corsbie Park (Wicklow)," on 24th April, 1621—Roll of Nova Scotia Baronets, *Nova Scotia Papers*, pp. 121-122.

[3] *Register Royal Letters*, vol. ii. pp. 513 and 514.

mounted to the Earldom of Arran on the prestige acquired through his accusation of Morton—a Douglas—of complicity in the taking off of Darnley. And now Ochiltree was to date his own downfall to his accusation of another Douglas— the Marquis of Hamilton—of high treason.[1] He alleged that Hamilton harboured a design of employing the Scottish levies raised for the German wars in support of his claims to the throne. "The Lord Ochiltree," wrote the king to the Scots Privy Council from Hampton Court on 24th September, 1631, "having bene examined befoir our Counsell heir tuitching some information gevin by him reflecting upon some nobilitie of that our Kingdome, we have bene pleased to remitt him thither to be tryed according to the lawes thereof, haveing to that purpois sent you heirwith enclosed some depositions under his owin hand, and the authentic copies of others, whereof the principalls we cause reserve heir becaus they lykwyse concerne other persones : Our pleasur is, that haveing gevin ordour for receaving and committing him to safe custodie, you caus try and censure him according to our saids lawis befoir what Judicatorie and judges you shall think fitt and compitent for that purpois.[2]

The allegations made by Ochiltree were found, after a protracted investigation, to be baseless : "the story appeared to be a piece of the most notorious folly and forgery that ever was invented ; for which he was condemned to perpetual imprisonment in Blackness Castle."[3] In that gloomy keep by the tidal waters of the Forth he remained for twenty years. The Cromwellian invasion which brought gloom to many a leal Scottish heart, brought sunshine to the heart of Lord Ochiltree : the English invaders set him at liberty.

On his release he displayed an initiative and enterprise that showed that the failure of his Cape Breton colonial scheme was due to untoward circumstances and not to any defect of character on the part of Lord Ochiltree : it was now imperative for him to find some means of subsistence for himself and his family : "he took himself to be a Doctor of Medicine."[4]

---

[1] *Nova Scotia Papers*, pp. 54 and 55.
[2] *Reg. Royal Letters*, vol. ii. pp. 555 and 556.
[3] *Nova Scotia Papers*, p. 55.   [4] *Ibid.*

CHAPTER IV

"THE YEARS BETWEEN"

I.

IN the summer of 1632, the Chevalier de Razilly had anchored off the fort the Scots had built on the western shore of Port Royal, and presented the commission, signed by the British Ambassador at Paris, which authorised the surrender of the colony. Fully half a century was to elapse ere other systematic Scottish efforts should be made to establish a settlement in North America. It was a half century crowded with stirring and critical movements in Scottish history. The National Covenant and the Bishops' Wars; the Solemn League and Covenant; Dunbar and Worcester; Rullion Green, Drumclog, and Bothwell Brig—it was upon a weary and sorely wracked Scotland that the Revolution Settlement cast its anodyne of uneasy peace—a Scotland that had little leisure and little energy to spare for the planning of colonial schemes.

It is, however, in the controversies of those unquiet years of Scottish history that we find the motives that guided the Scots who in 1684 sought to establish the Presbyterian colony of Stuart's Town in South Carolina, and also, to a considerable extent, the Scots who a few years earlier had interested themselves in the Quaker-Scottish settlement of East New Jersey. Apart, however, from the influence they exerted on these later schemes, those troubled years of Scottish history are of interest in the general history of Scottish emigration. The troubles of these times cast many an unfortunate Scot ashore in the New World in a condition differing little, if at all, from that of the negro slaves who toiled in the tobacco and the sugar plantations.

This enforced migration was due to two main causes. In the first place, many of the Scots who fell into the hands of Cromwell after Dunbar and Worcester were transported to the Plantations. In October, 1651, for example, the Council of State directed the Committee for Prisoners to grant a license for transporting some Scots, prisoners, to the Barmudas, upon the usual security.[1] Such treatment was in general accord with the Cromwellian attitude towards " unruly men "—" A terrible Protector this ; no getting of him overset ! He has the ringleaders all in his hand, in prison or still at large ; as they love their estates and their life, let them be quiet. He can take your estate :—is there not proof enough to take your head, if he pleases ? He dislikes shedding blood ; but is very apt ' to barbadoes ' an unruly man— has sent and sends us by hundreds to Barbadoes, so that we have made an active verb of it : 'Barbadoes you.' "[2] In September, 1655, the Council of State directed the Commissioners of the Admiralty to give orders for the English, Scotch, Irish and Dutch mariners, prisoners in the castle of Plymouth, not thought fit to be tried for their lives, to be sent to Barbados.[3] Nine months later the Council of State were arranging for the transportation of 1200 men from Knockfergus in Ireland and Port Patrick in Scotland to Jamaica.[4] A generation later one of these exiles was encountered by the Scots settlers in East New Jersey : " I am just now drinking to one of them (*i.e.* the ' old Buckskin planters '), our Countryman who was sent away by Cromwell to New England, a slave from Dunbar. Living now in Woodbridge like a Scots Laird, wishes his countrymen and his Native Soyle very well, tho' he never intends to see it."[5]

After the Restoration the Cromwellian tradition of the disciplinary effectiveness of exile was continued. To the Scots Privy Council banishment to the Plantations suggested

---

[1] *Col. Cal.*, 1574-1660, p. 363.
[2] Carlyle, *Letters and Speeches of Oliver Cromwell*, part ix.
[3] *Col. Cal.*, 1574-1660, p. 363.   [4] *Ibid.* p. 363.
[5] Appendix E, Letter 14.

itself as a simple and effective procedure for ridding the country of recalcitrant Presbyterians. The practice which, when suggested by James I., had evoked the protest of the Scots Privy Council was freely employed by the Privy Councillors who governed Scotland on behalf of Charles II. The Covenanters sentenced to banishment were carried overseas by merchant ships, whose masters gave bond of 1000 merks for each prisoner to the effect that the prisoner would be duly transported and a certificate of landing would be obtained under the hand of the governor of the colony to which the prisoner had been taken. The number of Covenanters exiled to the Plantations has been estimated at seventeen hundred : [1] of these exiles two hundred, prisoners from the Westland rising, perished by shipwreck off the Orkneys.

Nor were Covenanters the only Scotsmen to be banished to the Plantations. In August, 1681, for example, the Privy Council received from Walter Gibson, merchant in Glasgow— an individual of considerable notoriety in Scottish colonial history—a supplication wherein he stated that he had a ship lying at New Port Glasgow about to sail for America, and signified his willingness to take with him " thieves or robbers sentenced by the Lords of Justiciary or other judges, to be banished thither, and all sorners, lusty beggars or gipsies," [2] declaring his readiness to find caution to transport them to Virginia, Maryland, or the Carribee Islands. As a result of this petition Gibson received a warrant, which was to endure for three months, and in which magistrates of burghs were ordered to deliver to him " all such strong and idle beggars, gypsies or other vagabonde persones who live by stouth and robbery and have no visible means to maintaine themselves and are sentenced by the said Magistrats and are presently imprisoned, to the effect they may be transported in the petitioners ships to the plantations and the country freed of them." [3]

[1] W. H. Carslaw, *Exiles of the Covenant*, p. 13.
[2] *Reg. P.C.S.*, Third Series, vol. vii. p. 178.
[3] It is of interest to compare the practice of the English government with that of the Scottish government in the matter of banishment to the Plantations : " The English government systematically deported to the colonies

In view of these practices, it is not surprising to find that in a proposal laid before the Scots Privy Council in the spring of 1681, " to erect a colonie of Scotish subjects in any part of America," one of the advantages urged in favour of the establishment of such a settlement was that it " would void the countrey of very many both idle and dissenting persones." [1] It is only fair to remark, however, that this *obiter dictum* represents the personal—and probably sycophantic—" humble opinion " of the Provost of Linlithgow, who was acting as spokesman for a conference of leading Scottish merchants summoned at the desire of the Committee of Trade " to give their advyse anent the causes of the decay of trade and what they should propose for the remeid thereof." [2] Of the penal usefulness of a settlement there is not a word in the finding of the Conference regarding colonial policy—a policy set forth with remarkable insight and sagacity in a memorandum entitled " Memorial concerning the Scottish plantation to be erected in some place of America." [3]

II.

Almost simultaneously with the transport of the Scottish prisoners to the Plantations, enterprising Scottish traders began to make their presence felt among the scattered settlements on the Atlantic seaboard of North America. In general, the presence of the Scots was resented by the inhabitants of these settlements. In the course of a petition addressed in

---

many undesirable elements in its population—political prisoners, religious nonconformists, delinquents and criminals. Thus in 1665, 126 Quakers in Newgate, as well as some others imprisoned elsewhere, were ordered to be transported to the colonies. In 1666, 100 Irish rebels were deported to Barbados, and in 1685, after the collapse of Monmouth's insurrection, 800 of his adherents were sent to enforced labor in the same colony, and some also were transported to Jamaica. Disorderly persons and convicts were regularly shipped to America. Virginia objected to this policy and secured exemption from it; but in 1684, St. Kitts sent to England a petition, which was granted, that the 300 malefactors long since ordered might finally be transported so as to strengthen the colony." G. L. Beer, *The Old Colonial System*, i. pp. 29 and 30, and authorities there quoted.

[1] *Reg. P.C.S.*, Third Series, vol. vii. p. 671.
[2] *Ibid.* p. 652.   [3] *Ibid.* pp. 664-665.

1657 to Governor Stuyvesant, the good burghers of New Amsterdam drew attention to the doings of the Scots : " They sail hither and thither to the best trading places, taking the bread as it were out of the mouths of the good burghers and resident inhabitants, without being subject in time of peace or war to any trouble or expense. . . . They carry away the profits in time of peace, and in time of war abandon the country and the inhabitants thereof." [1]

The complaints of the Dutch burghers were re-echoed at a later period in the English settlements. After the Restoration English colonial policy was regulated by a series of enactments " determined by the current economic theory of colonisation and by the ultimate end in view, which was the creation of a powerful self-sufficient commercial empire, dominating the seas and controlling the course of foreign exchange." [2] By the Navigation Act of 1660 and the complementary Statute, the Staple Act of 1663, Scots traders were debarred from trafficking with the English plantations. Efforts were made to enforce these restrictive regulations by the appointment in the colonies of the officials known as the " naval officers." " The naval officer early became a prominent feature of the local administrative system. . . . He was the personal representative of the Governor, and was entrusted by him with the detailed work of enforcing the commercial code : the giving of bonds, the examination of ships' papers and cargoes, and the entrance and clearance of vessels." [3] The appointment in 1671 of Commissioners of Customs in England—to replace the Farmers of the Customs—was soon followed by the establishment in the colonies of a hierarchy of Customs officials. Despite these precautions, however, illegal trade went on. The coast line was long. Secluded creeks and bays were frequent. The preventive service was on a relatively small scale. The gain from a successful venture—and most ventures proved successful—was considerable. Hence the illegal trade between Scotland and the Plantations flourished vigorously : to take one colony alone, between 1688 and 1695

---

[1] Doyle, *The Middle Colonies*, p. 47.
[2] G. L. Beer, *The Old Colonial System*, vol. i. p. 57.
[3] *Ibid.* pp. 267-268.

not fewer than fourteen ships, that had loaded tobacco in Pennsylvania for England, ... "do not appear to have delivered the same in England, Wales, or Berwick, as by their bonds they are obliged "; [1] while Mr. Valentine Prowse, late agent in Scotland to the Commissioner of his Majesty's Customs in London, reported that between 13th April, 1695, and 29th December, 1696, there had been in Scottish harbours not fewer than twenty four " ships and vessels trading to and from Scotland to the tobacco Plantations." [2] It is a significant fact that, if not in theory, at least in practice, the tobacco trade between the Plantations and Scotland was encouraged by means of a preferential tariff: " ... And seeing that Tobacco that comes immediatly from the Plantations, pays sixteen pennies Scots of Duty upon each pound weight, and that which comes from London and other ports, not immediatly from the Plantations, pays now two shilling Scots : We ordain, that the Duty upon Tobacco ; coming immediatly from the Plantations continue as formerly, but that Tobacco coming from other places pay eight pennies more, being two shillings eight pennies Scots upon each pound weight, in regard there is much native commodities Transported to the Plantations, but none to other places for Tobacco, but only ready money. ..." [3]

To the colonial government official, the Scot who settled in the Plantations appeared inevitably as the accomplice of the "brither Scot" who ran the illicit cargoes, and consequently the references to Scots settlers in colonial correspondence are generally couched in somewhat censorious terms. "There are several Scots men that inhabit here," runs a dispatch from the Governor of New Hampshire, dated 10th January, 1682, " and are great interlopers and bring in quantities of goods underhand from Scotland. I desire the Attorney Generall his opinion upon the Act of the 12th of the King ffor encouraging and increasing of shipping and naviga-

[1] *Manuscripts of House of Lords*, New Series, vol. ii. p. 462.
[2] *Ibid.* p. 464.
[3] "Proclamation for Regulating and Encourageing Trade and Manufactorees in the Kingdom of Scotland " : Advocates Library, *Proclamation of P.C.S.*, 11th April, 1681.

tion (*i.e.* the Navigation Act, 1660). Whether a Scotsman born can be permitted to inhabitt and trade as a merchant or factor, they pretending a right thereunto as being born within the allegiance of our Sovereign Lord the King. I humbly conceive Scotsmen are not privileged by that Act to exercise the trade or occupation of a merchant or ffactor in his Majtys plantations. Since my arrival here a Scot's vessel was seized by Mr. Randolph and condemned and sold for 120^l, of which Mr. Randolph will give yo. hon. a more particular account." [1] In the same strain is a dispatch of 31st August, 1686, from Mr. Mein, a Customs officer, reporting that " many prohibited goods are imported at East Jersey, the Governor being a Scotsman." [2]

Interesting testimony to the number of Scots settled at New York by the closing years of the seventeenth century is afforded by a passage in a dispatch of Lord Bellomont, dated from Boston, 26th October, 1699, and dealing with the arrival of two ships of force from the Scottish settlement at Darien. When the first Darien Expedition abandoned New Edinburgh in June, 1699, the fleet of three ships scattered, after working their way out of Caledonia Bay. The *St. Andrew*, after running aground on a rock in dangerous proximity to Carthagena, succeeded in reaching Port Royal in Jamaica. After an extremely trying passage, the *Caledonia* anchored off Sandy Hook. The *Unicorn* reached the Hudson estuary a few days later. When the Darien ships came to New York, the Governor, Lord Bellomont, was at Boston on duty. Under the influence of a letter received from a private correspondent Bellomont conceived the idea that his representative, the Lieutenant Governor, had not acted with sufficient firmness in handling the situation. " . . . I am the more particular in this acc^t of the ships from Caledonia, because I apprehend the Scotch that come in them, from a starving condition they were at their first coming, grew very Insolent, while they were at N. York . . . I have been cautious enough in my orders to the Lt. Governor of N. York not to suffer the Scots to buy more provisions than would serve to carry them home to Scotland,

---

[1] *C.O.* 1/51, No. 3.
[2] *Manuscripts of House of Lords*, New Series, vol. ii. p. 465.

and if he have suffered them to exceed that he is to blame. And for any Insolences comitted by them, it had been easy, I should thinke, to have put a check to that by comitting the officers and principall passengers belonging to those ships, till such time as they had made satisfaction for any Irregularities done by them, and till they had given security to the Government for their good behaviour. There are Scotch enough there to have been securities for them." [1]

III.

If in the English colonies that fringed the Atlantic seaboard of North America the Scot was regarded with suspicion and distrust, he received a cordial welcome in the English colonies among the Caribbean Islands. Nor is it difficult to find a reason for this difference of attitude. In these scattered islands the various maritime powers of Europe—Spain, France, England, Holland and even Denmark—had planted settlements wherever they could find, or make, a footing. During the first half of the seventeenth century a wholesome dread of the power of Spain, which in virtue of the Papal grant laid claim to all the West Indian islands, tended to keep the settlers belonging to the other nations on friendly terms with one another. English and French entered upon a joint occupation of St. Kitts, dwelt in amity, and even came to an understanding that should war break out between the mother countries there should be no fighting in St. Kitts unless express commands to commence hostilities were received from the home governments. In Santa Cruz, Dutchman and Frenchman settled down together, and St. Martin acknowledged the same dual ownership.

As the seventeenth century wore on, however, the early feeling of salutary respect for Spain wore off. The large island of Jamaica was wrested from the grasp of the Spaniard by Cromwell's expedition. Those cosmopolitan and picturesque marauders, the buccaneers, harried the coasts of the Spanish Main from Porto Bello to Maracaibo. When they had stripped the Atlantic coast towns of all available plunder

[1] *C.O.* 5/1043, No. 2, i.

they extended indefinitely the radius of their activities. One band under Morgan, acting under a commission obtained from a too complaisant governor of Jamaica, trudged through the jungles and toiled across the cordillera of the Isthmus, defeated a large Spanish force covering Panama, and sacked and burned that fortress of the Pacific. Other bands sought to emulate, on a smaller scale, " the unparalleled Exploits of Sir Henry Morgan, our English Jamaican Hero."[1] One band under Captain Sharpe and Sawkins made a raid on Santa Maria, paddled in canoes down the Santa Maria River, took unto themselves a squadron of Spanish warships, blockaded Panama, and thereafter flitted up and down the coasts of Peru and Chile, working havoc among the Spanish settlements and the Spanish coastwise shipping.

As the power of Spain in the Caribbean and the adjacent mainland grew gradually weaker, the other European settlers were less influenced by the common respect for Spain that had before kept Englishman, Frenchman, and Dutchman on terms of prudent friendship. In the history of the West Indies during the latter part of the seventeenth century and during the eighteenth century, there are political upheavals, resembling both in suddenness and in intensity those volcanic upheavals that wrecked West Indian towns and those hurricanes that overwhelmed West Indian fleets : " The West Indies," says Professor Andrews, " during our colonial era were the scene of some of the most varied and tempestuous struggles that we meet with anywhere in the New World. Here the navies fought many famous seabattles ; here islands were wrested at heavy cost of men and money, only to be rendered neutral or handed back with the signing of new treaties ; here pirates and privateers found favourable opportunities for their livelihood, until it could be said that it was more dangerous for a merchant ship to sail from one island to another than it was to sail to England."[2]

With the English West Indian islands but thinly settled and constantly exposed to the danger of raids by Frenchman or Spaniard, it was but natural that the Scot should be

---
[1] Part of sub-title of English (1684-5) edition of *Esquemeling*.
[2] Andrews, *The Colonial Period*, pp. 18, 19.

welcomed in the Caribbean islands, where he had proved himself not only a sturdy workman but also a stout fighter. Nor were external dangers the only ones the English planters had to take measures against. The rapid development of the sugar plantations had brought into the islands a very large population of negro slaves. In Barbados, where economic progress had been greatest, the problem of the slave population caused no little anxiety. " In 1667 it was estimated that in 1643 there were in Barbados only 6400 negroes, as against more than 50,000 in 1666. . . . In 1668 Governor Willoughby stated that the total population was 60,000 ; of which 40,000 were negroes. Nicholas Blake in 1669 also estimated the slave population at 40,000. At this time the number of negroes in the other colonies was far less. According to Governor Willoughby, in 1668 there were in Antigua only 700 and in Montserrat 300. In 1670 it was estimated that Jamaica had 2500 negroes." [1] But if Jamaica had a relatively small negro population, it must be remembered that Jamaica had inherited from the days of the Cromwellian conquest a Maroon war which was to last for many generations.

" Of the West Indian dependencies of Great Britain the two which have played the most important part in history are Jamaica and Barbados. They stand at opposite poles, in size, in position, in mode and date of acquisition. Jamaica is large, Barbados is small, Jamaica lies inside the ring of islands, Barbados outside and beyond it ; Jamaica is British in virtue of conquest, Barbados is British in virtue of settlement ; Jamaica was acquired after British colonisation had taken root and spread in the West Indies ; the settlement of Barbados, on the other hand, was almost its earliest effort." [2] Yet these two islands, presenting so many features of contrast, had, in the seventeenth century at least one characteristic in common : each appreciated the virtues of the Scot as a colonist ; each made strong efforts to secure contingents of Scottish settlers.

Among the hindrances to the development of Barbados the Governor, Lord Willoughby, notes, in a dispatch of the

[1] G. L. Beer, *The Old Colonial System*, part i. vol. i. p. 320 *n*.
[2] Lucas, *Historical Geog. of Brit. Colonies*, vol. i. p. 122.

summer of 1667, " First the want of free trade with Scotland, by wch formerly this and the rest of the Islands was supplyed wth brave servants and faithful subjects as by experience they have here been found." [1] In the official correspondence of Barbados at this time the desire to secure Scottish settlers is repeatedly expressed.[2]

To the good repute in which the Scots stood as settlers the Jamaican correspondence of this period also bears testimony. In his " Propositions for ye Speedy Settling of Jamaica " (sent to Secretary Lord Arlington on 20th Sept., 1670), Governor Sir Thomas Modyford urges " That all prudentiall meanes bie used to encourage ye Scotts to come hither, as being very good servants, and to prevent them from going to Poland and other nations, whereby they are absolutely lost to his Maties service." [3] A month later Modyford writes to the same effect : " His Matie may not doe amisse to suffer the Scots to come this way, who in 2 yeares will bring thousands of people and that will strengthen the place well, besides they are a hardy people to endure labour and (as I have heard say) have been the chief instruments of bringing Barbados to its perfection." [4]

The persistence of this desire on the part of the Jamaican authorities to obtain the services of Scots, is revealed a generation later, in the course of a letter concerning the Darien scheme, " I have letters to-day from Sir William Beeston of the 21st March," writes Secretary Vernon, on 8th June, 1699, to the Duke of Shrewsbury. " He speaks of the Scotch at Darien, that their provisions begin to fall short, and their money likewise fails them. . . . Sir William believes their want will make them run to Jamaica, which he wishes, as thinking they will be an additional strength to the Island." [5] Sir William was not disappointed : a considerable number of the Scots who survived the fevers of Darien and the hardships of the sea-passage to Jamaica settled in his colony.[6]

[1] *C.O.* 1/21, No. 89.
[2] See Appendix D.
[3] *C.O.* 1/25, No. 59, iii.
[4] *C.O.* 1/25, No. 77, i.
[5] *Letters Illustrative of the Reign of William III.*, vol. ii. p. 303.
[6] Bridges, *Annals of Jamaica*, vol. i. ch. 9.

IV.

The claims of the West Indies as a possible location for a Scottish colony were not overlooked by the Scottish merchants who, at the desire of the Committee of trade, assembled in the spring of 1681, " to give their advyse anent the causes of the decay of trade and what they should propose for the remeid thereof." The proceedings of this conference of merchants—its discussion on trade with Norway, France and the Baltic, its views on inland traffic, and its suggestions concerning shipping—are of the greatest interest in connection with all the later Scottish colonial schemes. They show a keen interest in commercial problems, and reveal a state of eagerness for commercial expansion that explains the success of the New Jersey enterprise, and accounts, to some extent, for the readiness with which Scotland welcomed the Darien scheme.

The views of the Conference regarding colonial policy are set forth in a memorandum entitled, " Memorial concerning the Scottish plantation to be erected in some place of America."[1] The " Memorial " does not seek to put forward in detail arguments in support of the benefits that may accrue from the establishment of such a colony : these are presumably regarded as self-evident : " it is thought the same, if effectual, may prove of great advantage to the country." After this brief exordium its composers concern themselves with two problems : the choice of a site for the colony ; the procedure to be adopted to ensure its effective foundation.

" It is aggried on by all who knows the tradeing of these places and have had occasions to navigate to most of these parts, both of the continent and isleands lyeing in the great and spatious Gulf of Mexico, that there are several isleands and continents wherein a Scottish plantatione might be erected and established, provydeing those who have the charge now from his Majesty of regulating trade will take unto their considerations the following proposals and consider seriouslie the severall circumstances in which the said plantatione

[1] *Reg. P.C.S.*, Third Series, vol. vii. pp. 664-665.

might stand involved and how the same may be rectified and the difficulties of erecting the said plantatione removed." The first location suggested for consideration is the coast of South America " from Surranam all along upon the coasts of New Andaluza . . . to the capeland of the Island Trinidat and from thence westward to Cape de Coquiboca " on " several islands," viz.—the Island of Margarita, Isle of Blanco [Blanquilla], Isle of Orshila [Orchilla], Isle of Rocka [Les Roques], Isle de Avis [Islas de Aves—Birds Islands], Isle Bonyra [Buen-Ayre], Coresaw [Curaçoa] (presentlie possessed by the Dutch), Isle Aruba [Oruba]. But to the occupation of any of the Colombian Islands there was one insuperable objection : " these lyeing all upon the coast of New Andaluza which is inhabited by the Spanziards who have considerable garrisons there, it is to be considered what inconveniences may be expected from so dangerous a neighbourhood."

After a reference to St. Lucia, St. Vincent, and Dominica and the remark that " all the rest of the Carribe Islands are already possest or inhabited be Dutch French or English to the Isle of Porto Rico and Santa Cruce," the " Memoriall " proceeds : " the consideration of them shall be waved and come to Jamaica, which is one Island possest be the Englishes but not on six pairt peopled or inhabited : so its thought the English for their own safetie would be content to allow a considerable pairt of that isleand for a Scotts plantation which (its thought) might serve our design."

" The next thing wee propose for a Scotts colony is Cape Florida or some pairt of it lyeing betwixt the 24 and 25 degrees of northern latitude, joyning with Carolina on the North, which is already ane English plantation, but the inconvenience the native Indians are there very numerous."

The " Isles of Bahama " are next commented on, but over them too is the cloud of Spanish jealousy : " The only inconveniences they lie along the coast of Cuba, which is possesst by the Spanzieards and lyeing in the mouth of the Gulf of Havana may be an eyesore to that nation who pretend to the empyre of the West Indies." It is instructive to compare the very evident dread of Spanish retaliation revealed in the " Memoriall " with the very different attitude towards Spain displayed by those responsible for the Darien Expedition.

After the consideration of possible sites the memorial proceeds to lay down "three preliminarie points to be maturelie and seriouslie advysed and thereafter putt to execution to the establishing of a colony there, viz. :

" First, to establish a sufficient fond for carrieing on of that designe.

" Seconde, to send some persone of knowledge, such as the comitee shall think fit to trust, expresse with a small vessell furnished for a tyme with instructions to navigate throw all these places where many Scotts gentlemen of qualitie and present planters there doe reside to take informatione from them where it will be most convenient and most for the advantage of the countrey to erect a Scotts plantatione, especially considering that there are many Scotts men alredie planted in these islands who, hearing of a designe of a Scotts plantatione for which they have longed these many yeirs, will be glad to remove themselves and their families to any place appointed, for that will be a considerable beginning to the said plantation, they being people acquainted and seasoned with these countries and will save much of the expense which the erecting of such a plantatione may occasion, and upon all these to make report to the comitee who may consider what is most expedient to be done for the advantage of the countrey.

" Also, for the more speedie satisfaction, its fitt to send for William Colquhoun, now resident in Glasgow, who hath been a planter amongst the Carribe Islands these 20 years and thereby hath acquyred a considerable fortune that hee hath now settled here in this country, is the onelie persone fitt for giveing information for further encouragement to the settleing of a colony."

To the note of suggestion and suspended judgment evident throughout the " Memoriall," the personal opinion [1] of the Provost of Linlithgow who acted as spokesman of the Conference affords a striking contrast :

" The last thing relating to improving our trade is to erect

[1] *Reg. P.C.S.*, Third Series, vol. vii. p. 671.

a collonie of Scottish subjects in any part of America, which truly if efficient, would be a great ease to the countrey and void it of very maney both idle and dissenting persones. The place in my humble opinion most proper for this collonie is Cape Florida, which is ane isthmuss of land joyning with Carolina in the north and butting on the Gulf of Havana southward, in length 360 myles and 250 in breadeth, lying betwixt the 24 and 29 degrees of northern latitude in a very temperat clim, it being (as I am credibly informed from those who have the charge of his Majestie's plantationes) in his Majestie's grant, being within the verge of the lands excepted out of the Spanish jurisdiction by the last treatie betwixt the two kings and, in effect, is upon the mater presentlie possessed by savages and so primi occupantis, being juris nullius. This project, in September, came the length of a patent, which was drawen at large and ready for his Majestie's hand, and now is remitted to this honourable comitee to consider if it were not advysable to be renewed for improvement of our trade."

When one bears in mind the fate of the Scots who settled a few years later at Port Royal in South Carolina, one trembles to think what might have befallen any of the Provost's fellow-countrymen who, relying too implicitly on the praepositorial interpretation of international law and treaty obligations, might have been rash enough to seek for peace and plenty in Cape Florida.

Yet in simple justice to the good Provost, who, if something of a visionary in matters relating to colonisation, was sincerely and earnestly devoted to the welfare of his native land, it must be admitted that there was no other tract of land on the Atlantic seaboard of North America to which he could direct the attention of his countrymen. Acadie, wrested from France by Cromwell, had been restored to the French by the Treaty of Breda. The New Netherlands, the Dutch colony on the Hudson and Delaware—thrust like a wedge between New England and Maryland—had in 1664 surrendered to Colonel Nicolls, and had become the provinces of New York, and East and West New Jersey—an arrangement that had survived the temporary success of the Dutch in 1673-4. The debatable land between Virginia and Florida had in 1663 been assigned to the Carolina Proprietors. Both in East New Jersey and in South Carolina the Scottish colonists who crossed the Atlantic a few years later made homes for themselves in the English plantations by arrangement with the authorities in control of the territory they had selected for their domicile.

V.

The Memorial concerning the Scottish plantation was presented to the Privy Council by the committee of merchants on 28th February, 1681, and marks the close of a week of discussion and deliberation of the highest significance in the economic history of Scotland. On the very next day the Privy Council issued a proclamation designed to prohibit imports of textile goods—" Discharging the Importing of Forraign Linen, or Woolen Cloth, Gold and Silver Threed etc. . . . Commodities which are either to be debarred as superfluous in themselves, or supplied by Domestic Manufactures or private Industry of our own subjects." [1] Thus with characteristic Caledonian impetuosity was inaugurated the intensive campaign for the stimulation of home industries, bringing in its train the inevitable retaliatory closing of foreign markets to the Scottish trader, and the consequent necessity of finding a new outlet for Scottish manufactures : and in this impulse to search for new markets is to be found one of the chief causes of the popularity of the Darien scheme.

The problem which the Privy Council sought to solve so hastily and peremptorily had in reality been engaging the attention of the Scottish government for two decades. In Scotland as in England the period immediately following the Restoration was marked by vigorous efforts to develop the commercial activities of the country. The first parliament of the reign of Charles II. " holden and begun at Edinburgh the first day of January one thousand six hundred threescore one years " was but eight days old when a Committee was appointed for " trade and complaints "—" the King's Maiestie conceiving it fit at this time for the more speedy

[1] *Reg. P.C.S.*, Third Series, vol. vii. p. 45 ; Advocates' Library, " Proclamations of Privy Council."

dispatch of business in this Parliament that some be appointed for prepareing of overtures for advancing of Tread Navigation and Manufactories and for hiering of private complaints betwixt parties." The Committee for Trade consisted of twelve representatives of each of the three Estates. To the Committee was given power "to meet advise upon and prepare such overtures and Acts as they shall think fit to be past for advancing of trade, navigation and manufactories, and for that end to call for the advice and help of understanding Merchants, or any who can give best information in those affairs." [1]

The same spirit of commercial enterprise inspired later on in the same year the framing of the "Act establishing Companies and Societies for making linning cloth stuffs etc." [2] Those who were concerned in the drafting of this Act—in all probability the Committee of Trade—looked before and after. As they backward cast their glance they found not a little that was disheartening: but they faced the future resolutely. "Oure Soverane Lord Considering that all the lawdable lawes and Statutes made be his Maiesties Ancestors anent Manufactories for enriching of his Maiesties antient Kingdome, putting of poore children, ydle persons and vagabonds to work for the maintenance and relief of the Countrie of the burden of such unprofitable persones, have been hitherto rendered ineffectual, and that many good spirites having aimed at the publict good, have for want of sufficient stocks councill and assistance been crushed by such undertakings doe conceave it necessar to create and erect companies and societies for manufactories, That what was above the capacity of single persones may be carried on by the joynt assistance Councell and means of many and therefor his Maiestie with advice and consent of his Estates of Parliament Doth establish particular societies and companies in the persones of such as shall enter themselves in the said Societies within any Shire or burgh, on or moe of this Kingdom."

The commodities to be manufactured by such companies were " lining cloath, worsted stockings, searges, baises, sayes,

[1] *A.P.C.*, vol. vii. p. 8.   [2] *A.P.S.*, vol. vii. p. 255.

callons, sempiterniums, castilians, perpetuancies, and all other wollen stuffs and cloaths." To facilitate the process of manufacture various concessions were granted to companies. They were allowed to regulate their own affairs. For a space of nineteen years they were to be free " of all custome, excise, or any other imposition whatsoever " either on raw materials imported for their use or on manufactured goods sent out of the Kingdom. The export of the above-named textiles was permitted only to those who were " Frie and of one of the societies forsaid."

To provide the skilled labour necessary for the carrying on of such manufactures as were contemplated two schemes, distinct but complementary, were devised. In the first place an effort was to be made to establish an elementary system of technical education in Scotland : " and that this pious charitable and proffitable design may be no longer frustrate, nor poore children, vagabonds or idle persons continew to be burdensome to the Countrie, It is Statute and Ordained That ther be in each paroche one or more persones provided and appointed upon the charges and expenses of the heritors thairof for instructing of the poore children, vagabonds and other idlers to fine and mix wooll, spin worstead and Knit Stockings." In the second place, inducements were offered to attract skilled craftsmen from abroad : " And that manufactories may be promoved and for the encourageing of skillful artizans from abroad for traineing up the persones foresaids and workeing for the use of the saids companies, It is hereby declared that all such as shall be brought home and imployed for the saids companies shall be frie to set up and worke in burgh and landward wher the companies shall think fit without paying any thing whatsoever to any person or persones under whatsoever culour or pretext for their freedom and shall be frie of taxes publict burdings or exactions during their lyfetime."

Emphatically this Act for Establishing Companies and Societies voiced a national desire for economic advancement. It was, indeed, merely the first of a series of measures passed in the year 1661 to stimulate Scottish industries. It was followed by an " Act discharging the exportation of lining

Yearne and regulating the breadth of lining cloath." [1] Then, as a counterblast to the English Navigation Act of 1660, came the " Act for Encourageing of Shiping and Navigation," designed for the protection of Scottish shipping and trade, " both which are much decayed if not wholly ruined by the late unhappie war and the said effects that have followed thereupon." [2] Closely akin to the ostensible purpose of this Navigation Act was the " Act for the Fishing and erecting of companies for promoving the same." [3] Then came a supplementary " Act for erecting manufactories," [4] followed by an " Act for planting and inclosing of ground." [5]

The supplementary " Act for erecting manufactories " reveals a keen desire on the part of the Government to protect and encourage textile industries. It confirmed the privilege of " masters, erectors, or enterteaners of manufactories " to regulate their own affairs. It forbade " all quartering or leveying of souldiers upon manufactories or the masters thereof." It protected the companies against attempts to tamper with their workmen, ordering " that no persone whatsoever intysse resset or interteane any of the servants or apprentices of the manufactories without consent of their masters under the paines contained in the acts of Parliament against coallhewers, salters, and their resetters." It sought to frustrate the wiles of the seventeenth century profiteer : " And also his Matie with advice forsaid Discharges all regraters and forestallers of mercats of wooll And that no merchant or persone whatsoever buy and keep up wooll to a dearth bot that they bring the same to be sold in open mercats under the paines contained in the Acts of Parliament made against regraters and forestallers. And in regarde ther is much deceat by wrapping up of wooll in the fleice by putting stones sand and other insufficient stuff in the same ; It is heirby declared that all such wooll shall be confiscat, the one half to his Maiesties use and the other halfe to the use of those who shall apprehend discover and persue the same."

During the two decades that followed this strenuous legislation a few companies were set up for the carrying on of

[1] *A.P.S.*, vol. vii. p. 257. [2] *Ibid.* [3] *Ibid.* p. 259.
[4] *Ibid.* p. 261. [5] *Ibid.* p. 263.

various industries, but in general the industrial horizon was heavy with ominous clouds when, in January, 1681, the conference of Scottish merchants was summoned, " to give their advyse anent the causes of the decay of trade and what they should propose for the remeid thereof." The result of the deliberations held during the week 21st-28th February between the merchants and the " Committee for Trade "[1] was the immediate adoption by the Government of a wholehearted policy of protection. On the first of March, 1681, the first steps were taken to put this policy into effect. The decisions of the Committee were "with all possible convenience and expedition to be formed into a Mature and Digested Proclamation, for Regulation of the Manufacture and Trade of the Kingdom." But this would take time, and therefore on 1st March was issued a premonitory proclamation . . . " because several merchants may either by mistake or upon a sinister design, give order for importing those goods which are prohibited ; Therefore to prevent all inconveniencies which may arise to this Our Ancient Kingdom by the Import of those Commodities which are either to be debarred as superfluous in themselves, or supplied by Domestic Manufactures or private Industry of Our own subjects, and to make the Importers thereof inexcusable ; We with Advice of Our Privy Council, do hereby discharge the Importation of all Silver and Gold Threed, Silver and Gold Lace, Fringes or Tracing, all Buttons of Gold and Silver Thread, all Manner of Stuff, or Ribbons in which there is any Gold or Silver Threed, all Philagram Work ; as also all Forraign Holland Linen,

---

[1] This Committee differed widely from Parliamentary Committees of Trade, such as the Commission for trade and complaints appointed 8th January, 1661 (see above, page 128). This was a Committee of the Privy Council : the members of the Committee were " His Royall Highness (the Duke of York) : Privy Seal : Queenberry : Argyle : Kintore : President of Session : Thesaurer Depute : Register : Advocat : Justice Clerk : Collintoun : Haddo (*Reg. P.C.S.*, Third Series, vol. vii. p. 652). " Forasmuch as the Lords of our Privy Council, having for encrease of Money and improvements of the Manufactures of this Kingdom, appointed a Committee who with the advice of the Merchants and other Persons experienced in these affairs have agreed upon several Conclusions " (*Reg. P.C.S.*, Third Series, vol. viii. p. 45 ; Advocates' Library, A Proclamation discharging the Importation of Forraign Linen, etc., 1st March, 1681).

Cambrick, Lawn, Darneck, Tyken, Bousten, or Damety, Tufted or Stripped Holland, Calligo, Muslin, Silesia and East India Linen, and all other Cloaths made of Linen or Cotton; as also, all Forraign Cloaths and Stuffs whatsomever, made of Wool-Yarn or Wool and Lint; all Forraign Silk and Woolen Stockings; all Forraign Laces made of Silk, Gimp or Threed, and all Manner of Laces and Paint of any sort or Collours; all Forraign made Gloves, Shoes, Boots, and Slippers; And do hereby discharge all merchants and others whatsomever to import unto this Kingdom any of the foresaid Commodities, after the date hereof: excepting only such as can be made appear upon Oath to have been ordered by preceding Commissions and shipped before the tenth of March."

The "Mature and Digested Proclamation," which was issued six weeks later,[1] is a pamphlet of twelve pages large quarto, confirming the principles of the premonitory manifesto and elaborating certain matters of detail. The reasons for the initiation of the new policy are explicitly stated—" there being severall Representatives made to Us and our Privy Council by diverse of the most considerable merchants of this Kingdom and others, that by the undue ballance of trade, occasioned chiefly by the Import of many unnecessary and superfluous Commodities, consumed upon vanity and luxury, a great part of the stock of the Money of the Kingdom was exported, and the improvement of the native Export and Manufacture of the Kingdom neglected, notwithstanding of the many good and wholesome Laws made by Us and Our Royall Ancestors for encouragement thereof." [2]

A wide range of industries came within the scope of this Proclamation. It sought to establish a ship-building industry: " Whereas it may be of great advantage to Trade, and improvement of Manufactorie that some encouragement may be given for building of Ships within this Kingdom; We have thought fit to ordain all Materials necessary for building and rigging of Ships in this Kingdom; such as

---

[1] Advocates' Library: "Proclamation of Privy Council, 11th April, 1681," *Reg. P.C.S.*, Third Series, vol. vii. p. 97.

[2] *Proclamation*, p. 4.

Timber and Planks for Shipping, Sails, Anchors, Cables, and Towes, to bee free of all manner of Duty; and do prohibite and discharge the buying or building abroad, any ships or Vessels, after the first day of June next, under the penalty of confiscation thereof." [1]

With true Scottish zeal for education it did not neglect the things of the mind: " And for encouragement of Learning and Manufactorie of Book-Keeping; we have thought fit to ordain ten of the hundred to be exacted off all bound-Books warrantably imported for publick sale, conform to the book of Rates; but that all Books warrantably imported in Sheets not bound, be free of all manner of duty." [2]

With Caledonian caution it envisaged the possibility of there being Scots in whom the flame of patriotism might be extinguished by the dross of self-interest: " And whereas divers un-frie men and others, who do not bear publick burthen within Burghs are in use to import prohibited Commodities in Noblemen and Gentlemen's Trunks to the great prejudice of Trade, the Tackmen or Collectors of our Customs, Surveyors, Collectors, waiters and their servants are hereby required to sight the Trunks of any person of what quality soever and to seize upon, burn and destroy the said prohibited goods." [3]

The wholesale prohibition of the import of goods, the permission to import certain commodities free, and the grant of an allowance for the excise of salt on fish exported, meant a considerable diminution of the revenue of the country, and to atone for this " an additional Excise " was decreed on French wine, brandy, tobacco, and " all Mum-beer, and other forraign Beer or Ale imported." But the cloud that thus lowered over old Scots conviviality was not without its silver lining. With paternal solicitude the Privy Council sought to calm ruffled minds by pointing to brighter days ahead: " And that our subjects may have no account to murmur of any new burden, we do declare that the additions foresaids upon wine, Brandy, Tobacco, Mum-beer, and other Forraign Beer and Ale, is only in compensation of the Detriment our Customs and Excise does suffer by the saids

[1] *Proclamation*, p. 9.   [2] *Ibid.* p. 9.   [3] *Ibid.* p. 8.

Prohibitions and are to continue and endure while the Prohibitions appointed by this and Our former Proclamation are in Vigour, and our Customs and Excise in collection, and no longer." [1]

Six months after the issue of the "Mature and Digested Proclamation" the "Act for encourageing Trade and Manufactures" [2] confirmed the privileges granted by previous statutes of similar import, consolidated the provisions of the spring proclamations, and added such amendements as prudence and reflection had suggested during the interval that had elapsed since the issue of the proclamations: the wearing of gold or silver thread, for example, was once more forbidden, but the sumptuary regulations were so far modified as to allow "to Officers and Souldiers of the King's whole standing forces the space of two years after the first of November next to wear out their Cloaths upon which ther is any gold or silver lace, threed, or Buttons."

. . . .

Of this strenuous and insistent legislation by Proclamation and by Statute, the Scottish desire to found a colony in America was the inevitable complement. The shrewd Scottish merchants who suggested to the Government the prohibition of foreign imports can hardly have failed to realise that this policy would inevitably close to Scots traders the markets where hitherto they had disposed of their wares. No man of ordinary prudence could fail to see the importance of securing new markets. In Scotland there had grown up a strong feeling that in colonial enterprise alone could there be found an effective solution for this pressing economic difficulty. The glimpses of the possibilities of the Plantation trade gained by the Scots, first during the Cromwellian Union, and later in the course of their systematic and persistent evasion of the English Navigation Acts, had made the merchants of the Northern Kingdom acutely appreciative of the commercial advantages possessed by England in the chain of settlements stretching from the icy wastes of Hudson Bay to the palm-fringed islands of the Caribbean. The desire on

[1] *Proclamation*, pp. 11 and 12.   [2] *A.P.S.*, vol. viii. p. 348.

the part of Scots traders for the foundation of a Scots colony found clear and emphatic expression in the memorial concerning the Scottish Plantation to be erected in some place of America. It was left, however, to William Paterson to give to Scottish mercantile ambitions a local habitation and a name.

VI.

Interesting as the "Memorial concerning the Scottish Plantation" is, as the expression of Scottish commercial aspirations, it is not less interesting in its approximation to the main principles that underlay contemporary English views on colonisation. From the various locations mentioned in the Memorial, it is clear that what the Scottish merchants had in view was a tropical or sub-tropical colony of the plantation type. Among Englishmen interested in commercial progress and in colonial trade, the tropical or sub-tropical plantation was precisely the type of colony that at this time was regarded with most favour. During the half century that had elapsed between the Union of the Crowns and the Restoration, the English attitude towards colonisation had, in one important respect, undergone a radical alteration. Colonisation was no longer favoured as a simple and effective means of blood-letting for the body politic. Gradually it had been borne in upon the minds of Englishmen that the surplus population for which, in Elizabethan and Early Stuart times, colonisation had seemed to offer itself as a valuable outlet, was in reality not a surplus population. The unemployment and the vagabondage then so rife were the inevitable concomitants of an era of transition. The dismissal of the bands of feudal retainers that followed on the enforcement of the Statutes of Livery and Maintenance; the tendency on the part of landowners, both lay and monastic, to substitute pasture for tillage; the dissolution of the monasteries; the enclosure of the common lands—all these had united to break up the communal habits of centuries, and to cause a serious dislocation of population. But, as the years passed, and men gradually adapted themselves to the new order of things, as trade expanded and new markets were found in East and West, the surplus population was gradually absorbed in home industry and foreign trade. In the battles and sieges of the Civil War had perished many of the best men of the country. In London the Plague had done its deadly work. The public conscience of the Restoration era, keenly alive to all that concerned commercial progress, saw clearly that a considerable portion of the land in England was as yet undeveloped [1] and that English trade was also capable of much improvement. The government that encouraged the immigration of Huguenot refugees was not likely to look with favour on the emigration of Englishmen to the American colonies; and it took no pains to conceal its view: "... this Kingdom hath, and doth daily suffer a great Prejudice by the Transporting great Number of the People thereof to the said Plantations for the peopling of them." [2] The view that " we have people enough and more than we can employ " is classed by Sir Josiah Child among the " vulgar errors " of the time.[3]

The most striking proof of the fact that at the time of the Restoration English industry was capable of giving employment to every Englishman in the country is found in the ease with which the Cromwellian army was absorbed into the civilian population. " Fifty thousand men, accustomed to the profession of arms, were at once thrown on the world : and experience seemed to warrant the belief that this change would produce much misery and crime, that the discharged veterans would be seen begging in every street, or that they would be driven by hunger to pillage. But no such result followed. In a few months there remained not a trace that the most formidable army in the world had just been absorbed into the mass of the community." [4] Not a little of this result was probably due, as Macaulay implies, to the sterling character of the Cromwellian soldier. Some of it must also be ascribed to the vigorous policy of the Restoration government as expressed in the " Act for inabling the Souldiers of

[1] See Preamble to 15°, Car. II. c. 7.   [2] 22 and 23, Car. II. c. 26.
[3] Child, Preface to *A New Discourse of Trade* (written circa 1669, first published 1693).
[4] Macaulay, *History of England*, chap. ii.

the Army now to be disbanded to exercise Trades."[1] But to us who have experienced the difficulties of the post-bellum settlement of an army which bore approximately the same ratio to the total population of Britain as Cromwell's did to the population of England, which had been under arms a much shorter period, and which had never lost its essentially civilian characteristics, it seems clear that the Cromwellian Army was absorbed so easily into the industrial population principally because there was abundant work to which the energies of the discharged soldiers could be turned.

Not only did it seem clear to many statesmen of the Restoration period that there was abundant work for Englishmen at home, but it was also evident that the general trend of foreign affairs suggested a policy of discouraging emigration. Despite the Francophile tendencies of Charles II., public opinion gradually came to look upon a struggle with France as inevitable. Clarendon's friendly attitude to France had been one of the demerits of his policy which were urged at the time of his fall. The Triple Alliance against France had been negotiated by the Cabal. Hostility to France had guided the policy of Danby, as far as his royal master would permit. In these circumstances anything that tended to decrease the effective numbers of the population could not but meet with disfavour. The widespread objection to emigration to the Colonies was a subject which closely engaged the attention of the chief contemporary writers on colonial policy, such as Sir Josiah Child, Dalby Thomas, Dr. Charles Davenant and John Cary.

---

[1] 12°, Car. II. chap. 16. This measure gave permission to all soldiers actually serving under General Monk on 25th April, 1660, to exercise Trades though they had not served their time as Apprentices, and it also enabled all who had entered upon their apprenticeship before joining the army, to enjoy all Immunities as if they had completed their apprenticeship. Stringent measures were framed to make these provisions effective. In case of any action, the discharged soldier might plead the General Issue: " . . . . and such Persons who notwithstanding this Act shall prosecute the said Suite by Bill, Plaint Information or Indictment, and shall have a Verdict passed against them or become Non suite therein or discontinue their said Suite such Person or Persons shall pay unto such Officer or Officers, Souldier or Souldiers double costs of Suite. . . ."

"The trade of our English Plantations in America," wrote Sir Josiah Child, "being now of as great bulk, and employing as much shipping as most of the trades of this Kingdom, it seems not unnecessary to discuss more at large concerning the nature of the plantations, and the good and evil consequences of them, in relation to this and other Kingdoms; and the rather, because some gentlemen of no mean capacities, are of opinion that his Majestie's plantations abroad, have very much prejudiced this Kingdom by draining us of our people." [1] Dalby Thomas, a more sprightly controversialist, recognises equally the intensity of the feeling against the plantations, but is hardly so gentle towards the upholders of this opinion : " There is nothing more frequent amongst the Generality of Mankind than is the Drawing wrong conclusions from right Premisses, whereby the most concise and truest Maxims and Sayings that wise men upon solid thinking have contrived to guide us, like Landmarks, in the Search of Truth, are perverted by wrong Applications, to drown our Understandings in the Gulph of Error. Thus, because Truth itself is not truer than that People are the Wealth of a Nation, those who have not time, Experience, and Skill, to examine the Fund of that undeniable Verity, though, in other Things, Men of excellent Understandings, are apt to infer, that all, who set foot out of the Kingdom, are in some Degree a Diminution of its Wealth, and thence take for granted that the American Colonies occasion the Decay both of the People and Riches of the Nation ; when upon a thorough Examination, nothing can appear more erraneous, as I doubt not to make plain to every Man." [2] Similarly Davenant devotes the opening pages of his Discourse on the Plantation Trade to the critical examination of " The most material objections to our colonies in America. . . . 1st, That they drain this Kingdom of people, the most important strength of any nation, 2dly, That they are a retreat to men of notions opposite to the religion of their country, and to persons

---

[1] *A New Discourse of Trade*, Foulis Edition, 1751, pp. 133 and 134.
[2] *Historical Account of the Rise and Growth of the West India Colonies* (1690), Harleian Misc. Edition 1744, p. 342.

disaffected to the government."[1] "I will consider one Objection" wrote Cary, "it having been a great question among many thoughtful men whether our Foreign Plantations have been an advantage to this Nation; the reasons they give against them are, that they have drained us of Multitudes of our People who might have been serviceable at home, and advanced Improvements in Husbandry and Manufactures; that the Kingdom of England is worse Peopled by so much as they are increased; and that Inhabitants being the Wealth of a Nation, by how much they are lessened, by so much we are poorer than when we first began to settle our Colonies."[2]

The objection to emigration was both widespread and strongly rooted, and in meeting it the advocates of colonial expansion laid stress upon the benefits of the colonies as sources for the supply of materials which could not be procured at home, upon the advantage to English industries of the colonial markets, and upon the importance of the plantation trade to the shipping of the nation. "The men of that day argued in a circle of sea power, commerce, and colonies."[3] Such a line of argument tended to bring out the prominence of the West Indian plantations in a policy guided by the idea of finding in the possession of colonies solid advantages to counterbalance the loss sustained by the mother country through emigration. Indeed Sir Josiah Child laid down, diplomatically but firmly, decided objections to New England, from the standpoint both of commerce and of politics. Of his twelve propositions embodying his views on plantations, the eleventh one runs: "That New England is the most prejudicial plantation to the Kingdom of England."[4] "I cannot omit," he declares after a tactful compliment to the character of the people of New England, "to take notice of some particulars, wherein Old England suffers diminution by the growth of those colonies settled in New England, and how that plantation differs from those more southerly with

[1] Coll. Edition 1771, vol. ii. p. 2.
[2] *An Essay on Trade* (Bristol, 1695), pp. 65 and 66.
[3] Beer, *Old Colonial System*, vol. i. p. 16.
[4] *A New Discourse*, Edition 1751, p. 134.

respect to the gain or loss of this Kingdom. All our American plantations, except that of New England, produce commodities of different natures from those of this Kingdom, as sugar, tobacco, cocoa, wool, ginger, sundry sorts of dying woods, etc., whereas New England produces generally the same as we have viz. corn and cattle, some quantities of fish they do likewise kill, but that is taken and saved altogether by their own inhabitants, which prejudices our Newfoundland trade, where, as has been said, very few are, or ought, according to prudence, to be employed in those fisheries but the inhabitants of Old England. The other commodities we have from them are some few great masts, furs, and train oil. . . ." Other disadvantages of New England were, in Sir Josiah's eyes, the possible danger to the mother country that might arise from the maritime proficiency of the inhabitants of these northern colonies and the fact that, " the people of New England by virtue of their primitive charters, being not so strictly tied to the observation of the laws of this Kingdom, do sometimes assume the liberty of trading contrary to the act of navigation." [1]

Far otherwise was it with the island colonies : " The people that evacuate from us to Barbadoes and the other West India plantations do commonly work one English to eight or ten blacks ; and if we keep the trade of our said plantations entirely to England, England would have no less inhabitants, but rather an increase of people by such evacuation, because that one Englishman, with the ten blacks that work with him, accounting what they eat, use and wear, would make employment for four men in England, . . . whereas, peradventure, of ten men that issue from us to New England and Ireland, what we send to or receive from them does not employ one man in England."

" The Commodities they (the Plantations) afford us," wrote Cary, " are more especially Sugars, Indigo, Ginger, Cotten, Tobacco, Piamento, and Fustick, of their own growth, also Logwood, which we bring from Jamaica (though first brought thither from the Bay of Campeacha on the Continent of Mexico belonging to the Spaniard, but cut by a loose sort of

[1] *A New Discourse,* Edition 1751, pp. 160, 161.

People, Subjects to this Kingdom, Men of desperate Fortunes, but of wonderful Courage, who by force have made small Settlements there and defend themselves by the same Means), besides great quantities of Fish taken the Coasts of Newfoundland and New England; These being the Product of Earth, Sea, and Labour are clear Profit to the Kingdom, and give a double Imployment to the People of England, first to those who raise them there, next to those who prepare Manufactures here wherewith they are supplied besides the Advantage to Navigation, for the Commodities Exported and Imported being generally bulky do thereby imploy more Ships, and consequently more Saylors. . . ."[1]

. . . . . .

It was these advantages of the tropical or sub-tropical plantation as a source of supply, and as a possible market for the products of Scottish factories, that in 1681 attracted the favour of the Scottish merchants. Loss of population through emigration need cause Scotland no anxiety: the twelve proprietors who, in 1682 acquired East Jersey from the trustees of Sir George Carteret might well assert in their Brief Account that "the chief Reason against Forraign Plantations—the drawing too many Inhabitants out of the Nation, and so leaving the Countries at Home unfurnished of people "[2]—was of negligible force where Scotland was concerned; and three years later George Scot could declare without fear of contradiction that "this Kingdom hath plenty of Inhabitants whereof yearly it may cast a fleece without the least prejudice of the general interest of the nation."[3] But sugar-works had already been set up at Glasgow,[4] and despite the restrictions of the English Navigation Acts the city of St. Mungo had begun to anticipate the days of the Tobacco Lords. The protective measures designed in 1681 to stimulate Scottish industries made a search for fresh markets inevitable. And where might such markets

---

[1] *Essay on Trade*, pp. 67 and 68.
[2] *A Brief Account of East New Jersey.*
[3] *Model of the Government of East New Jersey.*
[4] Prof. Scott, Introduction to *New Mills Cloth Manufactory*, p. xxxviii.

be sought with better hope of success than in the region of the Caribbean Islands, where already the Scots had settled in considerable numbers, and whence manufactured commodities could easily be shipped—as the Scottish merchants well knew—to the English plantations on the mainland of North America?

It is true that both in English and in Scottish colonial history the actual course of events seemed on the surface to proceed uninfluenced by contemporary theories. In the decade following the Restoration England lost Lord Willoughby's sub-tropical plantation of Surinam, but acquired the continental territories that became New York and East and West New Jersey, and made a beginning with the planting of Carolina; behind the maritime frontier of the Jerseys, the boundaries of Pennsylvania were a decade later to be staked out. The Scottish colony of Stuart's Town in South Carolina was essentially a colony of refuge; the Quaker Scottish settlement of East New Jersey was at its inception inspired by a similar aim.

But though the English acquisition of the New Netherlands may have been inspired mainly by strategic considerations, economic reasons were not lacking in support of this extension of territory: through New Amsterdam not a little of the tobacco of Virginia and Maryland found its way in Dutch ships, directly to Holland. The hope of Penn that " good skill in our most Southern Parts will yield us several of the Straights Commodities, especially Oyle, Dates, Figgs, Almonds, Raisins, and Currans," bears testimony to the fact that the founder of Pennsylvania was not uninfluenced by contemporary theories regarding colonisation."[1] By these theories the Lords Proprietors of Carolina were also guided and " in South Carolina ultimately was developed the purest type of plantation colony that existed on the continent."[2]

And what is true of English colonial history is substantially true of Scottish colonial history. The Scottish enterprises in East New Jersey and South Carolina were on a very small scale, though the history of each enterprise has many features

[1] Beer, *Old Colonial System*, vol. i. p. 55.   [2] *Ibid.*

of interest. The logical outcome of Scottish commercial ambitions was the foundation of the Company of Scotland trading to Africa and the Indies. And the outcome of the efforts of " the Court of Directors of the Indian and African Company of Scotland to settle a Colony in the Indies " was —the Darien Scheme.

CHAPTER V

EAST NEW JERSEY

BETWEEN the surrender of Sir William Alexander's colony at Port Royal to the Chevalier de Razilly and the beginning of the next Scottish colonial enterprise—the establishment of the Quaker-Scottish colony of East New Jersey—there stretched an interval of half a century. The new scheme, however, was the lineal descendant of the old: Robert Barclay of Urie, the first governor of the Quaker-Scottish colony of East New Jersey, was the grandson of Sir Robert Gordon of Gordonstown, the first of the Nova Scotia Baronets.[1] And a further link with the earlier Scottish movement is found in the fact that George Scot of Pitlochie, the Fifeshire laird who played a prominent part in the one tragic episode of the New Jersey enterprise, was the son of Sir John Scot of Scotstarvit, to whom Captain Mason had addressed his "Discourse," and who had acted in 1625 as deputy for Sir William Alexander in connection with applications for Nova Scotia Baronetcies.[2]

The year 1684, which saw the emigration of a considerable number of Scots to East Jersey, saw also the foundation of the short-lived Presbyterian colony of Stuart's Town, situated at Port Royal in South Carolina. Both movements stood quite apart from the general trend of Scottish mercantile aspirations as revealed in the Memorial of 1681. The foundation of the Scottish colony in South Carolina was the result of the efforts of a group of prominent Covenanters: the establishment of the Quaker-Scottish colony of East New Jersey was effected chiefly through the efforts of the celebrated Quaker apologist, Robert Barclay of Urie.

[1] *Nova Scotia Papers*, p. 120.   [2] *Ibid.* p. 23.

I.

"In studying the history of the American colonies," says Doyle, "we are at once struck with a certain lack of biographical interest."[1] It is a defect which is nowhere apparent in the history of Scottish colonial enterprise. Meagre as the material results of that enterprise were, the lives of the men who inspired and guided the various schemes are full of the interest that springs from strength of personality. Sir William Alexander, Gordon of Lochinvar, Robert Barclay of Urie, Principal William Dunlop, William Paterson, the leading spirits of Scottish colonial enterprise, form a group of men of strong individuality, men whose careers are suffused with an interest that not infrequently becomes romantic.

Robert Barclay of Urie, the eldest son of Colonel David Barclay, soldier and Quaker, Covenanter and champion of distressed Royalists, was born in 1648 at Gordonstown in Moray, the house of his maternal grandfather, Sir Robert Gordon, second son of the Earl of Sutherland. During his student days at the Scots College in Paris, of which his uncle and namesake was Rector, Robert showed much ability, especially in debate: the child was father of the man. Withdrawn from the College at the age of fifteen Robert Barclay returned to Scotland, where the Restoration Government was doing its utmost to establish the royal authority on unassailable foundations. One of the activities inspired by this policy was the persecution of men who had been connected with the Cromwellian Government. Colonel Barclay, who had sat in two of the Protector's parliaments, was imprisoned in Edinburgh Castle. There his intercourse with a fellow-prisoner, the Quaker John Swinton, led the veteran of Gustavus's campaigns to become a member of the Society of Friends. Almost at the same time, and mainly through the same influence, Robert Barclay also joined the Society: he was then eighteen years of age.[2]

In Robert Barclay the Quakers were soon to find an able exponent and defender of their religious principles. Four

---
[1] Doyle, *The Middle Colonies*, p. 479.
[2] Cadbury, *Robert Barclay*, ch. ii.

years after his conversion he published a tract entitled, "Truth Cleared of Calumnies":[1] in 1676 he published at Amsterdam the Latin edition of *An Apology for the True Christian Divinity as the Same is Held Forth and Preached by the People, in Scorn, Called the Quakers*; the first English edition of the Apology appeared in 1678.

But Barclay did not confine his efforts on behalf of the Friends to doctrinal expositions. Much of his energy was directed to shielding his fellow-religionists against the persecution provoked by their opinions and their way of life. That persecution was local rather than national. The Scots Privy Council was too busy dealing with the Presbyterians to trouble itself greatly about a sect that was essentially non-militant. It is true that in 1663 the Privy Council, "taking to their consideration the great abuse committed by these people who take upon them the profession of Quakers," appointed a committee to inquire into the activities of three prominent Quakers, and directed the magistrates of Edinburgh to put down Quaker meetings. Two years later the Council again considered the question of dealing with the Quakers. On neither occasion, however, did any general persecution follow from the deliberations of the Council.[2]

Despite the absence of active persecution by the central government in Scotland, the Quakers were subjected to much capricious ill-treatment at the hands of local authorities. In December, 1672, for example, Barclay and John Swinton rode from Urie to Montrose to attend a meeting of Friends, many of whom had recently suffered imprisonment. While

---

[1] *A Short Account of the Life and Writings of Robert Barclay*, p. 79.

[2] *Wodrow*, vol. i. p. 377. "Had this good act," says Wodrow grimly, with reference to the measure of 1663, "been prosecute with the same vigour as those against presbyterians were, we might, in this land, soon have been freed from that dangerous sect; but as soon as the bishops come into the council, in a few days after this, I observe little more done against them. They gave the council so much to do against presbyterian nonconformists, that for some years I meet with little further against the quakers; and any thing that was done was so little prosecute, that they spread terribly during this reign."

Regarding the measures taken against the Quakers in 1665 Wodrow comments: "The laird of Swinton is dropped (*i.e.* from the process of enquiry), and I find very little effectually done as to others of them; so that in this reign they got deep rooting, especially in the northern shires" (vol. i. p. 428).

the meeting was in progress many of the Quakers were re-arrested and Barclay and Swinton were imprisoned in the Tolbooth of Montrose.[1] Barclay was also, at a later period, twice imprisoned in the Tolbooth of Aberdeen.[2]

In various ways Barclay sought to oppose this local oppression. To the *Apology* he prefixed a Dedication to Charles II., couched in terms of clear and courageous admonition, and in this Dedication he referred to the sufferings of the Friends: this treatment he condemned as unjust, on the ground that the Quakers had done nothing to embarrass the Government: they had always held their meetings openly, and in the various political movements against the Crown not a single Quaker had been implicated. In 1676 Barclay was able to enlist the sympathy of several useful allies. In that year he had taken the manuscript of the *Apology* to Amsterdam. Continuing his travels to Herford in Westphalia he visited a distant kinswoman, the Princess Elizabeth, daughter of the Elector Palatine and sister of Prince Rupert. From the Princess he received a letter of recommendation to Prince Rupert. "... I delivered thy letter to thy Brother," wrote Barclay to the Princess, " who was civill to me. I also took occasion from thence to employ him to be assisting to me in ane address I Intend to make to the King on behalf of my Father, and about forty more of our Friends that are about some months ago Imprisoned in Scotland for Conscience sake, in which he promised his concurrence...."[3] With the Duke of York, too, Barclay formed a lasting friendship, and the Duke's influence was enlisted on behalf of the persecuted Quakers in Scotland.

In furtherance of his policy of aiding in every possible way his fellow-religionists, Barclay in 1682 acquired an interest in the Province of East New Jersey. "His work as a controversialist was now over. The cause of Quakerism called for a different kind of service.... It was not enough for them [the early Friends] to preach the possibility that peace can be obtained on earth, they must at all costs labour to establish it."[4] Yet it is difficult, at the first glance, to trace the motives

---

[1] Cadbury, *Robert Barclay*, pp. 38-39.
[2] *Ibid.* pp. 50, 65.
[3] *Ibid.* p. 45.
[4] *Ibid.* p. 68.

that impelled Barclay, at this particular period, to take a leading part in the establishment of a colony " intended to be a practical application of the Quaker theory of toleration, and to provide an asylum for the persecuted." [1] For Scottish Quakers there seemed to be no need of such an asylum. For some years past the persecution of Quakers at the hands of the Scottish Government had entirely died away : not a single reference to Quakers appears in the Records of the Privy Council for the years 1678-1680 ; during the period 1681-1682 the sole reference to the persecution of Quakers occurs in a petition recounting the harsh treatment of one Thomas Dunlop, by the town authorities of Musselburgh.[2] Moreover, the Duke of York, with whom Barclay was on terms of cordial friendship, was in residence at Holyrood as Governor of Scotland, and his influence might be depended on to turn aside the persecuting energies of the Scottish Government if indeed the Government had time or attention for any persecution except that of the Covenanters.

It may have been that Barclay, with an insight into English politics derived from frequent visits to London, recognised that the Duke's tenure of office in Scotland might at any moment be terminated by his recall to the Court in London. It may have been, again, that Barclay was influenced by the colonising zeal of Penn, who had an interest in both East New Jersey and West New Jersey, and had but a comparatively short time before become proprietor of Pennsylvania. It is most probable, however, that Barclay's thoughts were directed to the establishment of a colony of refuge on account of the vindictive and unremitting persecution to which the Quakers in and around the town of Aberdeen were subjected by the local authorities. Then, as now, Aberdeen contained a strong body of Quakers. Then, as now, Aberdeen was a stronghold of the Episcopalians. In the persecution of the Quakers the Bishop of Aberdeen is a prominent figure. On 1st February, 1683, the Lords of the Privy Council considered a petition of the Bishop, " representing that the Quakers in the toune and shyre have most insolently taken upon them to erect publick buriall places for these of their perswasion

[1] *D.N.B.*, " Robert Barclay."   [2] *Reg. P.C.S.*, 3rd Series, vol. vii.

near to the toune of Aberdeen, after the same was dimolished by the magistrats, and in severall paroches have built publick meeting houses and schooles for traineing up their children in their godles and hereticall opinions, and have provyded mortificationes of lands and money to that end." [1] The Council directed the magistrates of Aberdeen and the sheriff to inquire into these matters, but the inquiry seems to have had little practical effect. It is noteworthy that the state of affairs that provoked the worthy prelate to most unworthy rage was obviously of long standing, and in the pressure exerted on the Quakers by the local authorities of Aberdeen is to be found the most satisfactory explanation of Barclay's desire to found a colony of refuge.

If, however, we find in the persecution of the Aberdeen Quakers the motive that first impelled Barclay to thoughts of colonial enterprise, it is not unpermissible to think that a man of his clear intelligence and quick sympathy was stirred, in addition, by a motive of broad philanthropy to take up a project that offered some relief to the wretched peasantry of his native country. " There is nothing more strange than to see our Commons so besotted with the love of their own misery, that rather than quit their Native Country, they will live in much toyl and penury so long as they have strength, being hardly able all their life to acquire so much Riches as can save themselves from begging or starving when they grow old : meantime their children (so soon as they are able to walk) are exposed to the Cruelties of Fortune and the charity of others, naked and hungry, begging Food and Rayment from those that either can not or will not help them : and yet can hardly be perswaded to go to a most profitable fertile and safe Country, where they may have everything that is either necessary, profitable or pleasant for the life of man with very little pains and industry." [2] This noteworthy passage occurs in a broadsheet of 1684 which bears every evidence of having come from Barclay's pen.

The view that Barclay desired to make the East Jersey scheme a national rather than a sectarian enterprise is confirmed by a consideration of some of the steps taken to further

[1] *Reg. P.C.S.*, 3rd Series, vol. viii. p. 37.   [2] *Vide* Appendix E.

the project. Among Barclay's fellow-proprietors were the
Earl of Perth and Perth's brother, John Drummond of
Lundie. It has been conjectured that " the inclusion of the
Scots was due either to allay jealousy of a government
composed entirely of Quakers, or to fortify their interest at
Court by engaging in the undertaking persons of influence." [1]
There is nothing to show, however, that in West Jersey, the
neighbouring colony, any jealousy was aroused by the fact
that the Proprietors were all Quakers : nor could the intro-
duction of Scottish influence be regarded in early colonial
days as a lenitive measure : nor, again, did the influence of
Barclay at the Duke's court at Holyrood and that of Penn at
Whitehall require in any way to be buttressed. Perth was
Barclay's cousin : and, in accepting the place at the head of
the East Jersey Proprietors, Perth was probably influenced
by at least three considerations : by the claims of kinship ;
by a desire to assist one who enjoyed the special favour of the
Duke of York ; and by the hope of adding some wealth to a
family treasure kist by no means well lined.

The inclusion among the list of Proprietors of the name of
the leading Scottish politician of the day could not but give
prestige to the scheme. Other prominent members of the
Government willingly lent their assistance : among those who
at Edinburgh were prepared to furnish information to intending emigrants to East Jersey were the Lord Thesaurer-
Depute and the Lord Register. In various public announce-
ments concerning the scheme considerable prominence was
given to the presence of Scotsmen among the Proprietors.
In the Letters Patent of Charles II., of 23rd November, 1683,
charging all persons concerned in the Province of East New
Jersey to yield obedience to the Government of the twenty-
four grantees, Scots Proprietors alone are mentioned by
name : " . . . And whereas His Royal Highness James
Duke of York, by His Indenture bearing Date the 14th
Day of March Anno Dom 1682 in the five and thirtieth year
of His Majesties Reign (for the Consideration therein mentioned) did Grant and confirm the said Province of East
New Jersey . . . unto James, Earl of Perth, John Drummond

[1] Whitehead, *East Jersey under the Proprietary Governments*, p. 89.

of Londine, as also unto Robert Barclay of Ury, Esq; Robert Gordon of Cluny, Esquire, and other His Majesties Loving Subjects in England, Scotland, and elsewhere, to the number of Twenty four Grantees." [1] And when in the spring of 1684 Barclay published his broadside intended to stimulate emigration, he made an appeal "To all Trades-men, Servants and others who are willing to Transport themselves into the Province of New-East Jersey in America, a great part of which belongs to Scots-men, Proprietors thereof."

The emigration from Scotland to East Jersey was influenced strongly by Barclay's policy of inaugurating a colonial scheme that would make a general appeal to his fellow-countrymen. Among the Scottish emigrants there is no definite record of the presence of Quakers. In the twenty-seven letters from Scottish settlers in East Jersey which are included in Scot's *Model* there is no trace either of Quaker sentiment or of Quaker phraseology. Indeed the general tenor of one of the acts passed by the East Jersey Assembly in 1686, by which time Scottish settlers were established in considerable numbers in the colony, implies that the newcomers had carried across the Atlantic certain well-marked tendencies characteristic of Scottish life in the unquiet days of the seventeenth century. The act referred to was one prohibiting the carrying of swords, pistols, and other arms, and the giving or the receiving of challenges. The preamble to this measure asserted that "many of the inhabitants of the province received great abuses, were put in great fear, and involved in quarrels and challenges by reason of so many persons carrying unusual and unlawful weapons." [2] To the prevalence of these bellicose activities in seventeenth century Scotland the Records of the Privy Council bear convincing testimony.

II.

Like Acadie East Jersey was a province with a history: and, like Acadie, it had been claimed, and fought for, by rival colonising powers. In 1609 Henry Hudson, in the

[1] *Penn MSS.* vol. i. p. 6; *Col. Cal.* 1681-1685, p. 554.
[2] Whitehead, *East Jersey under the Proprietary Governments*, p. 116.

Half Moon, had explored on behalf of the Dutch East India Company the river that bears his name. Next year Dutch merchants, eager to exploit the fur-trade with the Indians, established posts on Manhattan Island and at the point on the Hudson where Albany now stands. Over this region, as over Acadie, England claimed sovereignty, on the strength of Cabot's discoveries: and Captain Samuel Argall, who destroyed the French 'habitation' at Port Royal, troubled for a time the Dutch on the Hudson. Gradually, however, the Dutch established themselves firmly on both banks of the Lower Hudson—the North River. In the autumn of 1655, too, they became masters of the settlements established by the Swedes on the Delaware. The Dutch thus held all the seaboard territory between New England and Delaware Bay.

The Dutch settlements not unnaturally aroused the jealousy of the neighbouring English colonists and attracted the critical attention of the Restoration statesmen who were keenly interested in colonial affairs. The Dutch had a monopoly of the rich fur-trade of the Hudson Valley. They also commanded a most important strategic route to the Great Lakes and Canada. Moreover, the wharves of New Amsterdam afforded a convenient means of shipping the tobacco of Maryland and of Virginia direct to continental Europe in contravention of the English Navigation Acts. International jealousy was further inflamed by the rivalry between Dutch and English on the Guinea Coast. From the English settlers on Long Island came complaints of the greed and cruelty of the Dutch. The English Government were informed that New Amsterdam was without effective means of defence. On 12th March, 1664, the Dutch territory was granted by Charles to the Duke of York. Five months later (29th August, O.S.) New Amsterdam surrendered to Colonel Nicolls.[1]

On 24th June, 1664, while the fleet of Nicolls was speeding westward, the Duke of York made a grant of the lands between the Hudson and the Delaware to Lord Berkeley and Sir George Carteret, cavaliers who, in the dark days of the Civil Wars and the Interregnum, had rendered valiant service to the Stuart cause. The land so granted was called Nova Caesarea

---

[1] Channing, *History of the United States*, vol. ii. ch. ii.

or New Jersey, in appreciation of Carteret's stout defence of Elizabeth Castle on the Island of Jersey in 1649. Against this breaking up of the newly acquired territory Nicolls protested vigorously but vainly.[1]

By the grant of 1664 Berkeley and Carteret became joint-proprietors of the lands between the Delaware and the Hudson.[2] Along with New York this territory was retaken by the Dutch in 1673. When New York and New Jersey were restored to England fifteen months later, New Jersey was divided into two territories, and, by the fresh grants deemed necessary on account of the Dutch conquest, East New Jersey was assigned to Carteret. East New Jersey extended " Eastward and Northward all along the Sea Coast and Hudson's River, from Little Egg Harbour to that part of Hudson's River which is in Fourtyone degrees of Northern Latitude."[3] In 1674 West Jersey was acquired from Berkeley by two Quakers—Bylling and Fenwick; with these were soon associated three other Quakers, Nicolas Lucas, Gawain Lawrie, and William Penn. Eight years later a group of twelve Quakers, of whom the chief were Penn and Lawrie, acquired from the trustees of Sir George Cartaret, who had died in 1679, the Province of East New Jersey at a price of £3,400. Their deeds of lease and release bore the date of 1st and 2nd February, 1681-2.[4] Six weeks later the number of Proprietors was doubled,[5] and among the new Proprietors Scotsmen occupied a prominent position. As has already been pointed out, the Scots Proprietors were the only ones mentioned by name in the letters patent by which, on 23rd November, 1683, the king confirmed the grant of East New Jersey to the Proprietors.

It was no doubt his influential connection with many of the leading men in Scotland combined with the outstanding position he occupied among the Quakers that led to the selection of Barclay as Governor of East New Jersey. The confidence of his brother Proprietors in him is clearly revealed

---

[1] Channing, *History of the United States*, vol. ii. p. 45.
[2] *Penn MSS.* vol. i. 6.   [3] *Ibid.*
[4] Whitehead, *East Jersey under the Proprietory Governments*, p. 83.
[5] *Penn MSS.* vol. i. 6.

in the terms of his appointment : " Such is his known fidelity and capacity that he has the government during life : but that every governor after him shall have it for three years only." He was not required to visit the Province in person, but was allowed to exercise his authority through a Deputy Governor, whose appointment was in his hands. This first Deputy Governor was Thomas Rudyard, a London lawyer and one of the Proprietors.[1]

III.

Like the propagandistic literature of Sir William Alexander and Gordon of Lochinvar, the literature issued in connection with the popularisation of the East Jersey scheme in Scotland well repays study. The later literature is much more varied than the " Encouragements " of the Laird of Menstrie and of Lochinvar. It may be divided into four distinct types : a pamphlet entitled *A Brief Account of the Province of East Jersey in America*, issued in 1682 by the first twelve Proprietors ; individual letters from Deputy Governors and other early colonists ; Barclay's broadsheet of 1684 ; Scot of Pitlochie's *Model of the Government of the Province of East New Jersey in America*, with its valuable appendix of letters from Scots settlers in the Province.

The *Brief Account* of the original Proprietors is by no means an inspiring document. It gives the rates of passage and other practical details with precision but without enthusiasm, and its closing paragraph breathes an air of almost melancholy resignation : " Lastly, Although this country, by means of its being already considerably inhabited, may afford many conveniences to strangers, of which unpeopled countries are destitute, as lodging, victualing, etc., yet all persons inclining into those parts must know, that in their settlement there they will find their exercises ; they must have there winter as well as summer, they must labour before they reap, and, till their plantations be cleared (in summer time) they must expect (as in all those countries) the musketos, flies, gnats, and such like, may in hot and

[1] Whitehead, *E.J.* p. 91.

fair weather, give them some disturbance, where people provide not against them, which as land is cleared, are less troublesome."

Much more buoyant is the tone of the letters sent home by Thomas Rudyard, the Deputy-Governor, and Samuel Groome, Receiver and Surveyor General. Rudyard, writing on the 30th May, 1683, refers to the abundance of building materials available; to the erection of saw mills—"there is 5 or 6 Saw mills going up here this Spring, two at work already"; and is pleased to find "the people are generally a sober professing people, wise in their Generation, Courteous in their Behaviour, and Respectful to us in office among them." [1]

Samuel Groome, Surveyor-General in East New Jersey, is described as "Mariner of Deptford," and in his letter one gets an interesting glimpse of his professional interests. "Friends and fellow proprietors," he writes on 11th August, 1683, "Since my last I have now sounded the Channell from Amboy to Sandy Hook, and find it to be a broad and bold Channell, in no place less than three fathom at high water, in ordinary tydes 4, 5 or 6 fathom except in one short place. Rariton River is a good River, and hath a good tyde of flood overpowering the freshes about 30 miles above Amboy: after its flood the tyde hath no force against the Freshes which comes out of several branches of Rariton, and joyns in one 40 or 50 miles above Amboy.

"I have spent considerable time in making discovery. I have not as yet had time to lay out much land for you, only about 17 or 18 thousand Acres in one tract, good upland near Elizabeth Town. . . ." [2]

One letter from Groome, "after performing its journey to Scotland, and being there widely circulated, exerting considerable influence in inducing emigration, was brought back to the Province, and is now in the Rutherfurd Collection of Original Papers in a good state of preservation." [3] The presence among the papers of Sir John Gordon of Durno (who became a Proprietor in December, 1683) of a copy of a long letter from Gawen Laurie, who succeeded Rudyard as

---

[1] Whitehead, *E.J.* pp. 149, 150.   [2] *Ibid.* pp. 154, 155.
[3] *Ibid.* p. 96 *n.*

Deputy-Governor is probably due also to the influence such letters were found to have in stimulating emigration.[1]

In the spring of 1684 appeared a broadsheet which in its persuasive advocacy of the merits of East Jersey furnishes a piquant contrast to the Laodicean utterances of the *Brief Account*. The broadsheet, it is true, does not bear the signature of Barclay. But in the masterly handling of the subject matter; in the skilful marshalling of argument and counter-argument; in its restrained but incisive appeal, it reveals unmistakably the mind of the expert controversialist. Its practices of setting forth the stock objections to emigration to East Jersey and then refuting these by means of close-knit dialect is a favourite device of Barclay in the *Apology*.[2]

The broadsheet is an "Advertisement to all Tradesmen, Husbandmen, Servants and others who are willing to Transport themselves into the Province of New-East-Jersey in America, a great part of which belongs to Scotsmen, Proprietors thereof." The preamble bears testimony to the activity with which the design was being pushed forward: "Whereas several Noblemen, Gentlemen, and others who (by undoubted rights derived from His Majesty and His Royal Highness are Interested and concerned in the Province of New-East-Jersey lying in the midst of the English Plantations in America), do intend (God-willing) to send several Ships thither in May, June, July, ensuing 1684, from Leith, Montrose, Aberdeen and Glasgow. . . ." The general advantages offered by the colony to Tradesmen, Husbandmen, Servants, and others are set forth clearly and simply, and those "who incline to go thither and desire further information" are advised to apply to "any of the Persons underwritten, who will fully inform them anent the Country, and every other thing necessary, and will answer and satisfy their scruples and objections, and give them all other Incouragements according to their several abilities and capacities. . . ."

After the list of advisers come the poignant reflections already quoted on the misery of "our Commons" and their

[1] Dunbar, *Social Life in Former Days*, Second Series, pp. 106-110.
[2] Cf. for example pp. 296-298 (Edit. 1886) of the *Apology*.

reluctance to seek relief abroad. The principal objections to emigration to New Jersey are then examined :

" First, they alledge that it is a long and dangerous voyage thither ! To which it is answered that ordinarily it is not above 6 or 7 weeks sailing from Scotland, which in a good ship well victualled and with good Company in the Summer Time is rather a pleasant Divertissement than a Trouble or Toyl. . . .

" Next, they say, there is no Company to be had save Barbarians, Woods and Wilderness ! To which it is answered that this is a great mistake, for this Country has been Peopled and Planted these several years by gone. . . . Nor are the woods there anything so wild and inhospitable as the mountains here. . . . The natives are very few and easily overcome, but these simple, serviceable creatures are rather an help and Incouragement than any ways hurtful or troublesome : and there can be no want of Company, seeing there are many thousands of Scots, English, and others living there already, and many more constantly going over : and this summer there are several gentlemen going from Scotland, such as . . . and many others, who are all persons of good quality and estates, and go not out of necessity but choice.

" Lastly, they object that far fetcht Fowls have fair Feathers, and they do not believe the half that is written and spoken in Commendation of these Countreys. To which it is answered, they may as easily deny the truth of everything which they have not seen with their own eyes, for all these things are as verily true as that there is any such pleasant Country as France, Italy, Spain etc. The things being matter of Fact are confirmed by letters from persons of undoubted credit, living on the place, and by certain Information of many Eye-witnesses, who, having once been there, can never after be induced to live in Scotland, nor can it reasonably be imagined that the persons above-written are all fools, to be imposed on by lies and fancies ; on the contrary, there are none (save those that are wise in their own eyes, but are really Ignorant) that are not undenyably convinced of the excellency of the Design. Let such as condemn it be so just as first to hear it and know it, which they may easily do by applying to some of the foresaid Persons, who can best inform them, and then if they think it not below them to be convinced, they will be forced to homologat."

A similar note of counter-challenge is sounded in the Dedication of Scot of Pitlochie's *Model*: " . . . there are (to our shame) a parcell of people, who, whether out of Ignorance or Malice, I cannot well determine, decry the design ; I believe they have a share of both, and thereby weaken not a little the hands of a number of well-meaning people, who would gradually promote the same effectually, were they not imposed upon by the false rumors, industriously spread abroad to stifle any such inclination." [1]

Though Scot's name is associated with the one tragic episode of the Scottish emigration to East New Jersey, he was inspired by lofty ideals and by unflagging enthusiasm in the cause of colonisation. It can hardly be doubted that his interest in colonisation had been aroused primarily by the severe treatment he and his family had suffered at the hands of the Privy Council. On 25th June, 1674, he was fined in £1000 for being present at Conventicles conducted by the Rev. John Welsh ; for " alleged impertinent and extravagant carriage before the council " Pitlochie incurred an additional fine of 500 merks.[2] Charged a month later with being a party to " the harbouring and resetting " of Mr. Welsh he was fined £1000 " by and attour the sum he was liable to and fined for his being at conventicles." [3] On 8th February, 1677, Pitlochie, taken again into custody for being at conventicles,

---

[1] To the opposition encountered by the promoters of the New Jersey scheme Scot refers with greater vehemence and in greater detail on pp. 18 and 19 of the *Model*: " . . . I am abundantly sensible, there are not a few who take upon them to censure this undertaking, who have not the capacity to pry into the advantages which may rationally be proposed in prosecution thereof, the strongest argument they are able to bring against it being taken from the practice of our Ancestors, altogether innocent of any such design, though reputed abundantly wise in their generation : and therefore in their children it can be no less than folly to introduce such a novelty : the same appearing to thwart the verity of some of our old Scottish Proverbs, that ill bairns are best heard at home : Fools are fain of flitting : and a Bird in hand is better than two in the bush : esteemed no less by them than sometimes were the oracles of Apollo at Delphos. . . . I have heard some, whose pretensions to wit were so great that they were upon the borders of Commencing Vertuosi, snarling at this intention, who having been engaged in the debate, bewrayed their ignorance so far in the affair as to inquire whether the plan treated anent, as the proper seats for a Colonie from hence, were Islands or on the continent."

[2] *Wodrow*, vol. ii. p. 238.   [3] *Ibid*, p. 244.

was imprisoned on the Bass Rock,[1] and his liberation from that island prison on 5th October of the same year would seem to be due to his having given " bond and caution under ten thousand merks, to confine himself within his own lands, and not to keep conventicles."[2] While Pitlochie was a prisoner on the Bass his wife was fined 1000 merks for being present at a conventicle.[3] On 14th May, 1679, Scot was again before the Council on a charge of attending conventicles: the cautioners to his bond of 1677 were ordered to pay 3000 merks, while sentence on Pitlochie himself was reserved.[4]

These experiences led him to think—just as similar experiences led the Westland Covenanters of his own day to think—of seeking for liberty of conscience in the New World. "When people find themselves straitened in point of their opinion," he wrote in the *Model*, "no reasonable man will question their call to go where by law they are allowed that Freedom in this point which they themselves would desire; this is one great encouragement to any one so circumstanced to remove to any one of the new plantations: the interest of which obligeth to lay this as a fundamental, that no man shall be in any way imposed upon in matters of principle but have their own freedom without the least hazard."

A visit to London in 1679 and the opportunity there " of frequent converse with several substantial and judicious gentlemen concerned in the American plantations " did much to confirm Pitlochie in his inclination to go overseas. He made a thorough study of all available literature bearing on English colonisation and, seeking to arouse the interest of his fellow-countrymen in an enterprise which he considered highly advantageous to them, he published in 1685 his *Model of the Government of the Province of East New Jersey in America.*— " Printed by John Reid and Sold be Alexander Ogston Stationer in the Parliament Closs."

Dedicated to the Earl of Perth, his brother Drummond of Lundie, and Viscount Tarbet, Lord Clerk-Register, the *Model* takes a form familiar to students of colonial propaganda of the Darien epoch—" a letter from a gentleman at Edinboro

---

[1] *Wodrow*, p. 257. [2] *Ibid.* vol. iii. p. 10.
[3] *Ibid.* vol. ii. p. 361. [4] *Ibid.* vol. iii. p. 10.

SEAL OF THE SCOTTISH-QUAKER PROPRIETORS OF EAST JERSEY.

From Whitehead's "*East Jersey under the Proprietary Governors.*"

... to his Correspondent in the Countrey." In the length
of its historical introduction it follows the Alexandrian
tradition in Scottish colonial literature. In its discursiveness
and volubility it offers an interesting contrast to the succinct
analysis and polished dialectic of Barclay's broadsheet.
The essential information conveyed in the letter from the
gentleman at Edinburgh is, in all essentials, very similar to
what is found in the earlier broadsheet. Two subsidiary
differences, however, are worthy of comment. In the *Model*
the freedom of conscience offered by New Jersey to the
persecuted in the days when " the sadness of distractions of
this Kingdom anent matters of opinion is of greater weight
than any other " is emphasised more than once. No little
energy, again, is directed by Pitlochie to the disparagement
of that other Scottish settlement intended as a colony of
refuge for the oppressed—the Presbyterian colony of Stuart's
Town established in 1684 at Port Royal, in Carolina. The
climate of Carolina, he declares, is unhealthy; there is the
hazard of the Spaniards; little help can be expected from
Charleston. In New Jersey, on the other hand, the climate
and the work are exactly suited to Scots settlers; though the
Governor is a Quaker the defences of the colony are not being
neglected; these defences, indeed, are occupying the attention
of certain "very substantial citizens of London." New
Jersey again is partially settled, and for newcomers there is
already some accommodation. "Sir," quoth the gentleman at Edinboro to his correspondent in the country, "you
will be obliged to say we have, even upon this one consideration, a great advantage of our countrymen lately settled at
Port Royal in Carolina." In emphasising the disadvantages
of Port Royal, Pitlochie was certainly lacking in charity, but
he assuredly had reason on his side: the disadvantages to
which he gives special prominence—the unhealthiness of the
climate and the proximity to the Spaniards—were precisely
those that brought about the downfall of the Scots settlement
in South Carolina.

As an appendix to his own epistle, Pitlochie published a
collection of letters sent home by Scots settlers in East New
Jersey, and two semi-official reports from the Deputy-

Governors, Rudyard and Lawrie. These reports give a picture of a busy, thriving community, and of a land the only need of which is the influx of settlers in large numbers. The private letters are of very great interest, not only on account of the corroboration they give of the Deputy-Governors' statements, but also on account of the light they throw on the experiences of the early settlers. The incidents of the Atlantic voyage, the thoughts and feelings of the pioneers, their daily round of life and work—all the information for which one looks in vain in the records of the Nova Scotia enterprise are all here set out with that engaging realism that is brother to romance. "A Scotch peasant," R. L. Stevenson reminds us, " will talk . . . liberally out of his experiences. He will not put you by with conversational counters and small jests ; he will give you the best of himself, like one interested in life and man's chief end. A Scotchman is vain, interested in himself and others, eager for sympathy, setting forth his thoughts and experience in the best light." In its essentials this characterisation is applicable to the Scottish settler in East Jersey, whether gentle or simple : and to this Caledonian zest in life we owe one of the most remarkable collections of letters to be found in the colonial documents of the seventeenth century.[1]

The originals of the letters printed by Pitlochie were widely read in Edinburgh, and were " to be seen by any inquisitive thereanent at Captain Hamilton's lodging at the Sign of the Ship." To the influence of these letters on Scottish emigration striking testimony is supplied by a passage in a letter written from Edinburgh on 2nd September, 1686, by Mrs. Dunlop to her husband, William Dunlop (later Principal of Glasgow University), who was then in Carolina : " I apprehend there will be little comfortable living in that place, for thou wilt have no encouragement at all from this. All have deserted it, and frequent accounts coming from New Jersey engadgeth several more to it." [2]

[1] See Appendix E.   [2] *Wodrow*, vol. iv. p. 520.

IV.

In the year 1687 the Proprietors of East New Jersey, at a time when their interests were threatened by the aggressive policy of the Governor of New York, forwarded to the King a petition, in the course of which they pointed out that " relying on this grant as inviolable we ventured great stocks in it, have sent many hundreds of Scotsmen there, and mean to send more unless we are discouraged." [1]

By 1683 Scots emigrants were beginning to arrive in East New Jersey in appreciable numbers. " The Scots," writes Gawen Lawrie on 26th March, 1684, " have taken a right course; they have sent over many servantts, and are sending more; they have lykeways sent severall poor familys and given them a small stock; and these familys, some for seven years, some for ten years, allow halfe the encrease to their landlords, except the milke which the tenant has to himselfe. I have sett them out land, and they are at work, I believe they will have forty acres sown this spring; and this summer I am to sett them out more, so that in a short time they will have a great increase coming in." One of the Scots who went over to East Jersey in 1683 was David Barclay, brother of the Governor.

The year 1684, however, was the *Annus Mirabilis* of Scots migration to East Jersey.[2] The inspiration and the guidance of that emigration devolved mainly upon Barclay. It has been held that " apparently it was the weight of Barclay's name rather than his actual ability which was valued by his brother Proprietors."[3] But a study of Barclay's activities at this time shows clearly that the success of the settlement

[1] *Col. Cal.* 1685-88, p. 386.

[2] "There is a great meeting of the proprietors of the New-Eist-Jersey plantation" records Fountainhall, under date 13th August, 1684, " wher the Earle of Perth, Chancelor, is a main undertaker, (the Toun being called New Perthtoun); ther are sundry Quakers also ingadged; and particularly Robert Barclay of Ury, who has got from the King a Palatine power ther. The Lord Neill Campbell, finding no peace, but being jaloused heir, is mortgaging his owne fortune, and buying 80,000 aikers ther. Montgomery of Skelmorly for his principles is also thinking to transport himselfe thither; Mr. George Scot of Pitlochie etc. Fountainhall, *Historical Notices*, ii. 550.

[3] Doyle, *The Middle Colonies*, p. 404.

was due largely to his energy and enterprise. Though he never visited it he threw himself into the work on behalf of his colony with the same eagerness as he had shown in his studies as a youth at the Scots College in Paris, and with the same enthusiasm and practical skill as he had shown in his championship of his fellow-religionists. In the broadsheet of 1684 we have already seen the work of his persuasive pen. Nor did he fail, when occasion offered, to reinforce that work by a personal appeal. " I cannot but . . . much regrett my misfortune," writes John Forbes, brother to the Laird of Barnla, to Mr. James Elphingston of Logie, " in not seeing you and taking your advice before I came to this place. But my Resolution was so sudden, by the encouragement I received from the Chief Governor and some of the proprietors at Aberdeen : (having come in only to see my Sister with my Brother) and by the many Gentlemen that were going along in the ship, that I was induced to go along without so much as taking leave of any of my Friends, save only those that were then in Town." [1]

To Sir John Gordon of Durno, who in December, 1683, had bought a proprietory share in East New Jersey, Barclay wrote as follows from Urie on 4th March, 1684 :

" Dear Cousine,—I suppose thou hast wrott ere now to London, to thy brother George, and proposed to him to bring down his veshell here to carry passengers to East-Jersey. I doubt not but he may make as good a venter that way as any he can propose, and knows how to project a retourn for himself. There will not want passengers, besids those that fills another ship to be hired, and one that is goeing from Glasgow with Manyward, which will be the best way. And besids those George may carry upon thy brother's accompt and thine's, iff he want it, it is but getting men from Strathnaver, to carry over at a venter, which is as profitable a commodity as he can trade in ; the sooner something be done in this the better. I expect also from thee a speedy answere as to that part now in thy optione, that thou wilt determine it one way or other, that I may regulate myself accordinglie. If George com with his ship so as to be ready

[1] Letter 18, Appendix E.

to goe about Whitsunday, he will be sure to be full, for the other is to com afterwards. Desire him to call at London to William Bockura, at Litle St. Helen's, over against Leathersellar's Hall in Bishopgait Street, who will give him fuile informatione in what may be needfull for him.

"So expecting thy care in this, and that thou wilt lett no time be lost, which is the chief point in such caises, I rest thy affectionat cousine, B." [1]

Both in his letter to Gordon and in his broadsheet Barclay speaks of a ship intended to sail from Glasgow, but no evidence is available to shew whether in 1684 a ship did leave the Clyde bound for East New Jersey. It may have been the intention of the East Jersey Proprietors to ship emigrants for their Province on board the *Carolina Merchant*, a vessel of 170 tons burthen armed with 16 guns, which belonged to Walter Gibson, merchant in Glasgow.[2] This ship was advertised as "bound for the Bermudas, Carolina, New Providence and the Cariby Islands, and ready to set Sail out of the River of Clyd against the 20 of February in this instant year, 1684." [3] It was not, however, until the 20th of July that the *Carolina Merchant* cleared from Gourock Bay. As part of his merchandise for the Plantations Walter Gibson had shipped thirty-five prisoners—a gift to him from the Tolbooths of Edinburgh and Glasgow. The *Carolina Merchant* also carried the small band of colonists under Lord Cardross who were crossing the Atlantic to found a Presbyterian settlement on the shores of Port Royal in Carolina. But there is no trace of any emigrant for East New Jersey taking his passage aboard this Glasgow ship.[4]

During the summer of 1684 two ships cleared from East Coast ports for East New Jersey, one from Montrose the other from Aberdeen. The ship from Aberdeen carried about 160 passengers, a number of whom had joined the vessel at Leith,[5] where it had anchored, probably on its way round from London to Aberdeen. The Montrose ship had a long but

---

[1] Dunbar, *Social Life in Former Days*, Sec. Ser. pp. 105, 106.
[2] Erskine of Carnock's *Journal*, p. 69.
[3] *Vide* Appendix F.   [4] Erskine of Carnock's *Journal*, pp. 69-72.
[5] Scot's *Model*, p. 267.

comparatively uneventful voyage : " The Passengers did all very well, though we had some very rough gusts, and were very thronged in so small a vessel, being 130 Souls, besides Sea-men : of these 27 were women, 6 or 7 children only ; one man . . . called William Clark, standing carelessly upon the Forecastle tumbled over boards, and drowned, tho' we put out our boat and endeavoured in vain to save him." [1] Eighteen weeks after leaving Montrose, and nine weeks after leaving Killabeg in Ireland, this ship reached the American coast. " The first land we discovered was about the middle of Long Island ; it appeared at first like trees growing out of the Sea. Towards night we anchored in Sandy Hook." [2]

The other ship had a much shorter passage : " we were only 8 weeks betwixt land and land, and entered the Capes of Virginia the same day 9 weeks we parted from Aberdeen." [3] But it had a much more exciting passage, " occasioned by a mighty storm of wind (which happened upon the 12 day of September last) and which blew so tempestuously that, in short, it carried first away our Boltsprit, and afterwards our whole three Masts, Flagstaff and all, by the board, before the Sailors were able to get them out : it likewise took away the awning above our quarter-deck and left not so much as an yard of a rope above our heads, all of which was done in the space of half an hour. We lay thus distressed like a pitiful wreck all that night, (we having lost our masts about 12 of the clock in the day) and two dayes thereafter at the mercie of the waves (which being like mountains occasioned by the great storm of wind) without hopes of recovery, being then about 200 leagues from this land of America, tossing to and fro expecting that each wave should overwhelm us : Yet at last it pleased God to turn the storm into a calm : and having preserved all our lower Yards, we made all haste and made Jury Masts of them : with the help whereof (tho' very insufficient ones to drive forward the bulk of so great a vessel) and of God's miraculous Mercie and Providence Who—immediately after we had put our ship in any mean posture for plying out her Voyage—was pleased to send us such a fair and moderate gale of wind, as brought us in sight of the

[1] App. E, Letter 17.   [2] App. E, Letter 9.   [3] App. E, Letter 14.

Capes of Virginia, with 15 days after, or thereabouts, having never ceased for the whole time till it brought us thither in safety. So we came within the capes, and sailed up that great Navigable Bay, called Chessapeik bay, up through all Virginia to Maryland, where we landed at the place where our ship was bound to take in her tobacco, for her homeward loadning. But being thus Disabled, and not being able to ply out her Voyage to this place (where she ought to have landed us), we was necessitated to travel from thence by Land to this place, being upwards of 200 English miles, and having left our Goods behind us, (which was thereafter to come about in a Sloup)...." [1]

In view of the disastrous voyage of a later emigrant ship bound for East New Jersey it is noteworthy that the only complaints voiced by passengers in the ships sent out by Barclay, are those prompted by appetites sharpened by keen sea breezes. " We were all very well at Sea," wrote Thomas Fullerton, Brother to the Laird of Kinnaber, to John Johnstone, Drugist in Edinburgh, " only we had more stomachs than meat; to prevent which, if you or any other Commorad come this way, it will be prudence to fortifie themselves with good Cheese, Butter, Bisket, Cakes and Brandie." [2] And John Reid, "who was Gardener to the Lord Advocate," advises intending emigrants " to provide butter, bisket, wine, and especially beer and ale, for their Sea voyage, besides the Ships allowance." [3]

The land in which the Scottish emigrants found themselves on the conclusion of the Atlantic voyage was far from being an unpeopled wilderness. In the early colonial days the Dutch had established trading posts on the western shore of the Hudson. To this region, which he called Albania, Governor Nicolls, before learning of the grant to Berkeley and Carteret, had directed a small but steady stream of colonists from Long Island and New England. The liberal terms of " The Concessions and agreement of the Lords Proprietors of New Jersey" had induced many families from the New England states to transfer themselves to the fertile, well-watered plains of New Jersey. When East New Jersey passed into the

[1] App. E, Letter 18.   [2] App. E, Letter 24.   [3] App. E, Letter 2.

hands of the Quaker-Scottish Proprietors the population of the Province amounted to about 5,000. About a third of this population dwelt on detached plantations scattered throughout the colony: the remainder dwelt in the villages or towns that had been set up after the New England model.[1] The capital and seat of government, Elizabethtown, contained about 700 inhabitants. The system of government established by the " Concessions " of Berkeley and Carteret provided for a council " of advice and consent " to be nominated by the Governor, and for an assembly of twelve representatives to be chosen annually by the freemen of the province.

In a populace imbued with democratic ideals derived from New England and accustomed to a considerable measure of self-government, the autocratic transfer of the province from the trustees of Carteret to the twenty-four Proprietors might be expected to arouse some degree of resentment. Of this Deputy-Governor Rudyard was certainly apprehensive, " . . . the people in general were not a little satisfied with thy late visit," wrote Rudyard to Penn, 13th January, 1683-4, " and bear thee very reverend Respect—And by thy inoffensive obliging Carriage thou layd the foundation for an amicable Complyance on their parts to the Proprietors, that the work cannot prove so difficult as hath been imagined."[2] The Proprietors, three months before the date of this letter, had obtained from King Charles Letters Patent " Charging and Commanding the Planters and Inhabitants and all other persons concerned in the said Province of East New Jersey, That they do submit and yield all due obedience to the Laws and Government of the said Grantees, their Heirs and Assigns, as absolute Proprietors and Governors thereof. . . ."[3]

Among one section of the population the resentment against proprietorial autocracy showed itself in a slight measure of hostility to the Scots, who were the protégés of the new Proprietors: " As to the number and nature of these Quit-renters," wrote Robert Fullerton, to his brother the Laird of Kinnaber, " they are about 2 or 300 Families, some civill and Discreet, others rude and Malcontent with the late

[1] Whitehead, *E. J.* pp. 91-93. [2] *Penn MSS.* vol. i. 7.
[3] *Penn MSS.* vol. i. 6.

Purchassers, and need some thing of austerity to make them Complaisant."[1] Yet this hostility to the newcomers was by no means universal: "The Countrey is very settled with People, most part of the first settlers came out of New England, very kind and loving people, kinder than in Scotland or England...."[2]

With the Indians, who had been conciliated by the just and faithful treatment accorded to them by the representative of the original proprietors, the Scots were soon on very friendly terms: ".... and for the Indian Natives, they are not troublesome any way to any of us, if we do them no harm, but are a very kind and loving people; the men do nothing but hunt, and the women they plant Corn and work at home: they come and trade among the Christians with skins or Venison, or Corn, or Pork, and in the summer time, they and their wives come down the Rivers in their Canoes, which they make themselves of a piece of a great tree, like a little Boat, and there they Fish and take Oysters."[3] "The Indians are a harmless People, and very kind to us," wrote John Cockburn, servitor in East Jersey, to his uncle, James Brown, Shoe Maker in Kelso, "they are not a hairie People as was said to us in Scotland."[4]

With the soil of East Jersey the Scottish settlers were well pleased: "The soyle of the country," wrote the ex-gardener to the Lord Advocate with professional precision, "is generally a red marle earth with a surface of black mould (nor doth it appear what realy it is to their eyes who cannot penetrate beyond the surface) full freighted with grass, pleasant herbs and flowers, and in many places little or no wood, but most places full of large timber, as walnut, especially oak; there be some places here and there in the woods, they call swamps, which is low Ground amidst or betwixt rising ground full of bushes, which holds water in winter, tho' most of them be dry in summer, but these being cleared, and some of them that needs being drained, are the richest land.... As soon as any of the land here comes to be cultivated, it over-runs with small Clover-grass, by the pasturage and dunging of cattle,

[1] App. E, Letter 18.
[2] App. E, Letter 7.
[3] App. E, Letter 7.
[4] App. E, Letter 26.

and so supplants the natural grass and herbs, not withstanding of their quick and strong growth. Fruit trees also prosper well here. . . . Here they sow most Indian corn and wheat; some Rye, Barley, Oates: Indian corn the first year that they break up or plough, the second they sow Wheat, because the spontaneous growth of the weeds is done away by howing the Indian corn, as we do cabbages. . . . There are a great store of Garden herbs here, I have not had time to inquire into them all, neither to send some of the many pleasant (tho to me unknown) plants of this Countrey, to James Sutherland, Physick Gardener at Edinburgh, but tell him, I will not forget him, when opportunity offers."[1] Another settler, accustomed in Scotland evidently to a more strenuous kind of agriculture than had fallen to the lot of the Lord Advocate's gardener, wrote: " We are not troubled here leading our pitts, mucking our Land, and ploughing 3 times: one Ploughing with 4 or 6 oxen at first breaking up, and with 2 horses only thereafter, suffices for all; you may judge whether that be easier Husbandrie than in Scotland."[2]

With the climate the Scots were equally pleased. " I find it wholesome," wrote Charles Gordon to Doctor John Gordon, Doctor of Medicine at Montrose, " for I am not (blessed be God) troubled here with Defluction, head-akes, and coughs, as at Edinburgh, which is a great inducement for me or any valitudinarian man to stay in this Countrey; People come from Barbadoes, to York, and hither for their healths sake —If you design to come hither yourself, you may come as a Planter, or a Merchant, but as a Doctor of Medicine I cannot advise you; for I can hear of no diseases here to cure but some Agues and some cutted legs and fingers, and there are no want of Empericks for these already. . . ."[3]

Thus happily settled in a pleasant and fertile land the Scots were soon busy cultivating their plantations and building their homesteads. But the lighter sides of colonial life were by no means neglected: " I know you love a Gunn and a Dogge," wrote James Mudie to his cousin, " and here ye will have use for both. For Wilde Geese, Turkies, Ducks and Drakes, Partridges, Conies, Doves, and innumerable more

[1] App. E, Letter 2.   [2] App. E, Letter 14.   [3] App. E, Letter 21.

kinds of Fowls of which I do not know their names, are here to be seen every hour of the day, in flocks above Thousands in Number : And for your skieft which you use to fish with bring here with you, or one like her, for I assure you of good employment, and yet ye may catch more Fish in one hour here, than any Fisher in Montrose in two, excepting Podloes at the shore head." [1] Nor were intellectual interests uncatered for : " .... George Keith ... hath brought Mathematicks, and Benjamin Clark a Library of Books to sell." [2] Nor, again, were the delights of fashionable society quite unknown : " This place is not altogether boorish, for at New York you may have railing and Gallantry enough ; the inhabitants are generally great spenders." [3]

V.

During the year 1685, the year of Argyle's Rising—" this black year," as Wodrow calls it—a considerable number of political prisoners were transported to East New Jersey. The dispatch of these prisoners was carried out under the supervision of Lord Niall Campbell, brother of the Earl of Argyle ; of Barclay and his relatives the Gordons of Gordonstown ; and of Scot of Pitlochie.

Lord Niall Campbell had been harshly dealt with by the Privy Council. "August 1st (1684), that excellent person lord Neil Campbell, brother to the noble earl of Argyle, had been cited before the council, for no other cause I can hear of, but that he was the son of the excellent marquis, and brother to the earl of Argyle. Nothing worthy of death or bonds could be laid to his charge. ' The clerks of council are warranted to receive caution for him, under the penalty of five thousand pounds sterling, that he confine himself to Edinburgh, and six miles about, and compear before the council in a charge of six hours.' " [4]

Smarting under this tyrannous invasion of his liberty Lord Niall resolved to go abroad,[5] and in September, 1684, received

---

[1] App. E, Letter 15.   [3] App. E, Letter 14.
[2] App. E, Letter 10.   [4] *Wodrow*, iv. p. 48.
[5] Fountainhall, *Historical Notices*, ii. 550.

from the Council, a pass, "allowing him to transport any whom he could engadge to his Majesties Plantations in America, providing these persones so to be transported be not declared Traiters, rebells, or fugitives."[1] Acting on the strength of this pass Lord Niall entered into an agreement with some prospective emigrants, but the following spring he appealed to the Privy Council, stating that, of the people he had engaged, "some ... are since that time put in prison, and others are in these Circumstances who would oblidge themselves to goe with the petitioner if they were freed." Lord Niall besought the Council to "appoint some effectual method how those who are already engadged, or are about to engadge, may be freed from their bonds or Imprisonment, and may have access to goe about their affaires till there be a fit season of the year for their transport, they alwayes behaving themselves peaceably as becometh."[2] The Council acquiesced: "The Lords of His Majesties Privy Councill haveing considered the foresaid petition Doe grant warrant to the Petitioner to transport the persones craved they not being heritors above one hundred pound Scots of valued rent nor fyned, the petitioner having found caution to transport them betwixt and the ... day of ... under the penalty of ffyve hundred merks for ilk one of them that they shall in the mean time live peaceably, and to transport them betwixt and the said day under the like penalty."[3] Soon, however, a more serious check to Lord Neill's plans was encountered. His brother, the Earl of Argyll, had, while making for the West Coast of Scotland, anchored off the Orkneys, where he had made some of the islanders prisoners. The Scottish Government retaliated. "His (Argyle's) lady, and my Lord Neill his brother, and his sone James, were secured prisoners in Edinburgh, and they ware threatned, that as he used the Orkney prisoners, so should they be used."[4] After the crushing of the Rebellion Lord Neill was set at liberty. Under date 3rd September, 1685, Erskine of Carnock records in his *Journal*: "Lord Neill Campbell sailed about a month ago to the same place, [New Jersey], having got a considerable number of prisoners

[1] *Reg. P.C. Acta*, 14th March, 1685.   [2] *Ibid.*   [3] *Ibid.*
[4] Fountainhall, *Historical Observes*, p. 167.

gifted him by the Council." [1] As Lord Niall's name does not appear among the names of those who, like Barclay and Scot, received gifts of prisoners from the Council during the summer of 1685, it is highly probable that those who accompanied Lord Niall were those with whom he had engaged in terms of the permit granted to him by the Council on 14th March, 1685.

In the closing days of 1684 Barclay had sought in vain to persuade the Privy Council to allot some of the political prisoners to the East Jersey Proprietors. "23 Decembris 1684. At Privy Councell," notes Fountainhall, "a petition was presented by Robert Barclay, for the proprietors and planters in East New Jersey, desiring that such of the phanatiques as they thought fitt to banish, or who finding themselves uneasy at home, ather from poverty or principles ware willing to remove, might be delivered to them, they standing much in neid of tradesmen and labourers of the ground. The Chancelar and Register ware for it ; but the Treasurer stopped it, (being no freind to thisse plantations,) till they should consult the kings pleasure anent it." [2]

In the summer of 1685 Barclay and his friends again took steps to obtain a share of the prisoners distributed by the Privy Council. The Castle of Dunnottar, the scene of the worst prison atrocities of Covenanting days, was close to Barclay's home at Ury, and both the tenor of the petitions addressed by Barclay and his friends to the council, and the absence of any complaints from such prisoners as fell to Barclay's share, confirm the view of Barclay's latest biographer that, in securing a share of the prisoners, Barclay was actuated by motives of broad philanthropy.[3]

On 9th July, 1685, the Council considered a petition from Sir Robert Gordon, younger, of Gordonstown, and Sir John Gordon, his brother, " shewing that wher severall prisoners and others that ly under outlawries are in the castle of Dunotter who are not yet disposed of to any of his Majesties plantations. And it being usuall to the Councill to grant a

---
[1] Erskine of Carnock's *Journal*, p. 154.
[2] Fountainhall, *Historical Notices*, ii. 585.
[3] Cadbury, *Robert Barclay*, pp. 70, 71.

gift of severall of such prisoners And the supplicants haveing interest in the province of East New Jersie Did beg the Councill would grant order for liberation of so many of the saids prisoners as the supplicants should find caution to transport to the said province. And there being one Mr. Wm. McKie who is declared fugitive as the supplicants are informed for non Compearance before the Commissioners of Justiciary at Elgin in february last And the said Mr. William being content to compear before the Councell and declair upon oath that he was never a Minister or in orders, also will give his oath that he was never at a feild conventicle ather as preacher or hearer, Therefor humbly supplicating the Councill to grant the forsaid order for transporting of the saids prisoners And particularly of the said Mr. William McKy he performing the promise before any judge the Councill should please to appoint." This petition was granted: "The Lords of his Majesties privy Councill . . . Doe hereby allow the petitioner to have some of these prisoners in Dunnotar Castle lately banished to be by him transported to the above written plantatione upon caution to transport them thither, And report a certificate from the Governor of the place of their landing there betwixt and . . . under the penalty of . . . for each of them, sea hazard, mortality, pyrats, and fever being alwise exceptid." [1]

On 30th July, 1685, the Council considered a petition from Barclay himself, "shewing that where the supplicant has immediately lying on the road of Leith a ship bounding for East New Jersey in America And seeing there are severall prisoners now in the prisons who are troublesome to the government to maintain Therefor humbly supplicating the Councell to allow the number of twenty-four of them to be transported by the applicant to the said plantation on his finding surety in the ordinary terms and releaving the government instantly of the trouble of them." [2] In response to this petition twenty-four prisoners were given to Barclay. There is, however, no record of the actual grant of any prisoners to the Gordons.

Both by Lord Niall Campbell and by Barclay the

[1] *Acta*, 9th July, 1685.   [2] *Acta*, 30th July, 1685.

transport of political prisoners was conducted apparently on a modest scale. The complete absence of complaints from any prisoners sent out either by Lord Niall or by Barclay justifies the inference that their treatment on the Atlantic voyage was marked by due consideration for their comfort. By a stroke of tragic irony the party of prisoners whose sufferings fill the one dark page of the annals of East New Jersey was the party that in September, 1685, sailed in the vessel chartered by the author of the *Model*.

On the 1st January, 1685, Pitlochie received from the Chancellor official approval of his design in the form of a pass " Permitting and allowing Mr. George Scot of Pitlochie, with his Lady, Children, and Family ; and such other Persons as he shall ingage, to pass from this Kingdom, either by Sea or Land, to any of his Majesties Forreign Plantations, providing such persons to be transported by him be not declared Traitors, Rebels, Fugitives, and that without any Let Impediment or Molestation, from any person whatsoever ; they always behaving themselves peaceably and according to law." [1]

As an encouragement to brother Scots to accompany him, Pitlochie was able to point to certain inducements that in those days of religious dissension might well be considered to make a wide appeal :

" And for his further encouragement, the Lords of His Majesties Privy Council have been pleased by an Act to condescend That such as are under Bond, to appear before them when called, shall have up their said respective Bonds upon their going with him ; whereby they are secured from the Apprehension of any Process to be in their absence intented against them on that head.[2]

" Whereas there are several people in this Kingdom who upon account of their not going that length in conformity required of them by the Law, do live very uneasie ; who beside the other agreeable Accommodations of that place may there freely enjoy their own principles, without hazard or the least trouble : seeing there are Ministers of their own persuasion going along with the said Mr. George Scot ; who by

[1] *Model*, p. 270.   [2] *Ibid*.

the fundamental Constitutions of that Country are allowed the free Exercise of their Ministry, such as Mr. Archibald Riddel, brother to Sir John Riddel of Riddel, Mr. Thomas Paterson, late minister of Borthwick, and several other ministers."

Pitlochie's emigration scheme was wider in scope than any previous colonising effort: he had agents in Dumfries, Kirkcudbright, Ayr, Irvine, Kilmarnock, Glasgow, Stirling, Montrose and Aberdeen; at Edinburgh enquirers might consult either Pitlochie himself at his Lodging in Baillie Robinson's Land, or John Johnstone, Drugist at the sign of the Unicorn.[1] For the voyage Pitlochie chartered the *Henry and Francis* of Newcastle, a ship of 350 tons mounting 20 guns, Richard Hutton master. This ship was scheduled to "take in Passengers and Goods at Leith, and Passengers at Montrose and Aberdeen and Kirkwa' in Orkney, and set sail thence for East-New Jersey against the 20 day of July, God willing." Every effort was to be made to secure the comfort of the passengers: "It being resolved by those concerned in the fraight of the Vessel to Accommodate such Passengers as may conveniently [be] done without crouding themselves and their Families; the inconveniencies of which they are full resolved to avoid, as what is certainly very troublesome in such a voyage."[2]

In November, 1684, Pitlochie had received from the Council permission to transport a hundred prisoners to the Plantations. This grant was subsequently amended in such a manner as to exclude heritors of above one hundred pounds [Scots] yearly of valued rent. On 12th March, 1685,[3] Pitlochie intimated to the Council that he had chartered a ship for his voyage: "And seeing ... that by the Councills forsaid Act they had condescended that such as should find caution to transport themselves with the petitioner should be liberat thereupon to have some time to order their affaires, and the Petitioner being now to goe to Stirling, Glasgow, alswell as to the other prisons to intimat this to the prisoners And Therefor humbly supplicating the Councill would order the liberation of such as the petitioner shall engadge to

[1] *Model*, p. 272. [2] *Ibid.* p. 271. [3] *Acta of P.C.S.*

transport with him, they not being heretors above one hundred pounds yearly of valued rent."

Pitlochie lost no time in entering upon his visitation of the prisons, and the result is seen in an entry in the Acta of the Privy Council under date 17th March, 1685 :[1] "The Lords of His Majesties Privy Councill having heard and considered ane addresse made be James Armor, merchant, prisoner in the tolbooth of Glasgow, William Mair, prisoner in the tolbooth of Stirling and Halbert Wales prisoner in the tolbooth of Cannongate supplicating to be set at liberty, They being willing to goe off the kingdome to his Majesties plantations in America on or betwixt and the first of August next Against which time a ship will be ready to transport them thither, Doe hereby give order and warrant to the magistrates of the saids Burghs respective and keepers of the tolbooths thereof to sett the saids three persons at liberty, They having found caution to remove off this kingdom to the abovesaid plantations betwixt and the said first of August next and never to return thereto without his Majesties or the Councills licence, under the following penalties to witt, the said James Armor under the penalty of Two Thousand Merks, and each of the other two prisoners under the penalty of ffyve hundreth merks Scots money And that in the meantime to live peaceably and orderly and appear before the Councill if called under the foresaid penalty."

With this meagre response to his call for volunteers Pitlochie must have been bitterly disappointed, and, as spring passed into summer, it became increasingly evident that the number of people who were going to join him of their own accord would form but a small party. In the last week of July he received from the Privy Council the promise of a hundred prisoners. This was but the beginning of fresh trials. On August 7th [2] the Council had before it a petition from Pitlochie, "shewing that whereas the petitioner encouraged by the Councill and forwarding a designe he had of laying the foundation of a plantation from this Kingdome to America hath laid out his stock for promotting thereof, The Lords of the secret committee a fourtnight agoe came to

[1] *Acta of P.C.S.* [2] *Acta P.C.S.*

a resolution intimate to the petitioner that he should have fliftie prisoners here and ffiftie in Dunottar whereupon the petitioner did enter into ane aggriement with some tradesmen In their persones absolutely necessar for his said designe And gave them money to entertean them nor inquireing else where after them haveing them thus secured. And now the Councill haveing ordered one hundreth seventie and seven prisoners here to be transported to Jamaica In which number are these persons the petitioner trusted to whereby his designe will be altogether ruined be not haveing time to provyde himself of such otherwise."

As a result of this remonstrance twelve of the prisoners allocated to the Jamaica ship were transferred to Pitlochie. On 12th August he received from the Council " the benefit of the first prisoners ather yesterday sentenced or hereafter to be sentenced to his Majesties plantations abroad." At intervals small numbers of prisoners were added to Pitlochie's personnel, but on August 26th he complained that he was far short of the number he had expected, and that some of the prisoners put on board his vessel by the Council's orders were through age or other infirmity useless as colonists.

On 5th September the *Henry and Francis* cleared from Leith Roads.[1] Crowded under hatches and bringing with them the seeds of disease contracted during their confinement in the dungeon of Dunnottar, the prisoners were soon stricken by a malignant fever which also affected the other passengers and the crew. More than sixty of the ship's company perished, and among the victims of the epidemic were Pitlochie and his wife. His daughter, Euphemia, had married John Johnston (formerly a druggist in Edinburgh), to whom Pitlochie left the disposal of the prisoners. On arriving at New Jersey, Johnston sought to obtain from the prisoners " a voluntary declaration " that they would work for four years as indentured servants. This the prisoners refused to make, and they were supported by the New Jersey law courts. The jury summoned by the Governor " to sit and cognosce upon the affair " found that " the pannels had not of their own accord come to that ship, nor bargained with Pitlochie for money or

---

[1] *Wodrow*, iv. p. 332.

services, and therefore they were assoiled." Many of them made their way to New England. The Rev. Mr. Riddel settled at Woodbridge in East Jersey, but returned to Scotland after the Revolution.[1]

VI.

The Scottish settlers, many of whom were men of good education, soon formed an important section of the population of East New Jersey. Three of them—Captain Andrew Hamilton, David Mudie and John Johnstone—formed one-third of the Governor's Council. Consideration for the interest of the Scots guided the Proprietors in the choice of Lord Niall Campbell, who in August, 1685 had purchased the proprietary share of Viscount Tarbet, to succeed Gawen Lawrie as Deputy-Governor. Lord Campbell published his commission on 5th October, 1686, and appointed his council a fortnight later.[2] Within two months he delegated his authority to Andrew Hamilton. Lord Niall was obliged to take this step "by the urgent necessity of some weighty affairs being about to take a voyage to Britain."[3]

Hamilton published his formal commission as Deputy-Governor in March, 1687. Two years later, when the Proprietors had surrendered their governmental rights, Hamilton sailed for Britain, but in 1692, after the Proprietors had resumed their authority, he returned to East Jersey as Governor.

Hamilton governed with intelligence and tact, but his care for the interests of the Province, and in particular for those of his fellow-countrymen, did not commend itself to the Surveyor-General of the Plantations, Edward Randolph. In the course of a report laid before the House of Lords on 20th February, 1696-1697, Randolph stated: "East Jersey had several Scotchmen to be the Governors, who usurped a government over the inhabitants; and now, after great chopping and changing they are the estate of the present Proprietors, who have appointed Col. Andrew Hamilton, a Scotchman, to be their Governor. . . . He raises money upon the inhabitants, and is a great favourer of the Scotch traders his countrymen.

[1] *Wodrow*, iv. 332-334. [2] Whitehead, *E.J.* p. 117. [3] *Ibid.* p. 118.

He sat Judge in the Court last year at the trial of a vessel with goods from Scotland, and dismissed the case upon the Master's sham petition." [1]

Hamilton was in the autumn of 1697 deprived of his office of Governor under circumstances which could not but arouse keen resentment on the part of his fellow-countrymen settled in East New Jersey. As part of the English counter-offensive to the Act of 1695 of the Scots Parliament establishing the Company of Scotland trading to Africa and the Indies there had been passed by the English Parliament the Act 7 and 8, William III. c. 22, "for preventing frauds and regulating abuses in the plantation trade," one of the provisions of which was that no public post of trust or profit in the colonies could be held only by any other than a natural born subject of England. Though it was ultimately decided that Scotsmen, on account of the allegiance they owed to the English crown, could not be legally debarred from holding office in the colonies, the East Jersey Proprietors interpreted the Act in 1697 as rendering Hamilton's position untenable, and in October of that year, much to their regret, they removed him from office.

His successor, Jeremiah Basse, arrived in the Province in the spring of 1698. If Governor Hamilton had shown undue favour to "the Scotch traders, his countrymen," the same charge could not be levelled against Basse. "I am too much discouraged," he wrote in June, 1699, "in my zeal for the common good and His Majesties services, in that I have nothing beyond a Proprietary Commission to support me, and even then persons seeming to desert me because of my discountenancing the Scotch and pirates." [2]

In East New Jersey the tidings of the settlement of the Scots in Darien caused much excitement. Tidings of a Scottish victory in a skirmish with the Spaniards—that of 6th February, 1699—raised high hopes. It was commonly reported that the Darien Scots had raised a fortress which mounted 150 guns, and would protect and encourage in every way all who would trade or correspond with them. A wave

[1] *H. of Lords MSS.* vol. ii. (New Ser.) p. 442.
[2] *Col. Cal.* 1699, p. 280.

of excitement swept over the New Jersey Scots. It was therefore with a certain grim satisfaction that on June 10th, 1699, Governor Basse penned the opening sentences of the dispatch to the Council of Trade and Plantations in which he acknowledged receipt of the instructions to forbid the furnishing of aid to the Scots in Darien: " I received yours of January 2, and immediately published enclosed proclamation. These orders arrived very opportunely to curb the endeavours of some gentlemen of the Scotch nation to promote not only the Scotch interest in general, but that particular settlement which they now call Caledonia." [1]

But the worthy Governor's satisfaction was short-lived. Some of the leading Scots of the Province were so little awed by the publication of the Proclamation that they asserted—in the hearing of Governor Basse and his Council—that King William's attitude towards the Scots in Darien might bring about a rupture between Scotland and England. In spite of the Proclamation, too, they continued to hold correspondence with their fellow-countrymen in Darien and encouraged the inhabitants of New Jersey to go to the Isthmus to trade.[2]

In their attitude of defiance the New Jersey Scots were, according to Basse, " emboldened by their expectation of the arrival of a gentleman of their nation to fill the seat of the government in these provinces by his Majesties speciall approbation." Governor Hamilton was indeed returning. From the Attorney-General and the Solicitor-General the Proprietors had obtained a ruling that a native of Scotland was not excluded from holding office in the colonies by the Act 7 and 8, William III. c. 22.[3] In 1692 he had been appointed Governor of East New Jersey and West New Jersey, and he now returned to rule over the combined provinces, as he had been doing when relieved of his office in 1697. In the rather stormy domestic politics of New Jersey during the period that elapsed between Hamilton's return and the formation in 1702 of the combined provinces into a Crown Colony the Scots, with Hamilton at their head, formed an important faction, upholding the interests of the Quaker-Scottish Proprietors.

[1] *Col. Cal.* 1699, pp. 281-2. [2] *Ibid.*
[3] Whitehead, *E. J.* p. 148.

VII.

If the Scottish settlers in East New Jersey played a strenuous part in the domestic politics of the Province, the Scottish Proprietors were equally prominent in the intercolonial controversy between New Jersey and New York. This was, of course, no new question in colonial politics. It dated back to the very earliest days of the Jerseys when the dismemberment of the Dutch territory and the grant of the land between the Hudson and the Delaware to Carteret and Berkeley had evoked a strong protest from Governor Nicolls.

By the authorities of New York the problem of the control of the Hudson navigation was envisaged purely from the economic and administrative standpoint. In May, 1685, in the course of a covering note to an address of condolence and congratulation to the king, the Mayor of New York wrote: "Pray also acquaint the King that since he separated Delaware and the two Jerseys from New York, the city has lost a third of its trade. We bear the burthen with willingness and submission, but we hope that the King will reunite these parts and enlarge the Government eastward."[1] On 25th November, 1686, the Secretary of New York wrote to the Earl of Sunderland: "It will be very difficult for this Government to subsist unless Connecticut and East and West Jersey be annexed. This place is the centre of the King's territory in these parts, and is therefore by situation the fittest to have them joined to it. . . . It is very inconvenient to the King's interest here, this side of the river paying customs and the other being free. The goods that come here cannot be consumed there, but are 'stolen' into this government to the great prejudice alike of the King and the merchants."[2]

In the correspondence of the Scots Proprietors, however, there is heard a strong assertion of punctilious nationalism. It is a note that is distinguishable also in the other Scottish colonising projects of this time: faint and a trifle querulous, perhaps, in the controversy between the Scots settled at Port Royal in South Carolina and the authorities at Charleston; but deep and passionate in the days of the Darien Scheme.

[1] *Col. Cal.* 1681-85, p. 667.   [2] *Ibid.* 1681-85, p. 289.

Within a week of the time of their acquiring an interest in East New Jersey the Scots Proprietors displayed their anxiety to have a government virtually independent of the English colonial system. " I did write you formerly," wrote the Lord Register of Scotland to Sir John Werden on 21st December, 1682, " of our desire who are Proprietors of East Jersey to have our Government rather holden by Charter of his R^{all} H^s just as it is at present by transmission from our authors without any augmentatōn of our privilege but only to be under ye D^{ks} imediate protection." [1]

Nor were the Scots slow to resent any policy on the part of the Governor of New York that seemed to threaten their interests. On 22nd August, 1684, the Earl of Perth, his brother Drummond of Lundin, and Viscount Tarbet addressed the following letter to " Collonel Dungan, Lieutănt to this R.H. In New York ": " Wee did promise our selves in you a good and kind neighbour both ; judging you would have so inclined to a colony wherein wee are so much concerned, And that the regard you have to your Maisters Honnour and interest would have obligded you to it, considering wee are such as have the hapinesse to claim an interest in his favour : Wee have discoursed with his Commissioners at London of these things y^t were by you proposed in relation to the bringing our Colony under the Government of New York ; And doubt not but wee have convinced them of the reason which induced us not to yeald to such a proposall : and wee Doubt not both the Duke and they are fully convinced of our Right in everie Respect, Both of Government, Pourts, Harbours, free trade and navigation And having spoke to the Duke wee found him verie just ; and to abhour the thoughts of allowing any thing to be done contrary to what he hath Past under his hand and Seall ; And wee persuade ourselves you will lay aside all thoughts of attempting what may reflect upon the Justice or honnour of your maister, or may give us just reason to complaine, Since there shall be no thing wanting on our Part that may lead to ane advantageous correspondence, which as wee expect from you so shall be seriously recommended by us to our agents, and always entertained." [2]

[1] *C.O.* 5/1112. Fol. 40.   [2] *C.O.* 1/55, No. 23; *Col. Cal.* 1681-85, p. 667.

From New York Dougan sent on February 13th, 1684-5, a spirited rejoinder, in which he disclaimed any intention of acting with unfairness, pointed out the disadvantages of the dual control of the Hudson, and censured the action of the agents of the New Jersey Proprietors in " dispersing printed papers to ye Disturbance of ye inhabitants of Staten Island." [1]

Once begun, the struggle went on unrelaxed. East New Jersey survived the issue against it of writs of " quo warranto " in the years of 1685 and 1686.[2] In the closing months of 1686 a more subtle strategy was employed. Writing to the Earl of Sunderland on 25th November, 1686, the Secretary of New York remarks : " The Lord Nial Campbil is Governor of East Jersey, and one Mr. Hamilton who is sent over by the proprietors to inspect and make a report to them of that province is convinced by me how disadvantageous it is to the proprietors to keep it. I have prevailed with the Lord Nial Campbil to write to that purpose and to motion the exchange of Pemaquid for East Jersey : and I believe they will petition either for an exchange or that his Majesty will be pleased to ac\ept of that Plantation." [3]

In the following July the Proprietors of East New Jersey did present a petition to the king. Its tenor, however, was very different from what the New York authorities had evidently been led to expect. The Proprietors pointed out that they had not received their province as a grant, but had bought it : the most considerable of them would not have been concerned in it had they not received from his Majesty assurance of the soil, free trade, and free navigation : relying on that grant as inviolable they had ventured great stocks in the enterprise, had sent many hundreds of Scots to the Province, and would send more unless they were discouraged. After a clear and dispassionate discussion of the interstate problems that had caused friction between East New Jersey and New York, the Proprietors put forward several suggestions, the first being " That East Jersey may not be annexed to New York, but be continued as a distinct government, or be joined with West Jersey, the King naming

---

[1] *C.O.* 1/57, No. 28. [2] *Col. Cal.* 1685-88, pp. 67, 73, 77, 173, 182.
[3] *C.O.* 1/61, No. 11 ; *Col. Cal.* 1685-88, p. 289.

one of the Proprietors governor, and allowing the rest or their proxies to be always of the Council." [1]

It was some reward to the pertinacity of the Proprietors that when, in the spring of 1688, in deference to the King's centralising policy, they made surrender of their authority,[2] East Jersey was joined not to New York but, in company with New York and West Jersey, to New England.[3] After the Revolution the Proprietors quietly resumed their authority. The earlier policy of the Proprietors, as evinced in the first Proposal of the Petition of 1687, was to some extent followed when in 1692 Andrew Hamilton became Governor of both East and West Jersey. In 1702 New Jersey became a Crown Colony. Among the Proprietors who signed the document that made the final surrender of East Jersey to the Crown were four Scots: John Johnstone, John Barclay, Thomas Gordon, Gilbert Mollison.[4]

[1] *Col. Cal.* 1685-88, p. 386.
[2] C.O. 1/64, No. 48.
[3] C.O. 5/904, p. 381.
[4] Whitehead, *E.J.* p. 153.

CHAPTER VI

STUART'S TOWN, SOUTH CAROLINA

OVER that part of the low, river-veined, island-fringed coast of South Carolina where in 1684 a band of self-exiled Covenanters planted their small settlement of Stuart's Town, there brooded dark memories of early colonial tragedies. On one of the waterways of Port Royal there was founded in the year 1562 the Huguenot colony of Charlesfort. A year later the garrison which Ribault had left there, full of hope and ardour, quitted these shores, a company of broken men, worn with famine and misery and discord, before whom lay the still greater horrors of a long Atlantic voyage in a small and wretchedly equipped vessel. In 1564 Laudonnière planted another Huguenot settlement, which he named Fort Caroline, some distance to the south of Port Royal. Its history of mutiny and famine offers a gloomy parallel to that of Ribault's fort. But its end was more drastic and more sanguinary. In the midst of a wild storm of wind and rain it was surprised by a Spanish force from St. Augustine. The garrison of Fort Caroline, together with a large body of reinforcements but lately arrived, was put to the sword—a ruthless deed ruthlessly avenged by the private crusade of a Gascon gentleman, Dominique de Gourgues.[1]

The strategic importance of the Florida coast had from early times been recognised by the Spaniards. It lay conveniently near the Bahama Channel through which the galleons, laden with the riches of Mexico and Peru, worked their way out from the Caribbean Sea to the Atlantic. When the Spanish merchantmen and treasure-ships began to attract

[1] Lescarbot, *Histoire de la Nouvelle France*, bk. i. chaps. 5-7, 8-18.

the attention of English and French privateers, the advantage of having on the Florida coast a seaport that would act as a depot for the warships that protected Spanish trade was clearly seen by the Spaniards. Two attempts to establish a colony on this coast were unsuccessful, but the Spaniards were stirred to fresh efforts by the arrival of the French in these regions, and St. Augustine was founded.

Although Port Royal lay within the territory granted to the Lords Proprietors of Carolina by Charles II. in their Second Charter, that of 1665, the Spaniards continued to regard it as within their sphere of influence. Traces of Spanish occupation were found, in the shape of a cross erected in an Indian village, by Captain Sandford when in 1666 he explored Port Royal. The decision of the colonists who arrived at Port Royal in April, 1670, but speedily moved on to the Ashley River, fifty miles farther north, has been attributed to a desire on their part to settle well away from the zone of effective Spanish occupation.[1] It is not without significance, too, that in the Treaty of America concluded between Britain and Spain in July, 1670, and confirming these powers in the possession of the territories they had effectively conquered, no attempt is made to define the Carolina-Florida frontier. As in Acadie, the Scottish settlers in South Carolina were going to set up an outpost in a debatable land.

I.

The territory of Carolina, granted by King Charles II. in 1663 to eight Proprietors, chief of whom were Clarendon and Ashley, and extended both to the north and to the south by a second charter granted in 1665, occupied a definite place in the English scheme of colonial expansion. It was to be developed as a colony that would furnish the mother-country with tropical and sub-tropical products. The colonists who sailed for Carolina in January, 1670, were instructed to procure indigo seed and cotton seed; cuttings of vines and of olive trees; sugar canes and ginger roots planted in tubs of earth. In the closing paragraphs of *An Account of the Province of*

[1] Doyle, *The English in America*, p. 473 n.

Carolina in America, a pamphlet published in London in 1682 which could hardly have escaped the notice of the Scots engaged in procuring the grant of land at Port Royal, stress is laid on the facilities afforded by the province for the production of Wine, Oyl, Silk, Tobacco, Indigo, Cotton, Sumack, and Drugs—Jallap, Sarsaparilla, Turmerick, Sassafras, Snakeroot. " This country," the *Account* concludes, " being of the same clymate and Temperature of Aleppo, Smyrna, Antioch, Judea and the Province of Nanking, the richest in China, will (I conceive) produce any thing which those Countreys do, were the Seeds brought into it."

It was not, however, the economic advantages of Carolina that turned the attention of the Westland Covenanters to this province. Worn out by long continued persecution, which year by year grew more stringent and more vindictive, they were attracted by those provisions of the two Carolina Charters which permitted the Lords Proprietors to grant freedom of conscience to colonists ; " they (the Covenanters) said they would now seek a country where they might live undisturbed as freemen and as Christians."[1] As early as 1672 a proposal of carrying over a plantation to Carolina had been put before the Covenanters by Lockhart.[2]

Among the Scots who were looking to the American colonies for a haven from the storms of politico-religious persecution, the claims of Carolina were by no means unanimously favoured. The elaborately planned Fundamental Constitutions of Locke, with their faded squirearchy of landgraves and caciques, aroused distrust, if not downright aversion. " They did not like the government of those *palatinates*, as they were called," declares Burnet.[3] Scot of Pitlochie was emphatic in his condemnation : " There is one further consideration obliging me altogether to close my Ears and Eyes against Carolina : whatever specious pretences may flee abroad in favour thereof, and be received by such who are not concerned to enquire farther than to hear-say ; and that is the consideration of the model of the Government, than which nothing can be more discouraging to any having the sense of a rational man, or spirit of a Gentleman. The offices of Honour and Trust, such as

[1] Burnet, *History of My Own Time*, i. 526.   [2] *Ibid.*   [3] *Ibid.*

Chancellour, Thesaurer, Admiral, Secretary, etc. are all Hereditably annexed to the Proprietors, by the constitution of their Government : so that let a Gentleman deserve never so well, however eminent his parts may be, he must in the first place purchase a property, ere he can attain to any of those places of Trust or Honor ; whereas, if you have so much Money as to make this purchase, you may then come to these preferments though you were the arrantest Blockhead in nature . . . so that when I have this consideration before my Eyes, I must conclude any who subject themselves to that model of Government are either ignorant of the constitutions thereof, or of very mean Spirit, to settle themselves in a place where neither Virtue nor Merit can neither raise them nor their Posterity. Let me add another ground of my dissatisfaction with the Model of that Government, and you may judge whether the same be reasonable or not. There are eight Proprietors ; by their Constitutions it appears clear to me that they are so many Sovereigns, seeing by one express Article of their Fundamental Constitutions, it is declared That the Proprietors are no wayes subject to Law, in so far as to be censured by any judicature there : So that be their Actings never so Illegal or unjust . . . they cannot be challenged upon account thereof in an Judicatory in Carolina." [1]

To the punctilious mind of the seventeenth-century Scot these considerations cannot have been without effect. By what counter-influence was this effect neutralised ? By the influence of Shaftesbury, who acted as liaison officer between Scotland and Carolina.

Both in Scotland and in Carolina Shaftesbury had acquired a commanding reputation. By the Covenanters he was regarded as their champion in the English Parliament ; of his speech made in the House of Lords on 25th March, 1679, on the oppression of Scotland by Lauderdale's Government, forty written copies were carried to Scotland by the next post.[2] One of the original Proprietors of Carolina, Shaftesbury, the " daring pilot in extremity," had taken charge of the affairs of the struggling colony after the failure to people it by settlers

---

[1] *Model of the Government of East New Jersey*, pp. 211-213.
[2] Roger North, *Examen*, p. 86.

from Barbados, and by his zeal and tenacity had laid the foundations of its prosperity. With public opinion in England hostile to migration to the colonies, Shaftesbury could not but welcome what promised to be the accession of a large number of Scottish settlers to Carolina. And what was more natural than that the Scots should look for a home in a territory where Shaftesbury wielded so much influence ? It is probably more than a coincidence that it was to Carolina that about this time a large number of Dissenters from the west of England turned their attention.[1]

II.

There has been a tendency among Scottish historians to ascribe the Covenanters' decision to establish a colony in Carolina to the panic produced among the Westland Whigs by the trial of William Laurie of Blackwood, who in November, 1682, was arrested on a charge of "harbouring and resetting fugitive ministers, and conversing with rebels who had been at Bothwel-bridge, and other intercommuned persons, and for receiving mail and duty from them." " According to the evidence of Monroe, in the Rye-House Plot," says Mr. Lang, " it was the treatment of Blackwood that set the Scottish lairds on the Carolina scheme, and by an easy transition on the conspiracy of 1682-1683."[2] As a result of long, ingenious and casuistical arguments on the part of the king's lawyers, Blackwood was on 5th February, 1683, condemned to death. "This," writes Burnet, "put all the gentry in a great fright : many knew they were as obnoxious as Blakewood was, and none could have the comfort to know that he was safe. This revived among them a design that Lockhart had set on foot ten years before, of carrying over a plantation to Carolina. All the presbyterian party saw they were now disinherited of a main part of their birthright of choosing their representatives in parliament : and upon that they said they would now seek a country where they might live undisturbed, as freemen and as Christians."[3] But in the midsummer of 1682, five months

---

[1] M'Crady, *S. Carolina under the Prop. Gov.* p. 193.
[2] A. Lang, *Sir George Mackenzie and his Times*, p. 247.
[3] Burnet, *History*, f. 526.

before Blackwood was even arrested, the Carolina project was afoot : [1] and on 16th September, 1682, two months before the arrest of Blackwood, Sir John Cochran, one of the promoters of the scheme, wrote from Edinburgh to the Earl of Aberdeen : [2] " Sir George Campbell of Cesnock and I have made a bargain for two Counties with the Lords proprietors of Carolina." [3]

Not, therefore, in the specific instance of the harsh treatment of Blackwood, but rather in the general desire of the Covenanters to escape from the ever-increasing stringency of repressive legislation is to be found the origin of the project of establishing a colony of refuge in Carolina.[4] The one

[1] Hist. MSS. Com. R. xv. app. viii. p. 184.

[2] *Letters to Earl of Aberdeen* (Spalding Club), p. 58.

[3] It should be noted that the evidence of Major Monroe is not to the effect that " it was the treatment of Blackwood that set the Scottish Lairds on the Carolina scheme." In his *Deposition* Monroe states : " I was engaged in that Commission concerning Carolina most innocently and with reluctancie, as is known to severalls of the undertakers. And I declare I knew of no other designe in it, bot to carry on a Scots plantation in that province, which was a thing very seriously intended by all the undertakers with whom I had occasion to speak concerning it. And if his Ma[ties] letter to the Councill hade not authorized the designe, I had never meddled in it.

" When in my journey to London I came to Ular I found Jerviswood ther, who told me that he was resolved to goe to London and did stay there to get my company hearing of my coming. He told me the reason of his going that journey was to shun the hazard that might follow upon the sentence ag[t] Blackwood which he believed no man in the west countrey could escape. And he found himself very ill stated with the late Chancellor."—*Deposition of Commissarie Monro*, A.P.S. vol. viii. app. p. 33.

[4] While these pages were passing through the press interesting corroboration of the view advanced in them came to hand in the form of the following communication made by Sir James Balfour Paul to the *Scottish Historical Review* for April, 1922 :

" SCOTTISH EMIGRANTS IN THE SEVENTEENTH CENTURY. Mr. George A. Taylor, of Boston, has sent me the following document, transcribed from the original in the Archives Department of the State of Massachusetts. . . .

J. BALFOUR PAUL.

To the Hon[rble] Gov[r], Dep[tie] Gov[r] and the rest of the Hono[ble] Magistrates and Dep[tys] now assembled in the Gen[ll] Court held at Boston 12[th] February 1679.

The Petition of Hugh Campbell, merch[t] in Boston, Humbly Sheweth that whereas yo[r] Petitioner at the time of his Departure from Scotland, was desired by sundry Godly Persons, inhabiting in the West Parts of Scotland, to informe myself of the customes, way of Gov[r]m[t] and priveledges of his Majesties subjects in these parts of y[e] world, and to give them an acco[t] thereof ; for that they did apprehend that the severity which was

American settlement of the Scottish Covenanters was indeed the meagre fruit of elaborate and ambitious designs. In its early days, too, the Carolina scheme aroused ardent hopes: " I find," wrote Sir George Mackenzie to Aberdeen, in the autumn of 1682, " the Carolina project encourages much our fanaticks, thinking they ar now secur of a retreat."[1]

In view of the close connection in 1683 between those who were prominent in the Carolina scheme and those who were prominent in the great Whig Insurrectionary plot, which was being elaborated at the same time as the Assassination Plot of Rumbold and Rumsey, the early stages of the Covenanters' project are invested with a significant interest. When the plots were discovered in the summer of 1683, the English

> exercised towards them by some in powre there, and other troubles would necessitate them to leave their Native Land, and to transplant themselves and famalyes into some of his Maj^{tys} plantaĉons where they might find acceptance. And I, having seriously considered their request, and taken the advice of sundry Christian Friends in this place doe apprehend none of his Maj^{tys} Plantations so convenient for them (all things considered) as amongst his Maj^{tys} good subjects in this colony: whereupon some time since I did acquaint the hono^{rble} Gov^t and Councill with the matter, who did signifie to me that a people of a Holy Conversation, Orthodox in matters of Religion and such as would be conformable to the Laws of England and of this Place would be acceptable to them. And since that ye Transportation of famelys into a Strang Land is a matter of so great concernment, and not to be undertaken in the place to which they shall come,
>
> Your Petitio^r therefore humbly Intreates the favour of this Hono^{rble} Court to take this matter into their serious consideraĉon, and for the Incouragem^t of such a People (so qualified as aforesaid, bringing with them an able and orthodox minister and schoolmaster) to grant to your Petitio^r for their use and account a convenient quantitye of Land sufficient to accomodate one hundred ffamilys or thereabout, so shall he ever pray as in duty bound st. [servant]
>
> HUGH CAMPBELL
>
> [endorsed]
>
> In answer to this petition the Magistrates Judges meet to allow to the petitioner on behalf of such as may on that account transport themselves hither, such accomodation to their number in the Nepmug Country as it will afford, provided they come within two years after this graunte
>
> 6 ffebr 29. The Magists have past this, their brethren the Deputys hereto consenting. Edward Rawson, secret.
>
> Consented to be the Deputys
>
> WILLIAM TORREY, Cleric."

Scottish Historical Review, vol. xix. 3, pp. 239, 240.

[1] *Letters to Earl of Aberdeen*, p. 69.

authorities pronounced very decidedly on the motives that had induced the Scots connected with the Carolina scheme to visit London : " . . . in order to a general insurrection by a correspondency with their party in Scotland and several counties of this our Kingdom, and because a correspondency by letter was thought dangerous, it was held necessary that some person should be sent into Scotland to invite the heads of the disaffected party in that our Kingdom to come hither under pretence of purchasing lands in Carolina, but, in truth, to concert with them, the best means of carrying on the designe joyntly in both Kingdoms." [1] Nor were the Scottish authorities less emphatic in the expression of their views. The Decreit of Forfalton against Sir John Cochran of Ochiltree declares that Sir John with others " went to Londone pretending to negotiat a setlement of ane scots Colonie in Carolina bot truelie and reallie to treat anent and carie on the sd. rebellione and conspiracie with the Earls of Shaftsberrie and Essex, Lord Russel and others in England." [2]

Against this charge of continuous dissimulation underlying the Carolina scheme, it is an argument of no little weight that in the autumn of 1684 a Scottish Presbyterian Colony was actually established in the district acquired two years previously from the Lords Proprietors of Carolina. The contract, too, between the Scottish Presbyterian leaders and the Lords Proprietors for the purchase of that land had been set forth with due legal formality.[3] A study of the earlier stages of the enterprise confirms the assertion of Burnet that " in the negotiation this year [1682] there was no mixing with the malecontents in England." [4] The scheme was primarily a colonising project.

Carolina was not the only colony to which the Covenanters had turned their attention. In the spring of 1682 a number of the leading Covenanters discussed carefully a proposal [5] for the purchase, for £15,000, of New York made to them on behalf of an English gentleman, a Presbyterian, " quho is

[1] Letter to Scots Privy Council, *Reg. P.C.* New Series, vol. viii. p. 214.
[2] *A.P.S.* vol. viii. app. 40 b.   [3] *Wodrow*, iii. p. 369.
[4] Burnet, *History*, f. 526.
[5] Hist. MSS. Com. *Fourteenth Rep.* app. iii. p. 113.

informed of a designe of maiking ane interest in America from this countrey and, by some agent of his, desyres wee bee acqwainted that he is willing the one halfe goe to ws, and that we erect quhat government best pleaseth ws and haive the halfe shaire in the government." A letter summarising the discussion bears the date 28th April, 1682. Lord Cardross, who had convened the meeting to discuss this proposal, and who eventually took out the colonists to Carolina, informed his friends that he had authority to state that if they became parties to this purchase, they might have Presbyterianism established, " and as to the civill ane joint interest in makeing of lawes and evrey things els relaitting to the government." After a minute and judicial analysis of the proposal, it was considered to be attended by too many difficulties to promise success, and the committee of Covenanters directed their attention to Carolina. The constitution of Carolina, which so aroused the ire of Pitlochie, proved " accomodate " to their minds. They were impressed also by the reputation of Port Royal harbour. Another meeting was arranged to discuss the Carolina scheme.

To negotiate with the Lords Proprietors of Carolina Sir John Cochran of Ochiltree and Sir George Campbell of Cessnock were sent to London. The Scottish deputation found a useful ally in Burnet : " those who were sent up were particularly recommended to me, and seemed to depend much on the advices I gave them. In the negotiation this year there was no mixing with the malecontents in England : only they who were sent up went among them, and informed them of the oppressions they lay under." [1] Among other Scots in London who were partisans of the Government, the activities of the commissioners not unnaturally aroused considerable curiosity. " I cannot imagine," wrote Hamilton to Queensberry on 13th July, 1682, " what of our countrey men are makeing court to Shaftesbery, unles it be those that are about the project of Carolina, wherein they say they are not like to agree becaus they will onely grant Presbyterian Government, but dureing pleasure." [2]

[1] Burnet, *History*, f. 526.
[2] Hist. MSS. Com. *Fifteenth Report*, app. viii. p. 242.

STUART'S TOWN, SOUTH CAROLINA 195

But the hope of obtaining a large number of Scottish settlers was an argument that carried great weight with the Carolina Proprietors and induced them to accede to the conditions formulated by the Scots.[1] The dispatches of the Proprietors to the Governor of Carolina of 21st November, 1682, give the salient features of the transaction. The Lords Proprietors had agreed with Sir John Cochran and Sir George Campbell for themselves and other Scots for the settlement of a county in Carolina. The land chosen by the Scots was to be purchased by the Proprietors from the Indians, and the Governor was directed to negotiate at once with the Indians for the acquisition of the land. The Scots had pointed out to the Lords Proprietors that it was doubtful whether the oppression of the people had been sufficiently guarded against by the system of administration then in operation in the province, and the Lords Proprietors, taking to heart the criticism of the Scots, had made certain changes in their Fundamental Constitutions.[2]

On his return to Scotland Sir John Cochran on 16th September sent to Lord Haddo, the Chancellor of Scotland, an account of the progress of the scheme: " Right Honorable my Lord—Sir George Campbell of Cesnock and I have made a bargain for two Counties with the Lords proprietors of Carolina, for our oune, and the use of such as shall undertake with us to plant their. Wee are oblidged to take up threttie six thousand aickers of land yearly for the space of eight years ; and this proportion of land being taken up, wee have right to als much more upon the same terms.

" In the manadgment of this affaire at London, wee did acquaint his Majestie and his Royall Highnes with the whol methods and steps of it. His Majestie hath been gratiouslie pleased to signifie to your Lordship, and the rest of the Lords of his Counsel heir, his approbation of the designe, which Letter I forbeare to present untill your Lordship come hither.

" So soon as I came into this countree, I went to my Lord Advocate, he being the only Minister of State upon the place, and acquainted him with what wee had done, and what wee were about to doe in prosecution of our designe. Accordingly

[1] Burnet, *History*, f. 526.   [2] *Col. Cal.* 1681-1685, pp. 338, 339.

when the Committee of the Counsel mett heir on Thursday last, I did acquaint their Lordships with the reson of our undertakers meeting heir.

"I shall not trouble your Lordship at present to give yow a speciall accompt of the methods and wayes aggreed upon to prosecut our designe: only to acquaint your Lordship that wee have appointed a vessel to goe from Greenock the first of October next; with whom wee send foure pilots and two gentlemen, to sound the best river in Carolina, and to take possession of the best land upon it for us, and so soon as is possible to return unto us; to the end that these pilots wee send may be able to guyde our ships into that river they make choice of. This is the substance of what wee have yet agreed on.

"Wee have aggreed that their shall be seventie two principall undertakers,[1] a list quhairof I have sent your Lordship heir enclosed. Wee have power to choose on Landgrave and tuo Cassicks for each Countie. Sir George Lockhart is to be Landgrave of the first Countie.

"I have reserved foure undertakers' places for your Lordship, and such of the Lords of the Session as inclyne to come into the undertaking. If their be anything in the bargain that your Lordship thinks may tempt you to come into it, the Societie will make yow very welcome; and I shall attend your Lordship upon your first coming hither, and give yow a scene of the wholl affaire.

"I will only in generall say that if this undertaking be actuallie prosecuted, it will tend very much to the honor and advantage of the nation in generall, and be as great ease into the Government. . . ."[2]

Sir John seems to have interpreted too favourably the attitude of his Royall Highnes to the project. Burnet was under no delusion: "The Duke encouraged the motion: he was glad to have so many untoward people sent far away, who, he reckoned, would be ready upon the first favourable conjuncture to break out into new rebellion."[3] When news

---

[1] The bond among the noblemen and gentlemen concerned in the enterprise contained "about thirty six" signatures. *Wodrow*, iii. p. 369.

[2] *Letters to Earl of Aberdeen*, p. 58.   [3] Burnet, *History*, f. 526.

reached London of Cochran's interpretation of the attitude of the Court, the Duke of York was at some pains to make his position clear : " In yours of the 27," he wrote to Queensberry on October 10, 1682, " you give me an account of Sir J. Cochran's pretentions. As to his affaires of Carolina, I wonder he should say I was satisfyd with all his proposals, for I told him I was not a competent judg of them, and gott them referd to the counsell, whom I knew would take care that nothing should be granted to him but what was consistant with his Majestys service, the interests of the church, and the peace of the country. 'Tis true, I told him I was glad he and others of his perswation thought of going there, because they would carry with them disaffected people." [1]

III.

The autumn of 1682—the time when Mackenzie "found the Carolina project encouraging much our fanaticks"—was a time of high and even of extravagant hopes among the Covenanters. But moderate counsel was not lacking. On 2nd August, 1682, a correspondent, who had a very just appreciation of the limited possibilities of Scottish colonial enterprise, thus advised Sir George Campbell : " . . . I think it will not be neadfull for you to be at the charge of procuring a license from the King for 10 ships, in that I believe some of them may not be employed upon transportation of people to Carolina. In that four or six vessels is all that you can expect to employ, thoe you were to transport a thousand persons next year, except the veshels were to be very small. . . . I believe it will not be for our advantage to transport a thousand next year ; in that it will cost us much more charge for transportation of people the first year then it will doe the following years, in that 200 or 300 going over the first year will make room for twice so many the next year ; and will make provisions for them ; neither doe I believe that those that counselled you to buy a 1,000 cows to plant your ground gave you good advice, in that perhaps a hundred or two may serve all the passengers you are to transport next year, by whom, or at

[1] Hist. MSS. Com. *Fifteenth Report*, app. viii. p. 175.

least by their overseers you may know whether it will be fitter to buy a 1,000 at the same rate or perhaps half so cheape." To help to defray expenses, it was recommended that the ships should be licensed to call at Virginia or Barbados, and to carry goods if necessary. The dispatch at once of a small vessel with an advance party was suggested, and useful information was furnished regarding the stores that should be provided for the new colony.[1]

The suggestion to dispatch a small vessel to explore the possibilities of Carolina was acted on. From Cochran's letter to Haddo we have seen that arrangements were being made for the dispatch of such a vessel, carrying two gentlemen and four pilots, from Greenock at the beginning of October. One of the Scottish commissioners, a certain Mr. Crawford—can it have been Crawford of Crawfordland, who was a year later to be sent down a prisoner from London along with Baillie of Jerviswood and others to be tried at Edinburgh?[2]—was provided with a duplicate of the agreement made with the Lords Proprietors and with a letter from Sir John Cochran to " Mr. Mortoum, Governour at Ashley River." " Wee have commissioned these men," runs the latter document, " to search out for us the most navigable river : and to acquaint themselves so well with the entries of quhat river shall be chosen that they may be able to navigate our ships. We sent you by Captain Adams from London, a letter direct from the Lords Proprietors, desiring you to furnish men and sloupes unto such as wee should commissionàt to sound the rivers and take up our land." After pointing out to the Governor the importance of the effect of such information as might be obtained by these commissioners, and suggesting the advisability of their being given all possible assistance, the Scots declare that if the reports brought back concerning the land and the rivers are favourable, they will enter heartily upon the work of plantation, and will bring with them " suche a considerable number of gentlemen and ministers, and such a strength of people provided of all things necessary, as will exceedingly raise the reputation of that province."[3] The

[1] Hist. MSS. Com. *Fourteenth Report*, app. iii. p. 114.   [2] *Wodrow*, iv. p. 72.
[3] Hist. MSS. Com. *Fourteenth Report*, app. iii. p. 114.

pioneer ship duly sailed, and next year the explorers returned to Scotland.[1]

In contrast with the general tone of the vigorous and progressive policy that guided the Carolina scheme in its early days, it is strange to detect a note of diffidence that is reminiscent of the days of Lochinvar and Sir William Alexander. " I have made offer," wrote Sir Patrick Hume, on 2nd October, 1682, to Cochran and Campbell, "of foure of the sex undertakeinges you wer pleased to trust mee with, in these three shires of Barwicke, Roxbrugh and Selkirk, to such persones whose concurrence others more judicious and I conceived might be of most use in the generall project, and did discover a prety good relish of the busines, but the whole affaire being new and unknowen to most in these pairtes, there is more time required to consider of a busines of this nature before positive resolutions can be fixt upon."[2]

IV.

The flame of colonising zeal, which burned so bright and clear in the autumn of 1682, was, ere many months had passed, to be obscured and wellnigh extinguished. During the spring of 1683 many of the Scots who had been most prominently identified with the Carolina project became involved in the political intrigues which Shaftesbury had left as a legacy to his party. The plan of using the Carolina scheme to cover the comings and goings of the Scottish sympathisers with the English Whigs has been ascribed by Burnet to the Duke of Monmouth.[3] Another important liaison officer was Ferguson the Plotter : " Ferguson was active in connection with this project and his abode in London was the rendezvous of many Scotsmen. It was observed that about him there flocked a society more various than even such a scheme of colonisation would account for. Highlanders, ' Society men ' or Cameronians, foreigners and sailors, were among his visitors : and by means of numerous Scottish pedlars, he could send news rapidly to the North."[4]

[1] Burnet, *History*, f. 541.
[2] Hist. MSS. Com. *Fourteenth Report*, app. iii. pp. 114-115.
[3] Burnet, *History*, f. 546.
[4] Jas. Ferguson, *Robert Ferguson the Plotter*, p. 68.

At first the complicity of the Scots with the English plotters was little suspected. " In the beginning of April," says Burnet, " some of them came up. The person that was most entirely trusted, and to whom the journey proved so fatal was Baillie. . . . He was my cousin german ; so I knew him well . . . I went to him as soon as I heard he was come, in great simplicity of heart, thinking of nothing but of Carolina. I was only afraid they might go too much into the company of the English, and give true representations of the state of affairs in Scotland : and that this might be reported about by men that would name them, and that might bring them into trouble. But a few weeks after, I found they came not to me as they were wont to do ; and I heard they were often with Lord Russell." [1] During the excitement into which London was thrown by the discovery of the plots, Baillie and the Campbells of Cessnock, father and son, changed their lodgings : this aroused suspicion and led to their arrest.[2] " Cochrane, another of those who had been concerned in this (the Carolina) treaty, was complained of, as having talked very freely of the Duke's government of Scotland : upon which the Scottish secretary sent a note to him desiring him to come to him ; for it was intended only to give him a reprimand, and to have ordered him to go to Scotland. But he knew his own secret : so he left his lodgings, and got beyond sea." [3]

During the months of plotting " their contracts for the project of Carolina seemed to go on apace." [4] A small number of the Scots who had gone to London in connection with the Carolina enterprise were, indeed, ignorant of the plotting, and were devoting their energies to expediting preparations in connection with the colonial scheme. " I was engaged in that Commission concerning Carolina," testified Major Monroe, one of the Scots arrested at this time, " most innocently and with reluctancie, as is known to severalls of the undertakers. And I declare I knew of no other designe in it, bot to carry on a Scots plantation in that province, which was a thing very seriously intended by all the undertakers with whom I had occasion to speak concerning it." [5]

[1] Burnet, *History*, f. 540. [2] *Ibid.* f. 549. [3] *Ibid.* ff. 549-550.
[4] *Ibid.* f. 541. [5] *A.P.S.* vol. viii. app. p. 33.

In the autumn of 1683, moreover, the Scots were once more negotiating with the Lords Proprietors of Carolina. On 30th September, 1683, the Proprietors sent to the Governor of Carolina a dispatch concerning the changes effected in the Fundamental Constitutions through the influence of "the Scots and some other considerable men that have a mind to become settlers."[1] The tenor of this dispatch corroborates the view regarding the division of labour suggested by Principal Story : "While Dunlop and his friends attended to the business of the emigration (and eventually went out and settled in Carolina) Carstares, Baillie of Jerviswood, Fletcher of Saltoun, and other patriots, prosecuted in London their correspondence with the revolutionary party."[2] The date of the dispatch indicates that, as soon as the confusion and excitement caused by the discovery of the plots had in some measure subsided, the work of Dunlop and his friends was quietly resumed.

V.

By the spring of 1684 the effects of the work of the steadfast minority began to reveal themselves. "There being severall Scotch going from Glasgow to Carolina," wrote the Proprietors to the Governor on 4th March, $168\frac{3}{4}$, "you are to permitt them to settle at Port Royall if they desire it and direct their Lands to bee run out to them according to our agreement with Sir John Corkran and Sir George Campbell, a Coppye whereof was heretofore sent you, the receipt of which you have acknowledged, or if they desire to settle among the English you are to direct the selling out of the lands to them, as wee have by our Instructions appoynted for all that come to settle among the English in our Province and to passe the grants to them accordingly. And wee desire that you will afford them all manner of countenance and advice in their undertaking."[3]

Another trace of the work of Dunlop and his friends is found in the publication in Scotland very early in 1684 of a

[1] *Col. Cal.* 1681-1685, p. 510.
[2] Principal Story, *William Carstares*, p. 65.
[3] *C.O.* 5/287, f. 129.

broadsheet entitled: "Prosposals / By Walter Gibson, Merchant in Glasgow, to such persons as are desirous to transport themselves to America, in a ship belonging to him, bound for the Bermudas, Carolina, New Providence, and the Carriby-Islands, and ready to set sail out of the River of Clyd against the 20 February in this instant year, 1684."[1] From the standpoint both of matter and of form, this broadsheet is far below the standard set by Barclay in the pamphlet issued on behalf of the New Jersey settlement; in point of interest to the historian, it is not for a moment to be compared to the earlier "Encouragements" of Lochinvar and of Sir William Alexander.

After detailing the cost of the passage and the grants of land to be allotted "to such as are willing to transport themselves with a design to settle in Carolina," Gibson's broadsheet concludes with a recital of the various inducements offered to intending emigrants: "The said Walter Gibson will give his best advice to all such as will Transport themselves, anent these things, which will be necessary for them, to carry alongst with them: and hath at Glasgow Patterns of some Tools which are used there, which shall be showed to them. And those who go in this vessel will have the occasion of good company of several sober, discreet persons, who intend to settle in Carolina, will dwell with them, and be ready to give good advice and assistance to them in their choice of their Plantations, whose society will be very helpful and comfortable, especially at their first settling there."

Of these "sober and discreet persons" the most important were William Dunlop and Lord Cardross. Dunlop, who was at this time thirty-five years of age, had grown to manhood in an atmosphere of religious persecution and civil strife. Both his father (who was minister of Paisley) and his mother had been imprisoned for their constancy in the cause of the Covenant: for his adherence to that cause, Dunlop's cousin and brother-in-law, William Carstares, had to seek refuge in Holland. Educated for the ministry of the Presbyterian Church, Dunlop was employed as tutor in the household of Sir John Cochran of Ochiltree. During the Westland Rising

[1] See Appendix, F.

of 1679 Dunlop was the messenger employed by the Moderate Whigs to lay their views before the leader of the Royal army. After the destruction of the Scottish settlement of Stuart's Town, Dunlop withdrew with the remnant of the Scots to Charleston. On his return to Scotland, after the Revolution, Dunlop was appointed minister of Ochiltree, and a little later Principal of Glasgow University.

In the dragonnades of those troubled days Lord Cardross and his family had undergone much suffering. During the winter of 1683 [1] and the following spring,[2] Dunlop and Cardross were together in Edinburgh. In the spring of 1684, too, Lord Cardross met in Edinburgh " one Mr. Gordon who had been several years in America, and gave a particular account of Carolina, and much commended the country."[3] On June 13th, 1684, Dunlop left Edinburgh for Glasgow " to prepare for his own and other persons' going to Carolina."[4] At the end of the month Cardross, accompanied by his half-brother, Erskine of Carnock, reached the northern shore of the Firth of Clyde. Among the company who rowed over from Greenock to welcome them was William Dunlop.[5]

In company with Carnock and Montgomerie of Skelmorlie, Cardross spent some days cruising about the Firth of Clyde. They visited Loch Long, and then coasted along the Cowal shore to Dunoon. "This morning," confides Carnock to his *Journal* under date 2nd July, "we came out of Loch Lung to the old castle of Denun, where we breakfasted, the people taking extraordinary prices for meat as £1. 4. for three little chickens fryed, with about twelve eggs." Later they went to Skelmorlie, rode along the shore to Largs, and then took boat across to the Big Cumbrae, where they lodged in the house of Mr. Alexander Symmer, a Presbyterian nonconforming minister.

Meanwhile Dunlop remained at Greenock, where Walter Gibson's vessel, the *Carolina Merchant*, a ship of 170 tons burthen, armed with 16 guns, was completing her preparations for the voyage. On board the *Carolina Merchant* were thirty-five prisoners destined for the plantations. Including

[1] Erskine of Carnock's *Journal*, p. 26.   [2] *Ibid.* p. 39.
[3] *Ibid.* p. 39.   [4] *Ibid.* p. 64.   [5] *Ibid.* p. 67.

prisoners, colonists, and crew, the ship's company numbered about 140 persons.

Day after day passed, and the *Carolina Merchant* swung at anchor in Gourock Bay awaiting a favourable wind. The evening of Saturday, 19th July, brought the long-desired breeze, and the skipper, Captain James Gibson (the owner's brother), resolved to sail next morning. But, unlike the Councillors of the Second Darien Expedition who scuttled out of Rothesay Bay leaving behind them their boats and landing parties, Captain Gibson's passengers refused to begin their voyage on a Sunday. On that day William Dunlop preached on shore " in a little garret . . . the lady not daring to be any way public." At seven o'clock next morning the sails of the emigrant ship were bent, and as she prepared to leave her moorings, Lord Cardross put off from shore in a small boat. Along with him was a trumpeter, who sounded several times, " which," says Erskine of Carnock, who witnessed the departure, " was truly pleasant upon sea." [1]

VI.

Lord Cardross and his company of emigrants sailed for Carolina at a time when the tension between the Spanish and the English colonists on the Florida-Carolina frontier had become peculiarly acute. During the seventeenth century the sphere of Spanish influence in North America had, both in the centre of the continent and along the Pacific coast, been steadily extended to the north. On the Atlantic coast, however, the territory to which Spain could assert an undisputed claim had been delimited, first by the English colonisation of Virginia and then by the establishment of English settlements in Carolina. The English settlement of Charleston was particularly resented by Spain. " This intrusion into the old Spanish province of Santa Elena was viewed with alarm by Spain, and, as always in the border Spanish colonies, the foreign danger was followed by renewed missionary activity on the threatened frontiers." [2] The missionary activity was

[1] Erskine of Carnock's *Journal*, pp. 67-72.
[2] Bolton and Marshall, *The Colonisation of North America*, p. 254.

followed, in turn, by desultory skirmishing between the English and the Spaniards, each aided by Indian allies. This border warfare began in 1680. In 1684 the Lords Proprietors of Carolina were decidedly apprehensive regarding Spanish designs on their territory. In the commission issued on 29th April of that year to Sir Richard Kyrle, Governor of Carolina, they emphasised the necessity of making adequate provision for defence : " The Spaniards have not always been very good neighbours, and we know not how soon they may attack you. You will therefore consult the Council and Parliament, and put the country into the best posture of defence you can, in order to which you will hasten the settlement of the militia and set good men in command. You will cause the companies to be frequently trained and agree upon the rendezvous of each company and regiment in case of alarm. . . . We hope that your preparations may make the enemy desist from attempts that are chiefly encouraged by carelessness in defence." [1] How far the military preparations of the governor acted as a deterrent it is impossible to determine, but the enemy certainly made no onslaught until fresh provocation was offered by the activities of the Scots settled at Stuart's Town.

VII.

Before sailing from Scotland the Carolina colonists had requested the Lords Proprietors to permit the Scottish settlement to be the seat of justice for the county in which it was situated. In a spirit of accommodation similar to that in which they had met the Scottish criticisms of the constitution of the province, the Proprietors signified their willingness to grant this supplementary request. There is, indeed, a note of almost paternal solicitude for the welfare of the Scots in the Proprietors' dispatch of 25th June, 1684: " The Scotts that are now going have desired that the town they pitch on may be the seat of justice for that county : we have no objection provided the site be healthy, the water good, the land high enough to admit of cellars underground and the situation far enough inland to render it safe from surprise by

[1] *Col. Cal.* 1681-1685, p. 623 ; *C.O.* 5/287, f. 126.

ships. The land must be reserved as laid down in our instructions, and you will direct all who settle in or near Port Royal to settle together as may be best for their defence and safety."[1]

From the benevolent attitude adopted towards them by the Proprietors throughout the negotiations, it might seem only natural for the Scottish colonists to expect that on landing at Port Royal they would be treated with similar consideration by the representatives of the Proprietors at Charleston. Self-interest, too, might have been expected to suggest to the authorities at Carolina the advantages of a policy of active and unremitting support of the settlement at Port Royal. Despite the fact that Britain and Spain were nominally at peace, there had flickered the desultory warfare on the Carolina-Florida frontier: at any moment this might leap up into a devastating blaze. At all seasons of the year Charleston lay open to attack by sea from St. Augustine. In the very year that saw the establishment of the Scottish colony there had been, as we have seen, considerable nervousness regarding the possibility of a Spanish descent on Carolina. The distance between St. Augustine and Charleston was little more than one-third of that between Charleston and Virginia—the nearest point from which effective aid could be expected. The Scottish settlement at Port Royal was therefore an outpost on the vulnerable flank of Charleston.[2] It had all the strategic advantages which such an outpost should possess. It was not too near to Charleston: no raiding force could overwhelm Port Royal and sweep on to Charleston before adequate warning could reach the latter place. Port Royal, on the other hand, was not too remote from Charleston to permit of the speedy arrival of reinforcements.

Yet, despite these incentives to co-operation and concerted action in the face of the common enemy, the relations between the Scottish settlers and the authorities at Charleston were far from friendly. This regrettable discord was due to two causes: the first was the uncertainty as to the legal status of the Scots in relation to the Governor and Grand Council of Carolina;

[1] *Col. Cal.* 1681-1685, p. 661; *C.O.* 5/288, f. 35.
[2] *C.O.* 5/287, f. 136; *C.O.* 5/288, f. 73.

the second was the apathy of the authorities at Charleston, despite repeated warnings from the Scots, towards the menace of a Spanish raid.

Lord Cardross interpreted his agreement with the Lords Proprietors as giving him " co-ordinate authority with the Governor and Grand Council at Charleston." [1] Once again the punctilious nationalism of the Scots was asserting itself. " Wee nothing doubt," wrote Cardross to the Governor on 25th March, 1685, " but you all know the contracts and treaties that have been made betwixt the Lords Proprietors and us, and other of our countreymen which as wee resolve to sincerely keep on our part, so likewise wee expect and resolve to have them faire to us." This remonstrance was evoked from Cardross by the receipt on the part of Caleb Westbrooke, one of the residents within his county, of a communication from Charleston authorising Westbrooke to arrest a man " within our bounds," and—" all this without notice to us "—citing Westbrooke to appear at Charleston " to give information respecting some transactions that have lately taken place to southward." [2]

So strained did the relations between Charleston and Port Royal become, that on 5th May, 1685, the Grand Council issued a warrant for the arrest of Lord Cardross.[3] When the marshal arrived at Port Royal with the warrant, Lord Cardross was suffering from fever. The Council interpreted his inability to come before them as contempt of their authority and on 2nd June issued a second warrant for his arrest,[4] and at the same time " ordered a party to bring him down sick or well." [5] Cardross challenged the legality " of the first paper that came from the council in the nature of a warrant," and expressed his surprise at his absence being treated as contempt of the authority of the Council : he was suffering from fever at the time of the serving of the first " warrant " ; he was still suffering from fever, which would prevent his attendance at the next meeting of the Council.[6] At the same

---

[1] M'Crady, *S. Carolina under Prop. Gov.* p. 214.
[2] *C.O.* 5/287, f. 134 ; *Col. Cal.* 1685-1688, p. 22.
[3] *Col. Cal.* 1685-1688, p. 40.   [4] *Ibid.* p. 47.   [5] *Ibid.* p. 68.
[6] *C.O.* 5/287, f. 135 ; *Col. Cal.* 1685-1688, no. 286.

time William Dunlop wrote unofficially and diplomatically to the Governor, corroborating Lord Cardross's statement and expressing surprise at the rigour with which the Council had proposed to act.[1]

The attitude of the Charleston authorities met with the disapproval of the Proprietors. On 22nd April, 1686, they wrote to the Governor: "We notice a violent run against Lord Cardross, which dissatisfies us much. We would have all persons of quality treated with civility and respect. We desire a report from you on the matter, and meanwhile you will stop all proceedings against him."[2] On 3rd March, 168⁶⁄₇, the Proprietors wrote to Cardross: "My Lord—We have seen your letters complaining of Ill usage in Carolina, And we are extreamly sorry that any there should soe farr forgett themselves as not to shew you that Respect that is due to your Quality. Wee doe noe way approve of those mens ill behaviour but believe that they themselves are now sensible of their Errors In this matter; Wee are heartily sorry for your Lordships Losses Recd. by the Spainyards and intend in fitting time to apply to the King for Reparation. Wee shall be ever Ready to doe your Lordship any service that lyes in our Power."[3] Before the descent of the Spaniards on Stuart's Town, however, Cardross, incensed at his treatment by the authorities at Charleston, had withdrawn from Carolina and joined the very considerable colony of Scottish exiles in Holland.

While the Governor and Council were devoting themselves energetically—and somewhat tactlessly—to the assertion of their authority over the Scots settlement, the important duty of strengthening the Scots against a possible attack from St. Augustine was persistently neglected. The knowledge that the land on which they were to settle was to be purchased on their behalf by the Charleston authorities from the Indians may have lulled the Scots into a sense of security before their arrival at Carolina; but once settled at Port Royal they did not long remain ignorant of the precarious nature of their tenure, in view of the ever-present menace of a Spanish attack.

[1] *Col. Cal.* 1685-1688, p. 68.   [2] *Ibid.* p. 118.   [3] *C.O.* 4/288, f. 109.

PRINCIPAL WILLIAM DUNLOP.
From portrait in Senate Room of Glasgow University.

Early in January, 1685, a party of Yamasee Indians brought to Port Royal a letter from the Governor of St. Augustine. Surmising that this message was in reality intended for the Governor of Carolina, the Scots forwarded it to Charleston. "As we be on their frontier," wrote Cardross in a covering letter, "it concerns us much to know the Spaniard's movements and intentions, and we beg therefore for a copy of the letter."[1] This eminently reasonable request was ignored. The same treatment was accorded to a requisition made by the Scots for six guns which the Proprietors promised would be supplied to them from the fort at Charleston.[2] Six months after the request for the guns was made, and fourteen months after the arrival of the Scots in Carolina, the Proprietors wrote to the Governor: "... and whereas we are told that there are divers Peeces of our Cannon that lye unmounted and useless at Old Charles Town, And having taken into our consideration that Stewarts Town at Port Royall is ye ffrontier of ye whole Settlement towards ye Spainard and most lyable to be hurt by them whenever they shall be disposed to disturb us, Wee doe therefore Order that you deliver ffive of ye aforesaid Peeces of Cannon to ye said Lord Cardrosse and ye said Alexander Dunlop or either of them or ther order (they giveing you security for ye transporting ye said ffive Peeces of Cannon to Stewards Town or some other Town in Port-Royal in Carolina) and there to mount ye same for ye safety thereof."[3]

In February, 1685, the inhabitants of Port Royal were alarmed by the arrival of Indians in such large numbers that it was a matter of some difficulty to find accommodation for them in the neighbourhood.[4] At first it was feared that this migration was the harbinger of a Spanish descent. In reality the Indians, who belonged to the Yamasee tribe, had flocked down to enter into an alliance with the Scots. Some years previously the Indian tribes of the Carolina-Florida border had been ordered by the Spaniards to move southwards in

[1] *Col. Cal.* 1681-1685, no. 2043; *C.O.* 5/287, f. 136.
[2] *C.O.* 5/287, f. 134; *Col. Cal.* 1685-1688, p. 22.
[3] *C.O.* 5/288, f. 73; *Col. Cal.* 1681-1685, p. 118.
[4] *Col. Cal.* 1685-1688, p. 5.

order that they might be withdrawn from English influence.[1] The Yamasees proved recalcitrant. The authorities at Charleston had, probably out of wholesome respect for the Spaniards, kept studiously aloof from all dealings with the Indians, but in the Scots the Yamasees found settlers with whom it was less difficult to enter into friendship. From their position in the debatable land and from their alliance with the Yamasees, the Scots were inevitably involved in the Indian border feuds. Their friendship with the Indians was viewed with disfavour by the authorities at Charleston [2] who, however, did little to render the Scots independent of their native allies. In May, 1685, several Yamasee Indians, examined by the Governor of Carolina, testified that " the Scots at Port Royal sent an emissary to persuade them to go to war with some neighbouring Indians who had a Chapel and a Spanish Friar, and gave them arms for the purpose. They did so, and brought back twenty prisoners as slaves to the Scots, and a manuscript of prayers produced." [3] The Scots' Indian allies had, in fact, raided the Spanish Mission of Santa Catalina.

The destruction of the Scots' settlement at Port Royal by the Spaniards has sometimes been regarded as provoked by this Indian raid.[4] The Lords Proprietors chose to adopt this view in order to excuse their public policy of forbidding the dispatch from Charleston of a punitive expedition.[5] But in view of the fact that sixteen months elapsed between the Indian raid and the destruction of Port Royal, the theory that the Spanish expedition against the Scots was a vindication of the claim of Spain to the territory on which the Scots had settled has much to commend it.[6]

The destruction of the Scots' settlement was effected in September, 1686.[7] The raiding party, composed of Spanish soldiers, Indians and Mulattos, numbered about one hundred and fifty.[8] Three galleys brought them north from St.

[1] Bolton and Marshall, *Colonisation of N. America*, p. 255.
[2] *Col. Cal.* 1685-1688, pp. 19 and 40.   [3] *Ibid.* p. 40.
[4] Bolton and Marshall, *Colonisation of N. America*, p. 255.
[5] *Col. Cal.* 1685-1688, p. 451.
[6] M'Crady, *S. Carolina under Prop. Gov.* p. 220.
[7] *Col. Cal.* 1685-1688, p. 295.   [8] *Ibid.* p. 336.

Augustine. The Scots, who had suffered from the fevers of the coastal plain, had only twenty-five men fit to oppose the raiders. The settlement was completely destroyed: the survivors took refuge in Charleston. At an earlier stage of the same raid the country house of the Governor of Carolina and that of the Secretary of the Province had been sacked, and from these residences much booty, including thirteen slaves, had been carried away.[1]

Stung into activity by this raid, the inhabitants of Charleston determined to retaliate by an attack on St. Augustine. Preparations were energetically pushed forward. The Parliament of Carolina passed an Act authorising the immediate invasion of Spanish territory, and appointed two Receivers to collect an assessment levied to finance the invasion. Two French privateers were hired. The crews of these mustered two hundred men. An additional force of three hundred colonists was raised.[2] A new Governor, however, arrived at Charleston and forbade the sailing of the expedition. The Lords Proprietors supported the Governor.[3] And Scotland sent out no Dominique de Gourgues.

. . . .

And so, in far-off Carolina, the curtain is rung down on the last of the one-act dramas of early Scottish colonial history. And, in Scotland, the stage is being set for the great drama of Darien.

[1] M'Crady, *S. Carolina under Prop. Gov.* p. 295.
[2] *Col. Cal.* 1685-1688, p. 295.   [3] *Ibid.* p. 336.

APPENDIX A

The French protest against the Scottish expedition of 1623 (*Public Record Office C.O.* 1/3, No. 13).

(Le Comte de Tillières arrived in England as French Ambassador about September 1623 ; he was recalled in June 1624.)

Le Memorial de Monseign[r] Le Comte de Tillières, Ambassadeur pour le Roy de France.

Mon[sr] Le Comte de Tillières Ambassadeur de France en Angleterre ayant receu Comandement de sa Ma[te] de poursuivre pres le Roy de la Grande Bretagne quelque ordre a ce que Ses sujets cessent d'entreprendre aux terres neufves autrement appellées La Nouvelle France entre le 40 et 50 degres, suivant l'information qui luy a este donnée des entreprises et actes d'hostilité des Anglois tant envers Le S. de Poutrincourt habitué au dit pays qu'envers les autres François qui y naviguent Led[t] Sr Ambassadeur a envoyé à Mon[s] le Secretaire Connové[1] le present mémoire pour le prier de vouloir representer a Sa Ma[te] de la Grande Bretagne combien ces troubles entre leurs sujets sont importans à leur bien comun et pourraient prejudicier avec le temps a la Paix et bonne Amitié qui est entre leurs Ma[tes], les[ds] Anglois ayant de la terre a s'estendre depuis la Virginia qui est au 36 degres jusqu'a vers La Floride plus de cinq cents Lieues loing jusques au Golphe de Mexique sans inquieter les[ds] François en la possession des[ds] Terres Neufves.

Partant led[t] Sr Ambassadeur requiet Sa Ma[te] de la Grande Bretagne de vouloir faire expedier quelques deffences à ses sujets de troubler les François qui naviguent aux[ds] terres

[1] Conway.

neufves et specialement le^{dt} Sr de Poutrincourt en ses possessions et domaines par dela, afin par devant luy Les^{ds} deffences de Lad^{te} Maj^{te} de la Grande Bretagne il le puisse signifier aux^{ds} Anglois quand occasion le pointera et par ce moyen les convoqer à se contenir dans leurs bonds pour n'estre obligez les uns et les autres à en venir aux extremites d'une petite guerre.

APPENDIX B

DATE OF THE SETTLEMENT OF SIR WILLIAM ALEXANDER'S COLONISTS AT PORT ROYAL.

HITHERTO the first settlement of the Scots at Port Royal in Nova Scotia has been ascribed to the year 1628 :[1] certain documents in the Egerton MSS. (B.M.) yield convincing testimony that the first Scots settlement at Port Royal was not made till the year 1629. The problem of the date of the settlement is both intricate and interesting, and the evidence bearing on it will repay study.

It is incontestable that the year 1628 saw a good deal of activity on the part of those who were interested in Sir William Alexander's colonial projects, and especially on the part of Sir William's eldest son, Sir William Alexander, the younger.

During the winter of 1627-1628 a considerable number of Scottish gentlemen had been induced to become Nova Scotia baronets—fourteen baronets were created between October 1627 and February 1628 [2]—and money was therefore available to finance an expedition.

Early in the year 1628 Alexander's ships departed from Dumbarton. The last entry in the Burgh Records referring to their presence at Dumbarton bears the date 28th January, 1628.

On 26th March, 1628, Sir William Alexander, the younger, received official permission to proceed on an expedition. The copy of that permission which is preserved is in the following terms :

"(Charles R.)

"Whareas the four schippis, called the . . . belonging to

---

[1] Rogers, *Mem. of Earl of Stirling*, vol. i. pp. 102 and 103.
[2] *Nova Scotia Papers*, p. 43.

APPENDIX B

Sir William Alexander, Knight, son to Sir William Alexander, our Secretairie for Scotland; whareof the . . . are to set out towards Newfoundland, the River of Canade, and New Scotland, for settling of Colonies in those partes, and for other thare laufull effaires : Theis are, tharefore, to will and require you, and everie one of you, to permitt and suffer the said schippes, and everie one of them, with thare wholl furneture, goods, merchandice, schips companies, and planties (plantees?) quietlie and peaceabillie in thare going thither, returning from thence, or during thare being further in any other parte whatsoever, till they shall happin to returne to any of our dominiones, to pas by you, without any of your lettes, stayes, troubles, imprestis of ther men, or any other men, or any other hinderance whatsoever : Wharef you shall not faill."

"Whitehall, the 26th March, 1628." [1]

A month later the fleet was in Scottish waters, and already Sir William Alexander, the younger, had entered upon the family inheritance of vexation and disappointment. The tale of woe is told briefly but significantly in the following extract from the Register of the Privy Council of Scotland :

"Forsamekill as it is understood be the Lords of Secreit Counsell that diverse persons who were conduced and tane on be Sir Williame Alexander, Knight, and his officiars, to have beene transported be thame for the plantatioun of New Scotland, have most unworthilie abandoned that service and imployment, refuising to performe the conditionis of thar agreement, to the disappointing of that intendet Plantation which his Majestie so earnestlie affects, ffor remedeing of which undewtifull dealing, the saids Lords recommends to the Shireffs, Justices of Peace, and Proveists and Bailleis within burgh, and thairwith all gives thame power and commissione, everie one of thame, within thair awin bounds and jurisdictioun, to take tryell of all and sindrie persouns who haveing covenanted with the said Sir Williame Alexander, or his officers, to goe with thame to New Scotland, have abandoned that service and runne away, and ather to compell thame to performe the conditionis of thair agreement, or otherwayes to doe justice upon thame, according to the

[1] *Register Royal Letters*, vol. i. p. 266 ; Rogers, *Memorials*, vol. i. p. 102.

merite of thair trespasse: And that the saide Shireffs, Justices of peace, provests and Bailleis within burgh concurre, countenance, and assist the said Sir Williame Alexander and his officers in all and everie thing that may further and advance the service foresaids: And for this effect, that the said Shireffs and others foresaids delyver the said personns to the said Sir Williame Alexander and his officers, it being first qualified that they have ressaved money from the said Sir Williame and his officers, or that they have beene in service and entertained by thame."

"*Apud Halyrudhous.*
"Vicesimo tertio die mensis Aprilis 1628." [1]

The extent to which this hue and cry may have proved effective it is impossible to determine, but that the fleet left Scotland soon after there is no reasonable doubt. The Earl of Stirling's biographer states emphatically that "the fleet left Scotland in May, carrying upwards of seventy colonists, who were safely landed at Port Royal." [2] For this statement he quotes no authority. Of the exact date of departure there is apparently no record. For the number of colonists—"upwards of seventy"—there is certainly one authority of some importance. But, as will be shown in the sequel, wherever these Scots colonists were landed, it was not at Port Royal.

The next evidence bearing on Sir William's expedition belongs to the autumn of 1628. On the 28th August, 1628, Sir Alexander Nesbitt of that Ilk, sheriff principal of Berwickshire, obtained from the Privy Council suspension of a decree of horning passed against him for his failure "to apprehend and imprison Sir James Home of Eckills and Sir George Home, apparent thereof, and Alexander Home his sons." In the course of the statement made in support of his plea for suspension of the horning, Sir Alexander Nesbitt declared that "it is notoriously known to all the country that long before the giving of this charge both Sir George Home and Alexander

[1] *Reg. P.C.*, Second Series, vol. ii. pp. 313-314; Rogers, *Memorials*, vol. i. pp. 102-103.

[2] Rogers, vol. i. p. 103.

Home his brother were out of the country, the former in service with Sir Williame Alexander to Nova Scotia, and the said Alexander with the Earl of Mortain in the King's service and that they are still abroad."[1] When we consider the position of the person who is making this assertion, and take into account the fact that the Privy Council were inevitably aware of the progress of the Nova Scotia expedition, we may assume that the fleet had certainly left Scotland on a transatlantic voyage.

During November, 1628, two interesting pieces of corroborative evidence became available. On the 18th of that month the Privy Council sent to King Charles a letter " anent a new patent of the lands of Canada and the trade thereof : "

" Most sacred Soverane, wee have been petitiouned in name of some interested in New Scotland and Canada holdin of your Majestie's crowne of this Kingdome humblie shewing that by virtew of rights of land made unto thame by your Majestie or by Sir Williame Alexander, your Majestie's Lieutennent of these bounds, they have alreadie adventured sowmes of money for setting furth of a colonie to plant there, and intending, God willing, to prosecute the same and that they understand that by reasoun of a voyage made by ane Captaine Kick (*sic*) thither this last sommer there are some making sute to your Majestie for a new patent of the saids lands of Canada and of the trade thairof, to be holdin of your Majesteis crowne of England, which in our opinioun will prove so derogatorie to this your ancient Kingdome, under the great seal whereof your Majestie hes alreadie granted a right to the saids bounds, and will so exceedinglie discourage all undertakers of that kynde, as we cannot but at their humble suite represent the same to your majestie ; humbly intreatting that your Majestie may be graciouslie pleased to take this into your princlie consideratioun as no right may be heerafter graunted of the saids lands contrarie to your Majesteis said preceiding graunt, but that they may be still holdin of the crowne of this your ancient Kingdome, according to the purport and trew intentioun of your Majesties said former

[1] *Reg. P.C. Scot.*, Second Series, vol. ii. p. 443.

graunt. And we aʳ verie hopefull that, as the said Sir Williame Alexander hes sent furth his sonne with a colonie to plant there this last yeere, so it shall be secunded heerafter by manie other undertakers of good worth for the advancement of your Majesteis service, increasse of your revenewes, and hounour of this your said ancient Kingdome. And so with the continuance of our most humble services and best prayers for your Majesteis health and happiness, we humblie take leave, as your Majesteis most humble and faithfull servants : "

" Subscribitur : Mar, Monteith, Hadintoun, Wintoun, Linlithgow, Lauderdaill, Tracquair, A Carre, Arch. Achesoun, Advocat, Clerk Register, Sir George Elphinstoun, Scottistarvett. Halyruidhous, 18 November, 1628." [1]

The note of this dispatch is anticipatory. News had reached Edinburgh of the attempt on the part of the Kirkes to obtain a grant of Canadian territory, and immediately on the receipt of this news, sent north it may be presumed by Sir William Alexander with all haste, the Council sent off their memorial. Within a very few days—not more than five—tidings came to Edinburgh of the settlement of Alexander's colony. On 23rd November, 1628, Mr. William Maxwell, writing from Edinburgh, conveyed this information to Sir John Maxwell of Pollok. A proper appreciation of the value of the information regarding Alexander's colony is impossible unless the passage referring to it is taken in connection with its context :

" Rycht honorable, since the wryting of my last lettre unto your worship, the articles of agreement betwixt the King of France and the Rochell heathe come in my hands : Quhairfair, seeing I receaved thame, I thocht I could not bot send a double of thame to your worship, quhilk your honor sall receave herein incloset ; verbally copiet off the English exemplar sent from the Court in the last pacquet. I heir nothing farder then quhat wes in my last lettre direct to your worship, except that the King's Majesty heathe promisit to pay all the Earle of Mortounes debt, albeit it were 40m. lib sterling. It is for certaintie that Sir William Alexander is

[1] *Reg. P.C.*, Second Series, vol. ii. p. 489 ; *Nova Scotia Papers*, p. 46.

come home againe from Nova Scotia, and heathe left behind him 70 men and tua weemen, with provisioun to serve tham be the space of ane yeir, being placet in a pairt of the countrie quhilk is a natirall strenthe ; togither with some cannoun, musket, pouder and bullet, in caice of some suddent invasiouns togither with all thingis necessar for thair present use, and is to go hither againe in the spring with a new plantation. Bot since he came home the Englische men are suiten of his Majestie a patent to plant and possesse quhatsumever lands thairof quhilk they please, and these to be holden of the Crown of England. Quhat salbe the event I know not. These only haive I heard since the dait of my last letter ; and withe what heirafter sall fall furthe, I sall not faill to acquent your worship. . . ." [1]

William Maxwell was evidently well in touch with all the information concerning political affairs that was in circulation in influential circles in Edinburgh. There is ample corroboration of his assertions regarding the intention of Sir William Alexander, the younger, to return to Nova Scotia and regarding the English attempt to secure a patent of lands in Canada. In view of the access William Maxwell had to important information, and in view of the general trustworthiness of his assertions regarding colonial questions, there is no reason to doubt the substantial accuracy of his statement regarding the planting of a colony. The detailed nature of his information regarding the colony leads one to suspect that he is quoting from an official dispatch—in all probability part of the papers " sent from the Court in the last pacquet," the pacquet which had supplied him with the copy of the articles of agreement between the King of France and the Huguenots of La Rochelle. It should be observed, however, that despite his detailed information regarding the colony he does not specify its exact location. The significance of this omission will become apparent at a later stage of our discussion.

Finally, we have for the year 1628 the evidence of Stirling Kirk Session Records that on 25th December Sir William

---

[1] Mr. William Maxwell, Edinburgh, to Sir John Maxwell of Pollok, 23rd November, 1628 (reproduced in *The Maxwells of Pollok*, vol. ii. p. 199).

Alexander, the younger, " efter his returne from his sea voyage, gave to the puir of Stirling fiftie aught pundis money." [1]

. . . .

Until the summer of 1921 I had been content to regard the year 1628 as the date of the first Scots settlement at Port Royal. The evidence in favour of that year was strong, though not wholly conclusive, and I had met with no contradictory evidence, except the demand of the French ambassador quoted below. In the summer of 1921, however, while working through Egerton MS. 2395 and Harleian MS. 1760 in the British Museum, I came upon evidence which forced me first to reconsider the whole subject, then to dismiss the date 1628 as untenable, and finally to accept the date 1629 as indisputably the correct one.

With regard to the evidence that follows, certain facts should be borne in mind.

(a) By the Peace of Suza, which terminated hostilities between France and England, it was arranged that all conquests made after the 23rd of April, 1629, should be restored, and that Port Royal was claimed by the French on that ground; on 1st February, 1629-1630, the French ambassador made his demand:

" The Ambassador of France prays his Majesty of Great Britain that he may please to ordain and consent to what has been promised and granted by the Articles of the 23rd April last, to Captain Querch and Sir William Alexander and certain others of his subjects, who are resident, or shall hereafter reside, in New France; that they withdraw themselves therefrom, and restore into the hands of those whom it may please the King his Master to send out, and who shall be the bearers of his commission, all places and spots which they have occupied and inhabited since the last troubles, and, in particular, the fortress and settlement of Quebec, Coast of Cape Breton, and Port Royal, taken and occupied; to wit, the fortress and settlement of Quebec by Captain Querch, and the Coasts of Cape Breton and Port Royal by Sir William

[1] Quoted Rogers, vol. i. p. 205.

Alexanders, the Scots noblemen, since the 23rd April last. ...." [1]

(*b*) Extracts I. II. and III. from the Egerton MSS. are taken from papers that have for their purpose to urge the king to retain what had been taken from France, and if the Scots settlement of Port Royal had been effected in 1628, *i.e.* before the conclusion of hostilities, this certainly would not have been ignored.

Extract I.—William Alexander's information touching his Plantation at Cape Breton and Port Royal.

" ... The said Sir William resolving to plant in that place sent out his son Sir William Alexander this last spring with a colonie to inhabite the same who arriving first at Capbritton did finde three shipps there, whereof, one being a Barque of 60 Tunnes it was founde that the owners belonged to St. Sebastian in Portugall and that they had traded there contrary to the power graunted by his Majestie for wch and other reasouns according to the process which was formallie led, he the said Sir William having chosen the Lord Ochillrie and Monsieur de la Tour to be his assistants adjudged that Barque to be lawfull prize and gave a Shallop and other necessaries to transfer her Companie to other Shippes upon that coast according to their owne desire, as for the other two which he found to be french Shipps he did no wise trouble them.

" Thereafter having left the Lo. Oghillrie with some 60 or so English who went with him to inhabit there, At Cap britton, the said Sir William went from thence directly to Port Royal wch he found (as it had been a long tyme before) abandoned and without any signe that ever people had been there where he hath seated himself and his Companie according to the warrant graunted unto him by his Matie of purpose to people that part." [2]

[1] *C.O.* 1/5, No. 50 ; *Col. Cal.*, 1574-1660, p. 107. (The ambassador's note is quoted in full, Rogers, vol. i. pp. 120-121.)

[2] Egerton, 2395, f. 23.

On Extract I. the following comments fall to be made :

(*a*) The date of the landing of Lord Ochiltrie and his sixty colonists at Cape Breton was 1st July, 1629.[1]

(*b*) Clearly the expedition which reached Port Royal under Alexander was not a reinforcing one : the Scots were making the beginning of a settlement.

(*c*) The essential accuracy of the narrative contained in Extract I. is confirmed by testimony from an important independent source.—" Relation du Voyage fait par le Capitaine Daniel de Dieppe en la nouvelle France, la présente année 1629 " (*Champlain's Voyages*, Edit. 1632, Part II. pages 271-275). "Etant le 28 jour d'Aout entré dans la rivière nomée par les Sauvages ' Grand Cibou ' j'envoyais le jour d'après dans mon batteau dix de mes hommes le long de la coste, pour trouver quelques Sauvages, et apprendre d'eux en quel état etait l'habitation de Quebec, et arrivant mes dits hommes au Port aux Balaines ; y trouverent un navire de Bordeaux, le maître duquel se nommait Chambreau, qui leur dit que le Sieur Jacques Stuart Milor Ecossais était arrivé au dit lieu environ deux mois auparavant, avec deux grand navires et une patache Anglaise, et qu'ayant trouvé au dit lieu Michel Dihourse de St Jean de Luz, qui faisait sa pêscherie et secherie de molué s'était le dit Milor Ecossais saisi du navire et molué du dit Dihourse ; il avait permi que ses hommes fussent pillés et que le dit Milor avait peu après envoyé les deux plus grands de ses vaisseaux, avec le navire du dit Michel Dihourse et partie de ses hommes vers le port Royal pour y faire habitation."

Extract II.—His Majesty's Right and Title to Port Royal.

" . . . They (the French) went out and seated themselves upon the North side of the River of Canada, at Kebeck . . . but small notice was taken thereof till during the time of the late war a Comm^n. was given by his Majesty to remove them from thence wch was according performed, the place being taken a little after the peace was concluded wch at that time

---

[1] *C.O.* 1/5, Nos. 46 and 47 ; *Col. Cal.*, 1574-1660, pp. 105-106.

APPENDIX B

had not come to the taker's knowledge ; and a Colony of Scottish people was planted at Port Royal." [1]

(As Quebec surrendered to Kirke on 19th July, 1629, and as Sir William Alexander was at Cape Breton on 1st July ere leaving for Port Royal, the capture of Quebec and the planting of the colony of Scottish people must have occurred almost at the same time.)

Extract III.—Propositions and Considerations for the Business of Canada.

" . . . Divers English merchants and others the last years during the warr with France sett out certaine shippes under the command of Captaine Kirke wth great coste and charges into those parts and their voyage succeeded soe well that they took possession of the Gulfe and the greatest part of the River of Canada (wch the ffrench for this 24 or 25 yeares last past had usurped) and took downe the ffrench armes wch were planted at a place wthin the River of Canada called Tadousack, and sett up the English Armes in their place.

" This yeare (*i.e.* 1629) during the warr likewise the said Companie being united with Sir William Alexander and divers of his Majesty's subjects of Scotland, who have the interest of a patent for plantation in those parts under the seale of that Kingdome have by the authority of his Maties Commission employed manie Shippes Land Forces and Marchandises att a very great charge for the regayning of the whole River of Canada, and setting of plantation there.

" Wherefore they are humble suitors that his Maties ambassadors may be so instructed that nothing in this treaty of peace with France may be yielded unto, to the prejudice of his Maties and their interest in those parts." [2]

Regarding Extract III. the following comments fall to be made :

(*a*) The propositions were obviously addressed to King Charles before news of the fall of Quebec had arrived.

(*b*) Neither the fall of Quebec nor the occupation of Port Royal would have been omitted hád tidings of them come to hand prior to the drawing up of the proposition.

[1] Egerton, 2395, f. 21.   [2] *Ibid.* 2395, f. 22.

(c) Tadousack—the only post occupied during 1628—seems to some extent unfamiliar to the London memorialists : it is referred to as " a place within the River of Canada called Tadousack."

From the cumulative evidence of the above three extracts it is quite clear that the settlement of the Scots at Port Royal was effected in the summer of 1629, early in the month of July. In addition to the evidence just quoted from the Egerton MSS., a valuable piece of corroborative evidence is available from another source, a diplomatic paper in the Harleian MSS. This is the copy of a dispatch from the King, " Given under or Signett att or Manor of Greenwich the twelfth of June in the seventh yeare of or Raygne," and addressed " to or trusty and well-beloved Sr Isaac Wake, Knight, or Ambassador Resident wth the French King." At this date (12th June, 1631) negotiations were in progress between the Courts of Britain and France regarding the giving up of Quebec and Port Royal to France. King Charles I., hard pressed for money, was endeavouring to use the British occupation of these two places as a lever to extract from France the unpaid half of the dowry of Queen Henrietta Maria. He declares " That wee thoroughly understand to be putt in ballance, yf not in contract, against the porton money is the rendition of Quebec in Canada, taken by verteu of a commission given during the late warre under o^r great Seale by a Company of o^r subjects of this o^r kingdome of England, and the retyring from Port Royal, a place adioyning upon New England, where a company of the subjects of our kingdome of Scotland were seated and planted by vertue of the like commission under the seal of that o^r Kingdome, given out likewise during the warre in consequence of one formerly given by the King or father of happy memory.

" Trew it is that one of these places was taken and the plantation was made in the other after the peace." [1]

. . . .

Clearly, then, the first settlement of the Scots at Port Royal belongs to the year 1629, not to 1628. Yet the precise,

[1] Harleian, 1760, fol. 11.

APPENDIX B

detailed nature of the information in the Maxwell letter from Edinburgh leaves one with the feeling that a Scots colony was certainly planted somewhere in Canada in the summer of 1628. If not at Port Royal, where was it ? At Tadoussac.

This solution of the problem is supported by evidence, the cumulative effect of which leaves no room for doubt.

(*a*) When the fleet under Kirke left England in 1628 it consisted of three vessels ; when he appeared off Tadoussac in July of that year, Kirke commanded a fleet of six vessels.[1] Where had the three additional vessels come from ? Kingsford surmises that " the additional three vessels must have been craft which he had seized of inferior tonnage, acting as tenders." [2]

It should be remembered that Kirke at this time had in view the prospect of an engagement with de Roquemont's squadron from Dieppe. Was he likely to weaken the fighting personnel of his ships by drafting into these captured vessels a number of his men ? The three additional ships, however, took no part in the action in which de Roquemont was defeated. Why ? It seems most probable that the three additional ships represented the fleet of Sir William Alexander,[3] and that they took no part in the action because they were in reality transports laden with colonists.

(*b*) Tadoussac, situated on the deep gorge of the Saguenay, some miles above its junction with the St. Lawrence, was obviously a place of strategic importance, controlling the channel of the St. Lawrence below Quebec. Kirke destroyed the French station at Tadoussac, but failed to induce Champlain to surrender Quebec. To leave Tadoussac unoccupied when he quitted the St. Lawrence would be merely an invitation for the French to reoccupy their station, and, in view of Richelieu's attitude, reoccupation would mean that the defences of the outpost of Quebec would be greatly strengthened. Where, however, was he to find a garrison for Tadoussac ? The crews of the three privateers had enough to do

---

[1] Kingsford, *Hist. of Canada*, vol. i. p. 86.   [2] *Ibid.*

[3] Although Sir Wm. Alexander, senior, opposed the Canadian merchants, the latter appear to have regarded Sir William, the younger, as one of themselves. Egerton, 2395, f. 25.

to take their own ships home and provide prize crews for the warships taken from de Roquemont. What more natural on the part of Kirke than to use Alexander's 70 colonists to garrison the station at Tadoussac in anticipation of a return to the St. Lawrence in the following year?

(c) It will be remembered that the Maxwell letter did not specify the place of settlement. Now Port Royal obviously cannot have come before William Maxwell in this connection, for the Scots were not there; and Tadoussac must have seemed as strange and outlandish a vocable to Mr. William Maxwell as at a later date Ticonderoga seemed to Campbell of Inverawe. Even to the English Merchant Venturers the name had about it something unfamiliar. Much more then would it be unfamiliar to the Edinburgh correspondent, and from his unfamiliarity with it he would fail to remember it when he came to write to his kinsman of Pollok.

(d) The situation of Tadoussac at the foot of its tall cliffs of granite and on the brink of its deep and swift river met the requirements of this description of the location of the Scots as "a pairt of the countrie quhilk is a naturall strenthe." And with Britain in command of the seas both in home waters and in the St. Lawrence, the "cannoun, musket, pouder, and bullet" with which the Scots were provided "in caice of some suddent invacioun" were designed as a protection against a raid on the part of the French garrison that still held Quebec.

(e) Finally, it should be remembered that in the official mind of those days Nova Scotia was sharply differentiated from Canada: Nova Scotia was the seaboard province, Canada was the Valley of the St. Lawrence.[1] When this distinction is borne in mind the significance of the preamble to the grant made to Sir William Alexander on April 11th, 1629, of land at Largs to form a port for transatlantic trade, becomes immediately apparent: " Rex pro se et tanquam princeps et senescallus Scotie—pro magnis servitiis sibi et patri suo prestitis per D. Gulielmum Alexander de Menstrie militem principalem suum secretarium Scotie et ejus laboribus in fundanda colonia in Nova Scotia et Canada. . . ."[2]

[1] Egerton, 2395, f. 25.
[2] *Reg. Mag. Sig.*, vol. 1620-1633, p. 476, No. 1404.

APPENDIX C

THE following document, *Public Record Office C.O.* 1/6, No. 38, has a threefold interest: it reveals the determined spirit in which Kirke and his friends carried on their task; it gives an interesting glimpse of the military situation; it stirs our imagination as did the tales of adventure of the days when the *Boys' Own Paper* was the bright particular star of our youthful firmament.

" A note of all suche things as the Company hath in Canada and the nomb^r of men.

" In primus (*sic*) they have above 200 persons in the fort and habitation of Kebec and gone som 400 Leages in the Contrey for further discovereys.

" In the fort there is 16 peices of ornance and 8 murderers 75 musketts and 25 fowling pieces and 10 arkebusses, a Crooke and 30 pistolle 8 dozen of pikes and 24 holbeards and 40 Corseletts and 20 armors of proofe and 6 Targetts.

" In the sayd fort there is 2000 (rounds ?) of powder for the ordnance 300 (barrels ?) of musketts powder and one hundred and halfe of fowlinge powder, Round shot and burd shott, hanger shott and Crossebar shott and enough for the use of these powder and 10 barells more wch she (*sic*) may have of the store. Of 3 pinaces wch are there furnished wth 6 pieces of ordnance apiece and 6 murderers a peece and five barills a powder a peece and all thinges convenyent for there Rigginge and munition of war: the sayd 200 pso^{ns} vittled accordinge to his Maties allowance att sea for 18 monthes besides what They found upon the ground wch is able to find them 6 months more soe that the are very well vittled for 2 yeeres—and wch towe yeares if they worke as the have began they wil bee able to subsist of themselves.

"There is goods for to Trade wth the natives of that Contrey more then wee are able to vent in 2 yeeres : wch goods are no wheare vendable butt in that Contrey and wch goods stands to gain 6000 starlinge besides charges wch doth amount toe 6000 more.

"All sort of Tooles for smithes millers masones plastirers Carpenders joyners bricklers whellors bakers brewers ship carpenders shoemakers and taylors.

"To shallops fitted with cages for the head and all other furnyture.

"All sort of tooles belonging to the fortification.

"The above sayde fort is soe well situated that the(y) are able to wth stand 10,000 men and will not care for them, for whatsoever they can doe, for in winter they canott staye in the contrey soe that whoesoever goes to besige them they canott stay there above 3 months in all wch time the Musskeets (mosquitoes) wil so torment them that noe man is able to bee abroad in entry or threnches daye nor night w^thout loosinge there sights for at least eyght Dayes.

"Soe if it please his Matie to keep it wee doe not care what frenche or any other can doe thoe the have a 100 sayloe of ships and 10,000 men as a bove sayd."

APPENDIX D

Barbados Correspondence

The following documents reveal emphatically the high estimate in which in Barbados the Scots were held as colonists, and the eagerness with which their services were sought.

(a) C.O. 1/21, 102. Petition—the Address from the Barbados—5th September, 1667.

". . . (2) That wee may have a free trade and a supply from y^r Kingdome of Scotland of Scotch servants with whom being supplyed in good numbers (as experience heretofore hath been had) will render both Comodity and security to the Planters, and that they also of that Nation may have a free trade wth this Island. And because of late years many thousands have been drained hence,[1] and at present ye Planter lyes under great charge and duty without much produce for want of such servants (wch cannot be long continued upon this without supply therein), Wee humbly beg that yor Matie will please to command or permit the present transport of one or two thousand of English servants to us, though but for 2 yeares service, for ye charge of their passage wch if published will induce many frankly and freely to come over and Accomodate o^r Necessities; And then yor Matie will please to condescend to this free trade wth Scotland, it will be found that it will much weaken yor Maties Enemies abroad, the Scottish being ye Generall traveller and soldier in most foreign parts."

(b) Brit. Mus., Stowe 755, f. 19. Private letter of Lord William Willoughby, who, in 1666, succeeded his brother

---

[1] It was principally by migrations from Barbados and St. Kitts that the smaller English Caribbean Islands were settled.

(drowned in a hurricane) as Governor of Barbados, to a Scottish nobleman. July 26th, 1667.

"My Lord,
Having by sundry dispatches given his Maj^{tie} a constant Accompt of his affaires and my way of proceeding here; and the success I have had with this divided nation (who are now pretty well united), and knowing you are no stranger to these transactions I shall omitt any repeticoñ: but not the presenting my humble service to yor Lordp, who for an old Jockey, if not for Country sake, will assist me in a Request I have to Matie.

Some of yor Nation I find here and those good subjects. I wish there were more of them, the worst of whom would serve my turne, and live happily here and do the King good service three or 4000 servants would be upon honourable termes here entertained; and if in my time they can be supplyed, this country will be willing to pay for their passage and they shall be freemen after one years service: or if by the way of barter they will give good rates for them, obliging them to 4 years' service: by such a supply whether Peace or Warr I should be able to grapple with Mons$^{sr.}$ This I beseech yor Lord. to promote: I do assure you (tho' I decline yor Royall Company in that point who will destroy these plantations if not regulated) I shall willingly be yor Factor or to any person of honour of yor Nacõn. My Lord Broodall, I presume, may endeavour to promote this proposall, to whom I beg my humble service. This Island if rightly supplyed with men and ships may give Checkmate to Don Hanns and Mons^{sr} when my Master pleaseth, and should we have peace (wch is here hoped for) I am keeping my horse in case to chop up a Match at my best advantage. If you understand not the Language Suffolk doth, but I take yor Lordp to be a generall well read person.

We have more than a good many Irish amongst us, therefore I am for the down right Scott who I am certain will fight without a crucifix about his neck. I am troubled with an effeminate disease at present called a felloe on my forefinger of my right hand. I beseech you let that excuse this scribble

APPENDIX D

wch as it might have been longer so fairer written : but considering to whom I write, this is so large a Diversion from yor more serious affaires. However I must beg your Lordp for Pardon for adding this one word more,

That of a certaine I am,

WILL. WILLOUGHBY."

(c) *C.O.* 1/21, No. 162. Governor Lord W. Willoughby to Lords of Trade, Dec. 16, 1667.

" . . . There yet remains that I acquainte yor Lopps with the great want of servants in this Island, which the late [1] war hath occasioned, yf Labour fayle heere, his Maties Customs will at home, and yf the supply be not of good and sure men, the safety of this place will be always in question ; for though there be noe enemy abroad the keeping of the slaves in subjection must still be provided for. If your Lopps shall open a trade in Scotland, for transportation of the people of that Nation hither, and prevent any accesse of Irish in the future, it will accomodate all the ends propounded and abundantly gratify his Mat^{ys} good subjects here. . . ."

(d) *C.O.* 1/21, No. 20. An Account of the English Sugar Plantations, Barbadoes (23 Jan. 166).

" . . . Heretofore the Collonys were plentifully supplyed with Negro and Christian Servants, which are the Nerves and Sinews of a plantacoñ, the most of which latter they had from Scotland, who being excellent Planters and good Souldiers and considerable numbers coming yearly to the plantations kept the Collonys in so formidable posture that they neither feared the Insurrection of their slaves, nor any invasion from a forreigne Enemy, but are now by the Act of Navigation forbidden to have trade with Scotland, whereby they can have no servants from thence, and those Scotts now wander into Poland and Germany and manie other provinces which heretofore by their transporting to the Collonyes did increase the wealth and defend the dominion of his Matie."

(e) *C.O.* 1/67, No. 95. Barbadoes, Feb. 28, 1668 (O.S.).

" . . . And for as much as of late times wee are often alarmed with Rumors and reports of attempts and Invasions intended

---

[1] The war brought to a conclusion by the Treaty of Breda.

agaynst us (especially of late months much hath been taken as if the french were preparing this way) if y^or Maj^tie would permit wee might have a free trade with Scotland, wee should from thence bee quickly recruited and increase with lusty and able men, wch would bee a great strengthening to the place and bee beter for us then Soldiers because the one are workers and help to mentayne them selves when out of Martiall Employ but the others are lazie all the yeare and must relie for maintenance on the sweat of other men's labours wch wilbee very distructive for the Island and at the long run gnaw ye people to the bone; besides another advantage will accrue by incouraging the coming over of many Scotts and white men for in 4 or 5 yeares after their being here this place will so abound that it wilbee most Convenient for the supernumeraries to fix on some other island, of wch heere are store near us that if settled might become fruitfull and beneficiall. . . ."

APPENDIX E

Scotland and East New Jersey

(A) *Advertisement* [1]

" To all Trades-men, Husbandmen, Servants and others who are willing to Transport themselves into the Province of New-East Jersey in America, a great part of which belongs to Scots-men, Proprietors thereof.

" Whereas several Noblemen, Gentlemen, and others who (by undoubted rights derived from his Majesty and his Royal Highness) are Interested and concerned in the Province of New-East-Jersey, lying in the midst of the English Plantation in America, do intend (God-willing) to send several Ships thither, in May, June, July, ensuing 1684, from Leith Montrose, Aberdeen, and Glasgow. These are to give notice to all Trades-men, Husbandmen and others, who are willing and desirous to go there, and are able to Transport themselves and Families thither, upon their own Cost and Charges, to a pleasant and profitable Country, where they may live in great Plenty and Pleasure, upon far less Stock, and with much less labour and trouble than in Scotland, that as soon as they arrive there, they shall have considerable quantities of Land, set out Heretably to themselves and their heirs for ever, for which they shall pay nothing for the first four or five years, and afterwards pay only a small rent yearly to the Owners and Proprietors thereof, as they can agree: And all Trades-men, servants and others, such as, Wrights Coupers, Smiths, Masons, Millers, Shoe-makers, etc., who are willing to go there and are not able to transport themselves, that they

[1] *Bannatyne Miscellany*, vol. iii. p. 385. (From a printed broadside.)

shall be carried over free, and well maintained in Meat and Clothes the first four years, only for their Service, and thereafter they shall have considerable quantities of land, set out to themselves and their Heirs for ever, upon which they may live at the rate of Gentlemen all their lives and their Children after them : Their ordinary Service will be cutting down of wood with Axes, and other easie Husband-work, there being plenty of Oxen and Horses for Plowing and Harrowing etc. Let therefore all Trades-men, Husband-men, Servants and others who incline to go thither, and desire further Information herein, repair themselves to any of the Persons underwritten, who will fully inform them anent the Country, and every other thing necessary, and will answer and satisfy their Scruples and Objections, and give them all the Incouragements according to their several abilities and Capacities, viz:

" At Edinburgh let them apply themselves to the Lord Thesaurer-Deput, the Lord Register, Sir John Gordon, Mr. Patrick Lyon, Mr. George Alexander, Advocates, George Drummond of Blair, John Swintoun, John Drummond, Thomas Gordon, David Falconer, Andrew Hamilton, Merchants ; at Brunt-Island to William Robinson, Doctor of Medicine ; at Montross to John Gordon, Doctor of Medicine, John Fullerton of Kinaber, and Robert and Thomas Fullertons his brothers ; in the Shire of Mearns, to Robert Barclay of Urie, and John Barclay his Brother : at Aberdeen to Gilbert Moleson, Andrew Galloway, John and Robert Sandilands, William Gerard, Merchants ; in the Shire of Aberdeen, to Robert Gordon of Clunie and Robert Burnet of Lethanty ; in the shire of Pearth to David Toshach of Monyvard and Captain Patrick McGreiger ; in Merss Shire to James Johnston of Spoteswood ; at Kelso to Charles Ormiston merchant ; in the Lewes to Kenneth McKenzie Younger of Kildin : and if any Gentleman or others be desirous to buy or purchase any small shares or portions of Land in the said Province, they may referr to any of the foresaid Persons, who will direct them how they shall be served, providing they do it timously, because many more persons are dayly offering themselves to buy, then can be gotten well accommodated.

" There is nothing more strange than to see our Commons

APPENDIX E

so besotted with the love of their own misery, that rather than quitt their Native Country, they will live in much toyl and penury so long as they have strength, being hardly able all their life to acquire so much Riches as can save themselves from begging or starving when they grow old; meantime their Children (so soon as they are able to walk) are exposed to the Cruelties of Fortune, and the Charity of Others, naked and hungry, begging Food and Rayment from those that either can not, or will not help them: and yet can hardly be perswaded to go to a most profitable, fertile and safe country, where they may have everything that is either necessary, profitable, or pleasant for the life of man, with very little pains and industry: The woods and Plains are stored with infinite quantities of Deer and Roe, Elcks, Beaver, Hares, Connies, Wild Swine and Horses, etc., and Wild-honey in great abundance: The Trees abound with several sorts of Wine-grapes, Peaches, Apricots, Chestnuts, Walnuts, Plumbs, Mulberries, etc. The Sea and Rivers with Fishes, the Banks with Oysters, Clams, etc. Yea, the Soil is so excellent and fertile, that the Meadows naturally produce plenty of Strawberries, Purpy, and many more tender plants, which will hardly grow here in Gardens: Wheat, Barley, Oats, Pease and Beans etc., when sown yields ordinarily 20 and sometimes 30 fold Increase, and Indian Corn, which is a grain both wholesome and pleasant, yields ordinarily 150 and sometimes 200. fold: Sheep never miss to have two lambs at a time, and for the most part three, and these lambs have generally as many the next year: The winter lasts not ordinarily above two moneths: and one man's ordinary labour will with ease and plenty, maintain a family of ten or twelve persons: It was no wonder then that Ogilvie in his New-Atlas, calls this place the Garden of the World, and the Terrestrial Paradise: Why then should our Countreymen, in spite of those and many other Incouragements, be detained at home, either upon no ground at all, or upon such frivolous scruples and objections as these are.

"First, they alleadge that it is a long and dangerous Voyage thither! To which it is answered, that ordinarily it is not above 6 or 7 weeks' sailing from Scotland, which, in a good ship, well victualled, and with good Company in the Summer Time, is rather a pleasant Divertisement then a trouble or toyle, and it is certainly more dangerous to sail from Leith to London or Holland, then to New-East-Jersey.

"Next, they say there is no Company to bee had save Barbarians, Woods and Wilderness. To which it is answered, that this is a great mistake, for this country has been Peopled and Planted these several years by gone, so that Horses, Oxon, Cows, Sheep, Hogs, etc., are to be sold almost as cheap there as in Scotland, and surely they are much better, being all of the English Kinds. Nor are the Woods there any thing so wild and inhospitable as the Mountains here: Savage Beasts there are none save Wolfes, and those are onlie enemies to Sheep: The Natives are very few; and easily over come, but these simple serviceable creatures, are rather an help and Incouragement than any ways hurtful or troublesome: and there can be no want of Company, seing there are many thousands of Scots, English, and others living there already, and many more constantly going over; and this summer there are several gentlemen going from Scotland, such as David Toshach of Monyvard, with his Lady and Family, James Johnston of Spoteswood, Keneth McKenzie, younger, of Kildin, Captain Patrick McGreiger, Robert and Thomas Fullertons, Brothers german to the Laird of Kinaber, and John Barclay, Brother German to the Laird of Vrie, William Robison, Doctor of Medicine, and many others, who are all Persons of good quality and Estates, and go not out of necessity, but choice.

"Lastly, they object that far fetcht Fowls have fair Feathers, and they do not believe the truth of half of what is written and spoken in Commendation of these Countreys: To which it is answered, they may as easily deny the truth of everything which they have not seen with their own eyes, for all these things are as verily true, as that there is any such pleasant Countrey as France. Italy Spain, etc: The things being matter of Fact are confirmed by letters from Persons of Undoubted Credit, living on that place, and by certain Information of many Eye-witnesses, who, having once been there, can never after be induced to live in Scotland, nor can it reasonably be imagined that the persons abovewritten are all Fools, to be imposed upon by lies and fancies ; on the contrary, there are none (save those that are wise in their own Eyes, but are really Ignorant) that are not undenyably convinced of the excellency of the Design. Let such as condemn it be so just as first to hear it and know it, which they may easily do by applying to some of the foresaid Persons, who can best inform them, and then if they think it not below them to be convinced, they will be forced to homologat.

VIVAT REX."

(B) Letters from Scots settlers in East New Jersey. (From Scot of Pitlochie's *Model*.)

(1) A letter from George Mackenzie Merchant in Edinburgh, to Mr. George Alexander Advocate there.

" Elizabeth Town Sept. 1 1684.

Mr. Alexander.

I doubt not but you expect here a particular account of the province of New Jersey, but that I thought needless. The person, David Barclay, whom this comes alongst with, being more able to give you that satisfaction, as whose interest obligeth him to a more narrow observation of its natural advantages, and whose place being one of the Council, gives a larger liberty and occasion to inspect the concerns of this province. But in general its a healthfull, pleasant, fruitful Country, in many places of a most Luxurious Soyle, rewarding the labour of the Countryman sufficiently ; its well watered with many fair and pleasant Rivers and Creeks, stored with several sorts of fish, and most of the Rivulets convenient for mills, whereof there are severall, both for Sawing of wood and grinding of corn. They raise great store of Hogs and Cattle ; and fowls they have in abundance. The Countrey for ten or fifteen miles up from the River and Sea is generally plain, farther up Mountains. Besides the Towns mentioned in the publick paper since Governor Lawries arrivall, there is laid at Amboy-point 1000 acres for the City of Perth, divided into 96 Lotts, 9 Acres to a Lott ; the Remainder is for the streets, Market place, Governors house, and other public' conveniencies. How large the Countrey is, is a question hard to resolve, and how much bought by the Proprietors (if any), David Barclay can satisfy you. The Inhabitants are English, with a few Scots, French and Dutch, of sufficient number to defend themselves against any prejudice may be offered them by the Inhabitants. That Fancie of a Common Improvement will not take, but whoever expects profite from their Interests here, must Improve them a part. I have sold some of your Gloves at 2 shil and 6 pen: 3 shil and 4 pen: a pair; being what I could gett for them: the money five and a half parts less than English, and shall make an account thereof at meeting.

Present my service to all Friends.
I am Your very humble Servant
GEORGE MACKENZIE."

(2) A Double of a Letter from New Perth, date the 1 of the seventh month, 1684, from John Reid, who was Gardener to the Lord Advocate, to a Friend at Edinburgh.

"Seeing it hath pleased God to bring me and mine safe unto this port, I took upon myself as obliged to write something according to my promise of this countrey: indeed I must say its a brave place, but I have not had time to take such observations as I would, being so ingadged to attend my other businesse. Here is no outward want, especially of provisions, and if people were industrious they might have cloaths also within themselves; by the report of all, its the best of all the neighbouring Collonies, it is very wholesome, pleasant and a fertile land: there are also some barren lands, viz white Sandy land, full of Pine trees, it lyes betwixt South River and Barnegate or Neversink, (albeit there be also much good land in that precinct,) yet its a good place for raising a stock of cattle, providing they have large room to run in, for cattle finds good food there in winter, when none is in the best land, and therefore do the inhabitants provide little hay in winter. The soyl of the country is generally a red marle earth with a surface of black mould (nor doth it appear what really it is to their eyes who cannot penetrate beyond the surface) full freighted with grass, pleasant herbs and flowers, and in many places little or no wood, but most places full of large timber, as walnut, especially oak ; there be some places here and there in the woods, they call swamps, which is low Ground amidst or betwixt rising ground full of bushes, which holds water in winter, the most of them be dry in Summer, but these being cleared, and some of them that needs being drained, are the richest land. Here are great conveniencies of Bay, Sounds, Rivers, Creeks, Brooks, and Springs, all over the Province, but one of the best things is the large quantities of brave Meadowes, both salt and fresh, which makes the people here able to supply their Neighbours as they doe, throw the abundance of their cattle. I know one Planter who hath a hundred of cattle, not above three years settled ; and no wonder, for some of the grass is as high as my head. Its a pity to see so much good land as I have been over in this province lying waste, and greater pity to see so much good and convenient land taken and not improven.

As soon as any of the land here comes to be cultivated, it over-runs with small Clover-grass, by the pasturage and dunging of cattle, and so supplants the naturall grass and herbs, notwithstanding of their quick and strong growth. Fruit trees also prosper well here. Newark made about a thousand barrells of Sider last year (a barrel is 8 Scots gallons) this is like that of Woodbridge, who made 500 barrells of pork, in one year, before the law was made against the Swines trespassing.

Here they sow most Indian corn, and wheat ; some Rye, Barly, Oats : Indian corn the first year that they break up or plough, the second they sow Wheat, because the spontaneous growth of the weeds is done away by howing the Indian corn, as we do cabbage : here is one planter makes accompt, That he hath about three thousand bushels of wheat reapt this year : I suppose he hath above a hundred acres of it, but I doe not make these instances as so many precedents.

I know nothing wanting here, except that good Tradesmen, and good Husbandmen, and Labourers are scarce : a Labourer may have a bushell of Corn per day, when he is a little acquainted with the work of the Country, but Tradesmen much more. Smiths, Carpenters, Masons, Weavers, Taylors, Shoemakers, are very acceptable : any who comes let them bring some cloaths and their tools with them, as used in England, and provide butter, bisket, wine, and especially beer and ale, for their Sea voyage, besides the Ships allowance ; and they need not fear when they come here, albeit they have no more, yet they will be better if they have something either in money or Scots linnin and stuffs to buy a little provision at first, to set them up a house and buy a cow or two ; and tho a man be rich, I would not advise him to bring many servants, at least not to keep many at first, untill he see about him and know what he is doing.

I cannot tell what goods are best to bring, David Barclay can tell better ; But he who brings money may expect 15d for the English 5 shil : some may bring a little of the best wheat for a change of seed, and some barly and Oats, for the same use : also a little Scots field peas, there being none such here ; bring also some clover seed.

There are a great store of Garden herbs here, I have not had time to inquire into them all, neither to send some of the many pleasant (tho to me unknown) plants of this Countrey, to James Sutherland, Physick Gardener at Edinburgh, but tell him, I will not forget him, when opportunity offers.

I had forgot to write of Ambo, or New Perth, therefore I add, that it is one of the best places in America, by the report of all Travellers, for a town of trade ; for my part I never saw any so conveniently seated : this with my love, and my wife's to all friends, and acquaintances.

I Rest thy friend

JOHN REID."

(3) David Mudie's Letter to his Wife.

" New Perth, the 12 December, 1684.

My Heart,

  I hope this shall find you and your children in Good-health, and I wish in as much satisfaction as I and our Children are here : far beyond my expectation and others, my well wishers, who are with you. My last to you was upon my arrivall here, dated the 8th of November, and at that time I could give you but a small account of my judgment anent it, it would take a great deale of time to inform you of every thing, as it truelie is: But to be short, I have travelled through a part of it, and it is far larger than ever I heard it reported in Scotland, I dare say above a third more ground and there is abundance of brave Rivers through it all, better than ever I did see in any place, brave Meadows, alongst all the River sides, and lands above the Meadow ground: abundance of Fresh water Brooks, and Springs; plenty of Fishes in all the Rivers, in the Summer time, and that very good Fishes such as they preserve for Victual in the winter, and in very few days they use to take more than they make use of in Winter; as for wild Meat there is of all sorts. Cows, sheep, and Oxen as large as in England, and abundantly cheap, considering their goodness. Corns and all sorts of Fruit in great abundance, and no less than they are called in Scotland. Money within this three years is become pretty plentiful, servants dear and scarce. I have taken up Six Acres of Land in New Perth which pleases me exceedingly well, in regard it is good Land, and fit for building of a City, and Persons of Good Fortune are come from New York, and other places in the Countrey, and are very busy building and I am begun to build a house, and have near digged the ground, which is very hard, it being, under a great part of it, Oker, which is hard to digg, and the least deepness is eight feet. I have my two Wrights Squaring of Timber for it, and I resolve to have it a good Handsome House, Six Rooms off a floor with a study, two stories high above the Sellers, and the Garret above; And I doubt not if the Frost bide away, but I shall have the Sellers finished, and the gests laid above it, against the latter end of this month. For the land that lyes to the house, I resolve to fence in two Acres of it for an Orchard, and an Yard, and to have that done before the middle of February, and to have it planted with fruit trees; for I find a man in three years will have more Fruit in such an Orchard than he knows how to make use of.

And about the middle of February according as the Weather is, I resolve to go out where I have taken up my land, which is upon a River, called the South River, which is an exceeding pleasant River, and place; there goes onely with me there Mr. David Violent. I can go from New Perth to it in a Boat, in two houres and a half, let the wind blow as it will, and come back again in as much time. I wish I had as many Servants here as I could make use of; Any man that is frugal, and hath 300 lib Sterling in Stock, to come over here, and bring over 7 or 8 good Servants with him, I could assure him in 3 years time he should make a stock better than 1000 if not 1500 lib if he bestow his money right in Scotland, and take advice to bring all things here which is necessary for him to have in this Countrey. I am uncertain of the time I will be at Home, but I resolve you shall come over with me again, and ye will both think and say, when ye see the Countrey, that ye wish it had been done twenty years agoe. I thought it not fit to trouble my friends and relations, since I could not write [but] short letters to them, but any of them that desires to know the Condition of this Countrey, ye may shew them this letter, since there is no secret in it: you will find by William Burnet's Letter, that he desires some of his Sons to come over, and John Geddis writes for some of his Brethren; the which Letters cause (to be) delivered them carefully, and get an answer, that if they be to come over, ye may speak for their passage timely. He tells some of them are good Wrights:—which is all at present, but keep a good heart to yourself, and take care of your Children, and I hope to see you with more Comfort than we parted, and I am your ever loving Husband while I breathe.

DAVID MUDIE."

(4) James Johnstone of Spotswoodes Letter to his Brother, John Johnstone, Drugest in Edinburgh.

"East Jersey the 12th December, 1684.
Loving Brother.
I have taken up a part of my Land 9 miles from Amboy, and 4 miles from Piscataway, and as far from the nearest part of Rariton, on a Brook side, where there are exceeding great plains without any Timber, there is excellent Gunning for Deer and Turkies, of which there is great plenty

and easily shot. But I resolve to see a place called Barnegate which is 60 or 70 miles from this on the Southermost place of the Province, when there is a good River and Harbour, the best Fishing and Gunning in any place in America 30 or 40 miles from any Plantation. The Indians here are nothing to be feared, the Place being as peaceable as any where else. I had occasion to travel through Long Island, and Statten Island, and for many miles found as many towns and plantations in the way as in any so much Land in Lothean ; there are no Bears nor Ravinous Beasts but Wolves which are nothing to be feared, neither are the Countrey People afraid to be among them all night, in so much that I oft times going wrong, and lying out all night and hearing their yells about me, and telling that I was afraid of them, the Countrey People laughed at it : neither are the Snakes any thing to be noticed, for nothing can come near them, but they give warning with the ratling of their tail, so that People may either kill them, or go by them as they please.

Oxen are so well taught that they go sometimes in a Plough, or Cart, without Horse, or without a Gade-man ; Horses and Cattle are as cheap as in Scotland, considering their Goodness and the difference of the Money. All sorts of Scots goods sell well here, ye will be advised with the next occasion, what goods sell best in this place. I have great reason to thank God, that I am in a place which abundantly answers any thing I expected ; The Air is healthful and the Soil fruitful ; the Indian Corn yields commonly 2 or 3 hundred fold, Oats 20 fold as I am informed ; the Indian Corn is an excellent grain, I have eat it and like it very well in Pottage and Bread. There are several reasonable good towns in this Province : there are no poor persons here, but all are half idle in respect of what they work with you.

Flax, twice heckled, sold at 9d per pound ; Wool is very cheap, Only work is dear. The Liquour we most use is Sider ; we have great store of Fruit. In many places untaken up, there are many places and not a tree. I have never since last parting had any sickness to keep me from one Dyet, for which I render thanks to God. The Indians here make it their trade to kill Venison and sell it to us ; for a small matter,

I will have my Family served with Flesh all Winter; one of their Sachiams (which is their King) came to the Governor when I came first here, desiring he might be suffered to trade with us, and not be beat out of our houses when they were drunk, but only that we might bind them, and permit them to cut timber, and some such things. At New Perth we have a good Stationers Shop of Books. The land is no where difficult to clear, albeit the trees be 100 foot long, and 3 or 4 foot over; I would heartily wish and perswade any to come over that intends to live well, plentifully and pleasantly; Neither is there any tradesmen or Servant that could come wrong to this place, and I could wish my best friends no better but (to be) in the same place with me. The old Inhabitants are a most careless and infrugal People, their profession are most part Protestants, few Quakers, some Anabaptists, it is most desired there may be some Ministers sent us over, they would have considerable Benefices and good Estates; and since it would be a matter of great Piety, I hope ye will be instrumentall to advise some over to us; the place is abundantly healthfull, as any else. There is a great difference betwixt the people here, who are strong and vigorous, and the people more Southerly in Maryland. We have great store of Venison which is sometimes as fat as Pork, one good Buck is sold at 5 shil. and by the Indians at 2 shil. Oats are sold at 18 pence the Bushell. All sorts of Fish is here exceeding plentifull, the poorest Persons eat no meat that is Salt, except Pork; in Summer they live much on Milk. I would no more value the Sea coming through if I had occasion, than ye would riding of 20 miles; let me be remembered to all friends, to Patrick Fortune who most carefully disswaded me from this Voyage; which I doe not repent, but would as carefully perswade others, who study their own good. What I most earnestly desire of you, for the encouragement of this Plantation, is, (that) you would be Instrumental to send us over some Ministers, who I dare engadge shall afterwards ever be thankfull, and I oblidged to be, your ever affectionate Brother.

JAMES JOHNSTONE."

(5)
"Amboy : or New Perth in America,
9 of November, 1684.

Dear Brother,
Having accidentally met with the Bearer, had not time to give you any particular accompt of this Countrey, only assure you that it is beyond (not only) all our expectations, but all that you have ever heard spoken of it, we (praised be God) all of us arrived safely without the loss of any one Passenger; scarcely any of them was ever sick, only we had much trouble coming from Maryland by land, our Skipper having for his own advantage put in first at the Capes of Verginia : but we have had a brave Prospect of the Countrey, and all the way, as well as in this place where we now are, we found plenty of Corn, and all kinds of Fruit, with Fish, Venison, and wild Fowls, in such abundance, that a Deer may be had for 2 shilling Countrey money, and Turkies for 6 pence, which will be at least as big as any 2 Turkies in Scotland, and are really Turkies, only blacker than tame Turkies that you have seen. I shall give you full satisfaction with the next occasion, pray you fail not to write to me when you meet with any, otherwayes you disoblidge him who is ever yours,

D. McGregor."

Written to his Brother Munivard in Scotland.

(6) Patrick Falconer's Letter to Maurice Trent.

"Elizabeth Town in East Jersey,
the 28th of October, 1684.

Sir,
My last was dated the 22, Current, from Philadelphia, at which time I could give you but a small account of the Countrey; and as yet its but a small account I can give by reason that I have had but a little time as yet; I have travelled on foot more than a 100 miles in East and West Jersey, and Pensilvania. I have also travelled in Maryland, I cannot but say it is a good Countrey, but its possessed with a Debauched, Idle, Lasy People, all that they Labour for is only as much Bread as serves them for one Season, and as

much Tobacco as may furnish them with Cloaths. I believe it is the worst improved Countrey in the world, for the Indian wheat is that they trust to, and if that fail them they may expect to starve. I find Pensilvania and the two Jerseys are the places which set themselves out most for Planting of Corn; as for the Jerseys I need not insist in commending of them, for David Barclay, and Arthur Forbes, who had a longer stay here than I have had, will give you a more full account; for I intend to write no more than I am able to make good, I may say, that it is a pleasant Countrey, I did never see more pleasant Meadows, and Grass, then I have seen in both the Jersies; I have seen plains of good Hay consisting of about 50 Acres of ground, hardly one tree to be seen upon the whole spot: And there are several places so. I can say its a well watered Countrey, and good waters, and if they were desirous, they might have a very good Quarrie here for Stone of any sort, and Limestone likewise; but so long as Timber is so plenty, they will not be at the pains to seek after Stone; there are some houses in the Countrey built with stone, but very few. Having fallen in here, the end of the year, I cannot be capable to give an account what may be the product of the Countrey, but I hear that all sorts of Grain hath very good Increase, I see (the) Countrey abounds with Apples, Quinches, Peaches, Walnuts, and Chesnuts, and Strawberries in great abundance, wild Wine-Grapes are plentifull, wild-Fowl of all sorts, a great number of Deer, Turkie-Fowls wild, in great abundance and very big: I have seen these things in great plenty. I hope ye will excuse me because I am not capable to give an ampler account of the Countrey, for I have not been two dayes in one place; I will tell you this is a good Countrey for men who resolves to be Laborious; any who comes here they must resolve to work hard for the first two or three years, till they get a little Ground cleared, for this must be looked upon as a wood-Countrey, tho I must confess the woods are not so thick as people expect; and there are several places in the Countrey where there is little or no wood. People are generally very curious to have their land near Navigable Rivers, but when they are better acquaint, they will find that the farther back the better is the land.

There are abundance of Fish and Oysters here. This is not a Countrey for idle people, but such as will be at pains they need not doubt but to get Bread here in plenty—so I wish it be the Lords will that we may have a happy meeting again, his will be done ; I wish you may be protected by the Lord : this from

     Your affectionate Friend and
      humble Servant,
        PATRICK FALCONER."

(7) Abstract of a Letter writ by Peter Watson (who went over a Servant with David Barclay, in the year 1683) to John Watson, Messenger in Selkirk.

     " New Perth, the 20th of August, 1684.
Cusing,

  I could never write to you before now, because I was never rightly settled, and am not yet fully settled, but I am from among the rest of the Servants. One James Reid and I and our Families are together, set out to a Farm at Amboy ; we are to have some Land laid out to us, and we are Stocked with two Mares, four Cowes, two Sows, two Oxen : my wife and I and the Child Richard are very well in health, and hath been so ever since we came out of Scotland. Now as for this Countrey, it is a very good Countrey ; indeed poor men such as myself, may live better here than in Scotland if they will but work, a man can have Corn and Cattle or any other Goods for his work, and he can sell these goods to some hands for money, it is not for a man that hath a Familie to come bound four years, but young men, who have no trouble, they will do better to come and serve four years here than to serve in Scotland, for they are not so hard wrought as in Scotland, and when the four years are out they can gain abundance to work to other men ; or if they desire to settle upon Land of their own, they can have it reasonably cheap : the hardest work that is here, is clearing of the Ground, and felling of Trees and the like ; the first year is the worst, till they be accustomed with the work of the Countrey. My Neighbour and I did clear from the middle of February till the midst of May, five Acres of Land and have planted it with Indian

Corn, and Indian Beans, and Tobacco for our own smoaking, a man who lives here needs go no where to buy any things, here he can have Corn and Cattle and every thing that is necessary for mans use, if he be Industrious; only the thing that is dearest here is Cloathing, for there are but few sheep to this Countrey; but there are store of all other Beasts, such as Horses and Cows and Hoggs; there is here good Fishing, good hunting of Deer, and other kind of wild Beasts; the Countrey is very healthie as I have seen it yet, it is cold in the Winter like unto Scotland; But fra once the Summer breaks up, it is hotter than it is in Scotland. There are here very good Religious People, they go under the name of Independants, but are most like unto the Presbyterians, only they will not receive every one to their Society; we have great need of good and Faithful Ministers, and I wish to God, that there would come some over here; they can live as well, and have as much as in Scotland, and more than many get: we have none within all the Province of East-Jersey, except one who is Preacher in Newark; there were one or two Preachers more in the Province, but they are dead, and now the people they meet together every Sabbath day, and Read and Pray, and sing Psalms, in their Meeting-houses. This Countrey is very settled with People, most part of the first Settlers came out of New England, very kind and loving people, kinder than in Scotland or England; and for the Indian Natives, they are not troublesome any way to any of us, if we do them no harm, but are a very kind and loving people; the men do nothing but hunt, and the women they plant Corn and work at home: they come and trade among the Christians with skins or Venison, or Corn, or Pork, and in the summer time, they and their wives come down the Rivers in their Canoes, which they make themselves of a piece of a great tree, like a little Boat, and there they Fish and take Oysters. This Countrey is a very pleasant Countrey, with Rivers and Creeks to fish in; only it is full of wood, such as Oak and Walnut tree, Chesnut, Poplar, and Cedar. The only thing we want here is good People, I wish that all the poor Friends I or my wife hath were here. As for my Brother, if ye have a mind to come Brother, if you have but as much

in the world as would transport you hither and your Family,
I would desire you earnestly to come, and bring my Sister
with you ; if you have as much as will transport you sell all
and come, tho you had not a penny after your passage were
payed, you need not fear if you have a mind to work. I was
as little brought up with work as any man, yet blessed be
God, I can work now as my Neighbours, and live very con-
tentedly with my Wife, better than we ever did in Scotland :
show my Mother in law that my wife and I would be very
well pleased if she would come over, there are as old Women
as she comes here out of old England ; there was one came
alongst with us older than she : if she will come she shall live
with her Daughter and me, as easie, and as well as ever she
did live in Scotland, and I do know that was well enough.
My wife and I are well at present, as you could wish, God be
blessed ; I can say no more, but my love to my Brother, and
his wife, and all Friends.

      I rest your loving Cusin
           PETER WATSON."

(8) A Letter writ by John Campbell to John Dobie.

     "New Perth 8th of Nov. 1684.
B. John

  I wrote a line from Philadelphia to you, as we were
coming hither, your Cousin James Dobie the bearer is in such
haste, that I cannot write what I would say ; but in short,
we are come here to a good wholesome Countrey, in which
with little industrie a man may have a comfortable life. There
is good Wheat and Oats growing here, and Indian Corn which
our Servants like very well ; There is Fish and Fowl [in]
abundance, and of cows and Horses ; they labour with Horse
and Oxen. There is Deer through all the countrey, and
Turkies which some of our servants have killed a part of
already. There is Partrages and Quails very rife, that my
wife yesterday morning saw about 20 of them walking before
the door like Chickens. I shall say no more till I see further,
for I am with others going to the countrey on Monday to see
for the countrey lotts : for I have taken up the Towns already,
and cut down the trees of two Acres of ground with six men

in three days. My service to all friends. I am your most assured friend.

JOHN CAMPBELL."

(9) A letter from Thomas Fullerton, Brother to the Laird of Kennaber, to his Brother in Law Doctor Gordon in Montrose.

"Elizabethtown 4 January 1685.

Dear Brother,

By my last about a Month since, I dated from Amboy, you understand that we came to Sandy Hook 18 weeks after we sailed from Montrose, we were nine weeks at Sea from Killebeg in Ireland, we had many cross-winds, what other accidents we met with by the way were worth the telling, but not the writing: blessed be God we all kept our health very well, only one Boy fell overboard. What you expect, and I design by this, is a brief, but true accompt, of the Countrey. The first land we discovered was about the middle of Long Island, it appeared at first like trees growing out of the Sea Towards night we Anchored in Sandy Hook. The land is low and levell, that is the reason we were within 8 or 10 mile thereof before we saw it; the countrey appears all over woody; I landed on a Sandy-bank and close by the flood marsh where grew Bayes, sassafrax, and severall prettie shrubs I knew not: The Woods consist of severall kinds of Oaks, Chesnut, Hickory, Walnut, Poplar and Beech; Cedars grow on swamps and barrens, Firrs and Pines only on barrens. The ground generally is 2 or 3 inches deep of black dung as it were, below that is reddish mould. What you heard of the product of the Indian Corn, viz 100 or 200 fold; of 20 or 30 fold English wheat, of the abundance of deers and wild horses and severall turkies, and of the great plenty of fishes, are all true. There is very much cider here; In 13 or 14 years you may make 100 barrells from your own planting :—The best fleshes of all kinds ever I did see are here, tho this in respect of what you have heard, be generally tautollogie : yet I found myself obliged to write it, because I am witness to the truth thereof without Hyperbole.

Notwithstanding of all this, its very troublesome [and]

expensive to settle a plantation here, and when it is done I cannot promise you a man will grow very rich; but he needs want nothing, and it is not every one who will agree with the solitude of the Woods: those who can, and resolve to lead a countrey life, cannot doe better than come hither. A merchant who will come over and set up store in the countrey for a year, will make cent per cent of several commodities, with which I doe allow none to be acquainted but commerads. I wish I had some money of my stock so employed, and sent safely here. Johnstone of Spotswood and I have taken up, upon a river 6 or 8 miles [from] Amboy; your Brother Thomas and Robert are here also. Servants are not easily entertained here. I designed to have shot as many squirrels as would have furred a coat for you, but I am otherwise taken up. I have omitted to tell you that the weather here is constantly clear, the sun rises and setts free of clouds. I have observed none to have the cough in this countrey, tho' I have frequently lain in the woods, abundance of fire is an excellent counter charm. Now brother as to your own coming over it will be time to invite you when I have a good house and entertainment to treat you with unbought; for you must not feel any of the inconveniencies I have met with; we are all well, I pray God this may find you [so] also: present my service to all friends, Male or Female, this letter will serve that; present my service to my Grandmother; upon Christmas I drank her good health in Rhumb Madera and Fial Wine. If I can be frugall I may be soon rich here;—by my next I hope to ensure 60 or 70 lib. to the parson, for we want a minister, this from

    Your Affectionate Brother.
      THO: FULLERTON."

(10) A letter from the same hand to the Laird of Brotherstown in the Mairns of the same date—

" Kind Commerad.
  You were pleased so keenly to concern yourself with my welfare when I was by you, (and I find that absence augments true friendship,) that I am obliged to acquaint you with my present fortune, which I hope I shall be far

better than what I could expect by so much Stock in Scotland. This place is not altogether boorish, for at New York you may have railing and Gallantry enough, the inhabitants are generally great spenders. Dear Brothertown write to me, and give me an accompt of affairs, for I assure you, neither Governor nor Council will meddle with yours to me, nor mine to you : by my next I will write to Clunie and John Johnstone : in the mean time present my service to them. I am in haste to end writing, tho ever being

Your Oblidged Commerad and humble Servant,

THO: FULLERTON."

(11) Abstract of a Letter from Robert Hardie Merchant in Aberdeen, to his Son John Hardie Merchant there, dated from

" Elizabeth Town, the 8 of December 1684.

Loving Son

I have writ two letters already to you at our arrival, another shewing the death of your Brother William, and something of the countrey, but knowe not if they be come to your hands; and now, having this occasion, know that I am in good health, and your Brother Alexander, praised be God. Know that I intend to reside here, and should wish that I had all my children with me, but your convenience cannot permit, neither am I able to transport them as yet; however, I desire you to acquaint your sister Elspeth, that I desire her to come over if possible, with her first convenience. I intend before her coming to have a new house in New Perth, and a Plantation near by it; if I had gott a good accompt of that Little cargo I sent over, I would have lived upon it here, as well as upon 100 lib. sterling in Scotland; But I have got a bad accompt of it: however, I hope to Provide for you all with what is left, if the Lord bless. Shew my brother and brothers in law, that if they would come over with each of them two servants, they could have good land here at an easie rate, they might live better than masters, and with less trouble, if they took but half the pains they take in Scotland; for the Land is a brave and plentifull Land. Shew Andrew and David Hardie that if they can but pay their Passage and come to me, I shall make them to live in better condition than ever formerly. I doubt not but some of our neighbours will come over, to bring servants here, who will give you a true accompt how I and others can live here. He who comes first will have the best choise, and most profitable, as for idle-men who will neither work nor trade, (they) need never come here, for there are none idle here. I wish you all a blessing from God, and so rests—

    Your affectionate father

        ROBERT HARDIE."

(12) A letter from James Johnstone of Spotswood, dated the 13 of February 1685, from Piscattaway and East Jersey.

Dear Brother. These are to remember my kindest affection to you, my Mother, and all friends; we have kept our healths hitherto exceedingly well; Have endured a short but very severe winter, now the weather hath been for some time by-gone exceeding good, was a Bear-seed season with you. I have been throw several or most places of this Countrey of late, but am not yet resolved where my first Husbandry shall be: the Land is exceeding good which is yet to take up, much better than what is inhabited, only not so convenient; the difficulty of clearing many places is no wayes considerable; I find Land where Several hundred Ploughs may be presently set a work. I take all pains I can to be conveniently settled, and the Governor refuses us nothing we desire. I stand in need of 40 pound value of goods and some servants; hoping to have Corn for them, and others who come over: I could wish your self were here, we could live competently and quietly; but I doubt how affairs may permit. I wish any Land I had were sold that you might be furthered; present my love and service to my Mother and Sister, whom I hope to see here; I wish you would send over some Ministers, one or more, to us. I am

    Your Affectionate and ever

      mindfull Brother,

        JAMES JOHNSTONE."

(13) A Letter for Mr. Robert Paterson Principal of Marischal Colledge in the city of New Aberdeen, in Scotland.

" Woodbridge, in East Jersey
in America, March the 7th 1685

Sir, I hope you have heard of our Voyage and safe Arrival here. I thought it my duty to present my dutiful respects to you and all Friends at Aberdeen, and to acquaint you of mine own and all their welfares who came over the last year, all which intend to settle in the Countrey except ——, who has spent all his means already foolishly in drink, and is returning home for more. You have David Barclay and Arthur Forbes to inform you of this Countrey: when I have seen it through all the Seasons of the year as they did, I shall then give you my opinion, if you be desirous: only in short, what I have seen I may write,—that it pleases me better than Virginia, Maryland, Pensylvania, or West Jersey,—that it is pleasant to mine eyes, and I find it healthful to my body. I am not troubled here (blessed be God) with defluctions, head aikes, and coughs, as at Edinburgh :—that the land is furnished with all conveniencies of Nature, such as wood, Grass, Meadow, and abundance of fresh water springs, Brooks and Rivers, and plenty of Deer, Turkies, Geese and Ducks; many tender Herbs, Fruits, and Trees grow naturally here that will not grow in Scotland at all: these things are so notoriously known, that it is superfluity to write them, and no unbyassed person will deny them, or speak ill of the land. There is about a dozen or 14 houses in New Perth, and the half of those built since we came ; several others are building presently, and many others have taken Lotts to build; Mr. Mudie is building a stone house, and has a Horse Mill ready to set up; Governor Rudyard intends another Stone house this Summer. The Governors house, and the publick Courthouse are abuilding. It is the best scituate for a City of any yet I have seen, or for ought I can learn, of any yet known in America. There is great encouragement here for all kind of Tradesmen : I intend myself to follow mostly Planting and Fishing. Let this remember me to all my Friends, Relations, Comorads, and Acquaintances at Aberdeen ; I could not write

to them all, being busied about mine own settlement, and it is now far spent in the year, so that I do not expect to do much this year; neither could I settle sooner, by reason that my bed-cloaths are not yet come from Maryland, and the land I intend to settle on is not yet purchased from the Indians. I entreat to hear from you on all occasions, and what remarkable News abroad or at home, and how the Civilists place is disposed of. My service to yourself and bedfellow. I am Sir, Your most affectionate and
humble servant CHARLES GORDON."

(14) For Mr. Andrew Irvine Merchant, at his Shop, in the East end of the Lucken Booth in Edinburgh, in Scotland.

" Amboy in the Province
of East New Jersey in
America, March the 5th 1685.

Dear Andrew

I suppose ye have heard of our voyage from my Brother, and Governor Barclay. I shall only in short tell you that notwithstanding the loss of our masts, we were not only 8 weeks betwixt land and land, and entered the Capes of Virginia the same day 9 weeks we parted from Aberdeen. We sailed up Chessapeek bay to the head of Bohemia River in 2 sloopes, from thence we came to Elizabeth Town, partly by Land and partly by Water: the storm being the tail of a Hurricane, was not universall, for we heard of no ships which met with it but ourselves; nor the Montrose Ship did not meet with it. There is encouragement for several trades here; in the first place, Planting: for Wheat, Indian Corn, Beef, Pork etc., give all ready money in York and the Neighbour Collonies: Wheat 4 shillings the bushel, Indian Corn 2s. or half a crown. Pork and Beef etc to be had at an ordinary easie rate. And in the second place there may be Fishing: For the Inhabitants aver they swim so thick in the Creeks and Rivers, at certain seasons of the year, that they have hailed them out of the Water with their very hands. In the third place for one to have a Malt house, a brew house, and a bake house, to make Malt, brew beer, and bake bisket for Barbadoes and the Neighbour Collonies; providing he have a Ship of his own, and skill to manage his business would certainly be a good trade. Lastly for one to buy up the product of the Countrey, such as all kinds of grains, Beef Pork etc. and export them to Barbadoes, and import Rumm and Malasses, would certainly be a good trade ; as likewise change keeping would be a good trade in Amboy, for the highest designe of the old Buckskin Planters (I am just now drinking to one of them, our Countreymen, who was sent away by Cromwell to New England ; a slave from Dunbar, Living now in Woodbridge like a Scots Laird, wishes his Countreymen and his Native Soyle very well, though he never intends to see it. Pardon this Parenthesis,) is to acquire a piece of monie to drink in the change house. This Countrey and particularly the Town (showeth it to be the best scituated for a city of any here known in America) is but yet in infancie (it not being above 48 years at most since ever there was a Planter in the Province : and that occasioned by their changing so many masters) yet there are severall thousands of People already, and in no want of good company, and if ye please bad too, as in any place of the world : neither are we destitute of Books and Clergy, for George Keith (who arrived three weeks since with others, they were all winter in Barbadoes) hath brought Mathematicks, and Benjamin Clark a Library of Books to sell : so that you may see New Perth begins to be founded upon Clergy. Shew my Cusins, George Burnet and Richard Maitland, that I hope they will not laugh more at me, for saying in Edinburgh, I would line my house with Cedar-wood, for all houses here are covered with Cedar, and one just now built in Perth, altogether of Cedar Wood, it is reckoned a wood of no value here, except for its lastiness. I intend to follow Planting myself, and if I had but the small stock here I have in Scotland, with some more servants I would not go home to Aberdeen for a Regencie, as was profered me ; neither do I intend it ; however, hoping to get my own safe over. We are not troubled here leading our pitts, mucking our Land, and ploughing 3 times : one Ploughing with 4 or 6 oxen at first breaking up, and with 2 horses only, thereafter, suffices for all ; you may judge whether that be easier Husbandrie than in Scotland. But

I know you are no good Husbandman; But which of the aforesaid trades you will choose, if you will come here yourself is more than I can divine, or will advise you to; I have told you how things are, and in God's Name take your choice, as I have done. I shall tell you what I would do were I in your place, if it shall fall out you do come, I would get some trusty Comorads, Merchants, to joyn with me, and sett up a trade in Perth, for I think a mans own trade fitts him best: if you have 5000 merks it is enough, 4 in goods and one in Money. Let none come here destitute of money, it is of great request here, and gets cheape Pennyworths, and 25 per cent of advantage by it: but I doe not advise you, for if you should meet with such trouble and disappoyntments as we have done by being put by our Port, you would perhaps be discouraged, and give me the blame. All our baggage is not yet come from Maryland, and I want yet my bed Cloaths, and the land I intend to settle on is not yet purchased from the Indians; for after I have viewed all the Province, such of it as is yet habitable, I have chosen the South Branch of Rariton-River for conveniency of Fishing, Fowling, and Meadows; But all the best Land lyes back from the Rivers, and the Sea Coasts; the further back the better it is, which necessitates me to go a mile back. In brief what you heard of the countrey is all true, so I need not spin out long Descriptions of it: no unbyassed and indifferent Person will speak ill of the Land, it is both pleasant and wholesome; and industrious People, after some few years Labour, may lead a pleasant, easie Life, and want for nothing; and I am of opinion, may grow rich too, if they take pains for it, and follow Merchandising; and some are actually grown rich since they come here who had nothing before. If any shall miscredit what I have said, I shall not think myself baffled for that, but let them live in their opinion and I will live in mine; And if they please they may do with me as I did with John Skeen's wife, cast my Letters in mine own teeth, and when they come upon the place, I shall make good what I say, face to face, as she did to me: and if they come not themselves, they need not trouble themselves whether it be true or false. The goods fit for this Countrey are all kinds of house hold Plenishing, without which and a years provision in victualls, let none come hither, if they would wish not to be preyed on by the old Planters. All course cloth such as hodden grayes, and Plaiding, course stockings and Linning; no fine things for an infant countrey, except for a mans own use : course Bedding and Blankets :—Governor Barclay can give you full information as to this point. The Inconveniencies we have met with are great trouble and charges for want of our baggage; there is likewise trouble and charges for the first settlement in carting out one's goods to the woods :—fencing is the chief difficulty, and if there be many great trees the loggs must be drawn off with oxen and the branches burned, the trees are felled equal to a man's thigh high, but the roots are no impediments; where is much brush the roots must be plucked up with grubbing howes : any man may learn Husbandrie here who was not acquainted with it in Scotland, (Tobacco would grow here as well as in Maryland, but it is best for European graines) : I doe not intend to write more Letters to Edinburgh with this occasion, being busied about mine own settlement; therefore I entreat you will remember me to all my friends, Relations, Comorads and Acquaintances at Edinburgh, and shew them of my welfare that I had not my health so well these 7 years by-gone, as now (Blessed be God) and that I am not troubled with coughs and head aikes as in Edinburgh, which is likewise a great motive for me to stay in this Countrey. I intreat to hear from them all; you will not readily miss occasions from London every month to some place in America : And there is ordinarily occasions hither from the neighbour Collonies. I have received Letters from the Bissets and my Brother, from Mr. Alexander since we came : I intreat to hear particularly from the Professor of Divinitie and Mathematicks, Doctor Pitcairn, Mr. George Alexander, and any others who shall ask for me, wishing you and all your concerns well, I continue Dear Cusin,

    Your most affectionate Cusin,
     and humble Servant,
        Charles Gordon."

APPENDIX E

(Postscript by the foresaid hand)

" If any pleases to tell me what their scruples are, I shall endeavour to answer them, if Servants knew what a Countrey this is for them, and that they may live like little Lairds here, I think they would not be so shy as they are to come : and during their service they are better used than in any place in America I have seen. You may know my subscription by the sign I gave you of my Pistoles misserving in the Boat, or at least when you tell your mother, you may mind on me, for you will miss some pints of wine you spent with me (that Friday night, you conveyed me abroad) on the Shore and in the Ship. If there were a Caball of Merchants here to export the product of the Countrey to Barbadoes and the West Indies, and to Import Rumm, Malasses, Sugar and Cotton etc. it would do a great deal of good to this Countrey. I intreat to know what remarkable Revolutions has happened either abroad or at home since I came away. Any Merchants who settle here must take Lotts in the Town, and build houses. Mr. David Mudie is building a stone house, and hath already a Horse mill ready to set up presently in New Perth. Adieu."

(15) For Mr. James Mudie Merchant in Montrose.

" New Perth, the 9th of March, 1685.

Sir,

My Love ever being remembered to yourself, Lady and Children, these are earnestly intreating you to let my Wife have any little thing she stands in need of untill it shall please the Lord I return, and I shall pay you very thankfully, I have left Thomas Parson, and resolves to trade this Summer in the Countrey, and to come home with your Uncle the next Spring. I wish you were here and your whole Family, for I doubt not but the Countrey would please you well ; for there is abundance of much better land here than ever Arbikie was, and an Earldome to be bought far below in pryce the vallue of what such pettie Lairdships as Arbikie is sold for in Scotland ; without purging of the Lands of any incumbrances. For I hope to winn as much monie this year, as will bring a better Lairdship than Arbikie ; and if ye resolve not to come over, I resolve to buy Land before I come from this, and title it Arbikie But I shall be sorrie to take away your title, but if I do, it will be your own fault : and for your better incouragement, I know you love a Gunn and a Dogge, and here ye will have use for both. For Wilde Geese, Turkies, Ducks and Drakes, Patridges, Conies, Doves and innumerable more kinds of Fowls (of) which I know not their names, are here to be seen every hour of the day, in flocks above Thousands in Number ; And for your skieft which you use to fish with bring here with you, or ane like her, for I assure you of good employment, and yet ye may catch more Fish in one hour here, than any Fisher in Montrose in two, excepting Podloes at the shore head.

Sir, take this as no jest from me, for what is here written is a reall truth : but ye may think, it is not my dictating, but the writer and I have set it together the best way we can ; But yet not so full as I would have had it. Present my Love to your Sister, Uncle, and all Friends, and I am Sir,

    Your very loving Friend and
    Cusin JAMES MUDIE."

(16) A letter from David Mudie, Merchant in Montrose : For James Mudie of Courthill in Scotland.

      " New Perth the 9th of
       March 1685.

Loving Brother,

  I wrote you a lyne upon my arrivall here, and by my last to my wife of the date the 12 December, I desired her to let you see it, which I hope she has done if it be come to her hands ; I do now understand this Countrie, better than I did at that time, and the longer I travell in it I like it the better : for a frugall man with a small fortune may very soon raise a good Estate, which I wrote formerly to my Wife. In relation to the Countrie, I found it most certain and much better than I wrote : this Winter hath been exceeding hard and sharpe, the like not seen by those who have lived 20 or 30 years in it, which hath hindered me of a great deal of work: yet I have cleared three Acres of Ground to be an Orchard and a Garden, which lyes close to the house which I am building, which is all of stone work with Cellars under the ground, six Rooms off a Floor, two Stories high, besides the Garrat: and I have two Masons dayly working at it since the first of February: three Wrights working at an Horse Mill which will be clear against the latter end of this month: And I am told that the Mill will be worth 100 lib. a year, but I am sure she will be better than 50. of clear Money, for every Scots boll of Wheat or Indian corn pays here for grinding of it 2 shill: ster. This house and mill stands me a great deal of money, but there is none such in this Countrey, nor ever was. I resolve to go out to the Countrey to the Land which I have taken up, which is 2 hours going from my own house by water; I mind to settle some of my Servants there against the middle of this Month: I am provided with six course Horses, Oxen and Swine sufficiently in number, for any Plantation for the first year: the land I have settled on, in my Judgment is extraordinary good. If any friends or acquaintances hath any inclination to come over here, I can assure them, if they be frugall men, and have but 300 lib. Stir: Stock, they may live better than a gentleman with us of 40 Chalders of Victuall. I cannot now resolve to come home til this time twelve months, since Thomas Parson hath so much disappointed me, as I have written to my wife: but against that time, if the Lord preserve my health, I will come home then. Present my service to Arbikie, and to my Sisters, and to all our Friends, which will save me trouble to give them a line: my love to your wife, and children, I am,

Your loving Brother
DAVID MUDIE.

Let Arbikie, my sisters, and the rest of my Friends see this Letter."

(17) Abstract of a letter from Robert Fullerton Brother to the Laird of Kinnaber, to Brothers and Sisters, from Amboy the 6 of November 1684.

" Dear Brothers and Sisters,

By the Mercies of the Most High, we are safe arryved, after a long Demur by contrary winds : we encountered very happily at first with Long Island and the next day came to an Anchor in New Jersey. The Passengers did all very well, though we had some very rough gusts, and were very thronged in so small a vessel, being 130 Souls, besides Sea-men : of these 27 were women, 6 or 7 children only ; one man whom I hyred in your house called William Clark standing carelessly upon the Forecastle tumbled over boards, and drowned tho we put out our boat and endeavoured in vain to save him. This countrey pleaseth us very well, and appears to be nothing short of our expectation. We were yesterday, ranging about viewing our Land, whereof you shall have accompt by the next : the Land in general is good, and agrees with the accompt you have heard : the Trees are nothing so invincible as I did imagine, being neither so thick nor so great as we thought. The first plant that I touched was wild Bayes, which grow in abundance here ; the fruits are very excellent, such sorts as I have seen—apples the best I believe in the world, some I have seen of a pound weight. Cattle in generall are abundantly pleantifull, especially Horses and Oxen : the greatness and fatness of the Oxen will countervail the Difference of the price, being about 5 lib. Sterling. The Countrey is not altogether level, as some other Countreys here, but hath easie rysings and Vallies. My new experience cannot give you such an accompt as you may afterwards expect, but in generall the Countrey may satisfie any rationall ingenuous mind ; yet I find there be Novices who know no happiness save home, with a glass of wine, and Comorads in a change House : tho there be no want here of more noble divertisements as hunting wild Beasts, wild Horses, and Deer : yesterday I did see several droves of Deer, and wild Horses, as I did ride up in the Countrey. The Land which we were viewing is a large plain, under the blew hills, watered with

two or three little Rivers, about 8 or 9 miles from New Perth, four from Rariton River Northward: the land downwards is all taken up by the Quitrenters of Piscataway, Woodbridge, or Elizabethtown. There shall be nothing of care wanting in your affairs, and I do expect the like from you; I hope my Grandmother is in health—wish her from me long life, and good health and assure her she wronged the Countrey in her opinion: present my love to all my Friends—I am Your
affectionate Brother
ROBERT FULLARTON."

(18) A letter from John Forbes Brother to the Laird of Barnla. Directed to Mr. James Elphingston of Logie.
Writer to His Majesties Signet in
Edinburgh, in Scotland.

" From Amboy-point, alias New Perth,
in the Province of East New Jersey,
in America March 18. 1685.
Honored Sir,
I having the occasion of this Bearer Mr. Drummond, brother to John Drummond the Factor in Edinburgh, and who came Passenger with me to this place from Scotland, I could not omit my duty in acquainting you by this line of our safe arrival into America; tho being by the Divine Hand of Providence miraculously preserved from the cruelty of the tempestuous Ocean, occasioned by a mighty storm of wind, (which happened upon the 12 day of September last) and which blew so tempestuously that, in short, it carried first away our Boltsprit, and afterwards our whole three Masts, Flagstaff and all, by the board, before the Sailors were able to get them out: it likewise took away the awning above our quarter-deck and left not so much as an yard of a rope above our heads, all of which was done in the space of half an hour. We lay thus distressed like a pitiful wreck all that night, (we having lost our Masts about 12 of the clock in the day) and two dayes thereafter at the mercie of the Waves (which being like mountains occasioned by the great storm of wind) without hopes of recovery, being then above 200 leagues from this land of America, tossing to and fro expecting that each wave should overwhelm us: Yet at

last it pleased God to turn the storm into a calm : and having preserved all our lower Yards, we made all haste and made Jury Masts of them ; with the help whereof (tho very insufficient ones, to drive forward the bulk of so great a vessel) and of Gods miraculous Mercie and Providence Who—immediately after we had put our ship in any mean posture for plying out her Voyage—was pleased to send us such a fair and moderate gale of wind, as brought us in sight of the Capes of Virginia, within 15 days after, or thereabouts, having never ceased for the whole time till it brought us thither in safety. So we came within the capes, and sailed up that great Navigable Bay, called Chessapeik bay, up through all Virginia up to Maryland, where we landed at the place where our ship was bound to take in her tobacco, for her homeward Loadning. But being thus Disabled, and not being able to ply out her Voyage to this place (where she ought to have landed us), we was necessitated to travel from thence by Land to this place, being upwards of 200 English miles, and having left our Goods behind us, (which was thereafter to come about in a Sloup) we was necessitated to stay all winter in this New and young Citie, where we had but very bad Accommodation for Lodging, tho we knew of no want of Victuals of all sorts for money, tho at a considerable dear rate. This hindered us long from our falling to work about our husbandries, which was a great loss of time to us ; However when our Sloup came about—which did not hold half of our goods, so that every man yet wants half of his goods, But are dayly expecting them by the same Sloup which we fraghted thither back again—I went out to the Woods to the Land we had pitched upon, with several others of our Countreymen such as Tho: Gordon, and Mr. Char: his Brother, Brothers to the Laird of Straloch, Kinnabar's two sons Robert and Mr. Thomas Fullerton, James Johnstone of Spotswood and John Barclay the Governours Brother, with some others ; where we have all pitched near by one another, upon a piece of excellent land as we suppose ; whereof I judge I have not the worst (if not the absolute best) piece of Land in all the Tract, for we had it all at our own choosing and not by lots. This land lyes not on a Navigable River, but about 5 or 6 miles from Rariton

River, which is Navigable up the nearest place to our Plantations; For the best places of the Rivers are already inhabited by the old Planters of this Countrey who have been here some 16 or 18 years agoe. There are many places upon Navigable Rivers yet untaken, and some very near this place also, which is intended to be the Metropolis of this Province, But it is generally sandy barren land; and the best land is computed by all to be in the woods, back some several miles from the Navigable Rivers; So that we rather chuse land for profitableness than for Conveniencies of Towns and pleasure allenarly; For there is abundance both of good and barren land in this Province. So that a man may chuse some for pleasure and some for profit and conveniency, for I intend to take up about 4 or 500 Acres where I have now settled: which is on a very pleasant place and good land, and whereof I have, with two hands (not having had to get many servants away with me, having come away upon so short advertisement, and whereof I lost one at Maryland by sickness: so that now I have but two, and a woman for dressing our Victuals and cloaths, till I get more sent me this year) already cleared, or at least will clear, and (have) in Corn this year about 8 or 10 Acres of ground; tho it was prettie thick of stately tall Timber; and that since the 26 of January, at which time I went to the woods, I have 1,000 Acres to take up at this time, out of the first Division of 10,000 Acres, ordained to be laid out to every Proprietor I having bought a 10th part, whereof my Brother is half shares. I have also taken up 400 Acres of excellent fine land on Rariton River, about 20 miles above Amboy, whereon I design to set servants, that I expect over this ensuing summer: and so to divide our said parcels, and improve them for a year or two to the best advantage, and then to sell them off, If I design to come home, which we can do at good profit. Now for a general description of this Countrey;—it is a fine place for those who have a good stock, to let out upon a stock of Cattel of all sorts, which do greatly multiply here in a short time, and are sold at great rates, and may soon increase a stock greatly: or it is a good Countrey for an Industrious Frugall Man, that designs to follow Husbandries closely: providing he bring but some little stock to stock a Plantation withall : or it is very good for Tradesmen, as good Carpenters, Smiths, Tailors etc. who will get large wages a day : But it is not a Countrey for idle Sluggish People ; or those who cannot sometimes put too their hands, and encourage their servants. It is a place that produces many fine Fruits, and Physick Herbs ; The Woods are stored with wild Deers, Conies, Wolves, Bears, Racouns, some Beavers, and several other Beasts, which have fine Furrs ; and Fish, and Water Fowl for the killing. The Timber are mostly Oak of all sorts, Walnut, Chesnut, whereof there are great abundance where I have planted, tho they be scarce so bigg as these that comes to Scotland, yet large and pleasant. Strawberries grow very thick upon the ground amongst the Trees, so that some places of the woods are in summer as it were covered with a red cloth, As I am certainly informed. Fruit trees advance at a great rate in this place, for a Man may have an Orchard within a few years after the Planting, that may yield him a great quantitie of Cyder, which is the chiefest of their drink in this Province, even amongst the meanest of the Planters. So that this Countrey if well improved, may make a fine place ; for Nature has been deficient in nothing to it, either for pleasure or fruitfulness of the Soyl ; So that a man being once settled two or three years in it, and having Corn, Cattle, and all things necessary for the use of man within himself, And the trouble and hardship of his first settling by his hand, he may live as comfortably here as in any place in the world : Providing he could dispense with the want of his Friends and Relations, and the satisfaction of their Companie, which is the loss I most regrett in this place. And thus having given you a short description of the place, I cannot but in the next place, much regrett my misfortune, in not seeing you and taking your advise before I came to this place : But my Resolution was so sudden, by the encouragment I received from the Chief Governor and some of the proprietors at Aberdeen : (having come in only to see my Sister with my Brother) and by the many Gentlemen that were going along in the ship, that I was induced to go along without so much as taking my leave of any of my Friends, save onely those that were then in Town :

So that I came of resolution onely to see the place, and to settle onely if I found conveniency.—And having thus abruptly come away when I came here, I designed not to return till I took some tryal of the Countrey, that at my return I might be the more able to give a true accompt thereof. I am not as yet of any determined resolution as to my staying for altogether, as yet, but I resolved to stay this year, till I see what the ground produces, and to see how my endeavours take effect; and God willing, by that Time, I may in some measure be resolved what to do, for then the greatest hardship will be over my head; and by that time I will have up a prettie good house, which is near already framed, whereas hitherto I have dwell for the most part here in a Wigwam (as we call them here): accounting all our hardship in the beginning but short, in expectation of good success in the end. But however I may be resolved hereafter, I intend, God willing, life and health serving, to come home or start within this year or two, and see all my Friends, and apologise the best manner I can for my abrupt departure. Now having thus in some measure discharged a part of my dutyfull respects towards you by this line, in letting you know of my wellfare and present condition; Earnestly desiring ye will favour me with a return by the first occasion; where in I shall be glad to hear of your welfare, of your Kind Ladies and Children (To whom and others my nearest Friends and Relations, and Comerads, I desire the favour to be kindly remembered) begging pardon for this trouble and your patience to peruse this, when your leisure can permit: and afterwards to communicate it to my Uncle, Calder-hall and his Lady, or to my Cusins Harrie Lockhart, or George Erskine, if they call for it: I not having time at present to write to them at length, as I have in haste done to you. I shall forbear to give you further trouble at present; intreating you to remember me kindly to your Worthy and oblidging Lady and fine Children, and shall only subscribe myself, as I sincerely am, and shall continue to be, Sir,

   Your most affectionate Cusin
   and oblidged Servant, while
      JOHN FORBES."

(19) A Letter from Robert Fullerton, to his Brother the Laird of Kinnaber, dated from his new possession in the plains of New Caesarea : January, 7, 1685.

" Dear Brother.

You have, above, a transcript, containing the principal contents of an abrupt Letter, sent you three or four days after our arrivall : since that time we have possessed our Selves in the above mentioned plain 11 miles from New Perth, four from Rariton Northward and 12 from Elizabeth-Town ; we have the honour to be the first Inland planters in this part of America, for the former Settlements have been by the Riversides, which are all possessed by the Quit-renters ; the which I would have grudged at, had I not found the goodness of the Land upwards will countervail the trouble of transportation to the water. As to the number and nature of these Quit-renters, they are about 2 or 300 Families, some civill and Discreet, others rude and Malcontent with the late Purchassers, and need some thing of austerity to make them Complaisant. We have at present sharp frosts, and a good deall of Snow, three days of vitrifying frosts this winter, had not its match for cold these 16 years by gone, as the Inhabitants do inform us. Against this extream, we have a good Defence of Fire, and felling of Trees, and might live warm enough, were we not forced to travell for recruit of Provisions. I reckon the winter to consist only of nights, for the Suns appearance by day moderateth the cold and melts the Frost : I do not find the cold here to cause obstructions or coughs ; the Air is ever transparent. We have singular good stomachs, which if it continue as they say, it will require a fertile Countrey when peopled. I cannot find it necessary to give any particular account of this Countrey with its product, because ye have had already many, and some very ingenuous of this nature ; besides I have not yet proof of all the seasons of the year. We have the Deer to walk the round nightly about our Lodge ; this morning I shot a large Hart, and followed his bloody tract in the snow above two miles before he dyed ; I believe the fattest Deer in the world are here. We have made choice of your land next adjacent to mine, and have placed your Servants there, where they will settle, if we find convenient, when the snow is away : this is all at present from

    Your affectionate Brother
        ROBERT FULLERTON."

(20) Another Letter from the same hand dated the 10th of March 1685.

" Dear Brother.

 Before the despatch of the above written, of the date of this Instant, so that they may both go together ; the Winter is now past, and we are providing ground for the seed, the Fields being bare, we can better distinguish where is good land. We have chosen our chief Plantation and yours two miles further up in the Countrey, close under the blew Mountains, where you may reckon you have an Estate of 40 Chalders of Victual, with no more Wood thereon than yourself would desire, and it might yield no less yearly, presently, if it were all plenished after a little pains to root out the brush ; that which wanteth wood is open plain with short bushes, which we cut at the roots with a how : I wish the adjacent bounds were purchased, and possessed by our friends, who have any design this way ; for it is excellent land ; the mould in the Province in General, is either like that I possessed at the Northwater or more marly or clay ; but all of it hath 3, 4 or five inches of black rotten mould uppermost. I have not much to trouble you with, but my respects and love to all Friends ; if my Uncle or any other Friends send their Sons here, let them advert to this Maxim : A Gentleman that is not to work himself, must be well provided with a stock, and this must be more or less as he designs his Estate. I question not your care in my affairs ; neither need you question in your concerns the care of

    Yours affectionate Brother
        ROBERT FULLERTON."

(21) Abstract of a letter from Charles Gordon (Brother to the Laird of Straloch) to Doctor John Gordon, Doctor of Medicine at Montrose dated at

" Woodbridge in East Jersey, 7 of March 1685.

Dear Brother.
I design 100 pound Sterling for goods and servants; if Tradesmen and Servants knew they were better used here than in any Neighbouring Collonie, and that after their time is expired they may gain a stock by their work, and live like some of your Lairds before they dye, they would not so much scrouple to come hither. There are a number of queries proposed by our Brother Thomas to the Fullertons, which I remember you desired me to answer; the most materiall of them are answered, by this and my former Letters; I shall therefore superceed any long discription of it, till I see it throw all the seasons of the year; in short, I see it pleasant, and furnished with all conveniencies of Nature, such as woods, grass meadow, plenty of Fresh Springs, Creeks, and Rivers; I find it wholesome for I am not (blessed be God) troubled here with Defluction, head-akes, and coughs, as at Edinburgh, which is a great inducement for me or any valitudinarian man to stay in this Countrey; People come from Barbadoes, to York, and hither, for their healths sake.—If you design to come hither yourself, you may come as a Planter, or a Merchant, but as a Doctor of Medicine I cannot advise you; for I can hear of no diseases here to cure but some Agues and some cutted legs and fingers, and there are no want of Empericks for these already; I confess you could doe more than any yet in America, being versed both in Chirugery and Pharmacie; for here are abundance of curious Herbs, Shrubs, and Trees, and no doubt Medicinall ones for making of drugs, but there is little or no Imployment this way. Your Servants are settled on a pleasant plain beside the Fullertons on a brook; called the Vine or Cedar Brook, from a swamp of Cedars from whence it springs, and the multiplicity of vines which grow upon it. All your friends and Countrey men here are in good health, blessed be God: This hath been the hardest Winter that was almost since ever there were English

here ; the sound betwixt Jersey and Staten Island was frozen in January that carts and horses went upon it ; betwixt Martenmas and Christmas flying showers of snow with clear moderate frosts ; in January deep snow and most bitter frosts which ever I found, but did no wayes affect peoples bodies ; the Air being ordinary clear and serene ; about the 20 of January, the snow went off insensibly, and about 3 weeks in February it was almost like Summer in Scotland ; the end of February and beginning of March for the most part rain and wind. Acquaint me with the value of sweet-sent Gumm, which flowes from the wood, Gum-trees, of Sassafras, Sassaparilla, and such other things as the Countrey naturally produceth. Be pleased to send me some Medecins for Agues, and accidentall cutts, or sores, in case myself or Servants be overtaken with them. I hope with the blessing of God here to make a livelihood for myself. I entreat to hear what remarkable news, and revolutions are either at home with you, or abroad, and so continues

    Your most affectionate brother
    and humble Servant
      CHARLES GORDON."

(22) A Letter from Thomas Gordon, Brother to the Laird of Straloch. For Mr. George, Advocate in Edinburgh.

  " From the Cedar Brook of East New Jersey,
    in America, the 16 February 1685.

Dear Mr. George.
  This is the fifth time I have written to you since I came to America, some of which I am confident have come safe to your hands : so that I need not now resume them, for in them I gave you a full account of our danger by Sea and travels by Land, and therefore I shall now proceed and begin where I left last. Upon the eighteenth day of November I and my servants came here to the Woods, and 8 days thereafter my Wife and Children came also : I put up a Wigwam in 24 hours, which served us till we put up a better house ; which I made 24 foot long, and 15 foot wide, containing a Hall and Kitchen both in one, and a Chamber and a Study, which we put up pretty well (with Pallissadoes on the sides,

and Shingles on the roof) against Yuill, on which day we entered home to it; and have been ever since, and still am clearing ground and making fencing: So that I hope to have as much ground, cleared, fenced, ploughed, and planted with Indian Corn in the beginning of May, (which is the best time for ploughing it) as will maintain my Family the next year, if it please God to prosper it. Robert Fullerton and I are to joyn for a Plough this Spring consisting of 4 Oxen and two Horses, but if the Ground were once broken up, two Oxen and two Horses, or 4 Oxen alone will serve; so that the next Spring I intend (God willing) to have a Plough of my own alone. I intend to build a better House and larger, and to make a Kitchen of this I am in; which I will hardly get done this Summer, because I resolve to build upon my lot at New Perth. I am settled here in a very pleasant place, upon the side of a brave plain (almost free of woods) and near the water side, so that I might yoke a Plough where I please, were it not for want of Hay to maintain the Cattle, which I hope to get helped the next year, for I have several pieces of Meadow near me. The first Snow we had was about the midst of November, and went twice away again, and about the end of the month it came on, and continued with very great Frost and Knee deep Snow till towards the end of January; and then the Snow dessolved pleasantly and calmly with the heat and influence of the Sun, and now I judge it as warm here as it will be with you in May, and much more pleasant, for we are not by far so much troubled with winds here, as ye are in Scotland; the winter was generally very pleasant and calm, altho sometimes very vehement frost. I have spoken with several old Inhabitants here, who assure me they had not seen so hard a winter as this has been these 16 years bygone; and truly if I never see much worse I shall be very well pleased with this Countrie. We have great abundance of Deer, Turkies etc here about us; and as for the wild Beasts, and Natives, (whereof I was greatly affrayed before I came here) I find no danger, trouble, (or) inconveniency thereby at all: there are abundance of all sorts of Cattle in this Countrey to be had at very reasonable rates, I can buy a good Cow for 4 lib ster. a good Ox for 5 lib. ster., and a good Horse for 5 or

APPENDIX E   273

6 lib. ster: a Hog for 20s. ster: a Bushell of Wheat for 45s. ster: of Rye 356d ster. There are 8 of us settled here within half a mile of one another, and about ten miles from the town of New Perth, or Amboy-point, so that I can go and come in a day, either on foot or horseback, viz : Robert and Thomas Fullerton, James Johnstone of Spotswood, John Forbes, John Barclay, Doctor John Gordon his Servants, Andrew Alexander, and myself. This is the most of what I can say of this Countrey at present, for I intend to write nothing but what I either see or know to be certainly true, and for my part I am very well pleased with this retired Countrey life; and I love this Countrey very well as yet, altho I hear of some of our Countreymen who are not; neither can it be expected, that any Countrey in the World will please the different humours of all Persons. Blessed be God, myself and Wife, and Children, and Servants have been and are still in good health, which God continue : be pleased to communicate this to both yours and my Friends and Acquaintances, because I have not leasure to write at great length to every one ; and let those remember me to all others that give themselves the trouble to inquire for

                Your most humble and
                  oblidged Servant,
                            THOMAS GORDON."

(23) A Letter from David Mudie, of the date of the former, to Mr. Alexander Gairns, one of the Ministers at Edinburgh.

" Sir,
       I did write to you a line upon my arrival here, and my last the 12 of December, directed to John Graham ; I desired him to let you see his letter, and my wifes, which would inform you as fully as (if) I had written to you. Since that time I have travelled throw the Countrey, and informed myself of the conditions thereof, which still does the better please me : the Winter hath been exceeding hard, and sharp, which hath much hindered me of work ; yet I have cleared three acres of ground, to be an Orchard, and a Garden, which lyes at the back of my house, which I am building of stone, six rooms off a floor, Sellers all under the ground, two stories

high, and garrets, at which I have had Masons since the first of February; and I hope will have it fully Finished this Summer; I have also built a horse-mill: The house is 32 foot-wide, 40 foot long, the great wheel 30 foot Diameter, which I will have fully finished against the latter end of this Month; it is told me she may be worth 100 pound sterling a year; I am sure she will be better than 50 clear money: this from, Sir,

    Your humble and obedient Servant,

                DAVID MUDIE."

(24) A Letter from Thomas Fullerton, Brother to the Laird of Kinnaber, to John Johnstone, Drugist, in Edinburgh, dated the 9 of March, 1685, from East Jersey.

"Loving Commorad,—

Your Brother and I did write to you about three Moneths agoe, wherein we told you, that we were 9 weeks at sea, after we parted from Kellebegs, in Ireland; we were all very well at Sea only we had more Stomachs than meat; to prevent which, if you or any other Commorad come this way, it will be prudence to fortifie themselves with good Cheese, Butter, Bisket, Cakes and Brandie; I believe you are cloyed with discriptions of the Countrey: And therefore this in brief, the reports you hear of it are generally true, some it may be are Hyperbolick in magnifying its Goodness, but as many are detractive from what it really deserves. There is abundance of good Land for improving; abundance of Swine and Cattle for the raising; Deers for killing, houses for the building; But some expect all these without pains. Your brother and I and our servants, have had good Venison broth once a day all this winter; to be short, if a man please to live a Countrey Life to labour Land, plant Orchards, and such like; I believe he cannot come to a place that will better answer his expectations, and when he hath a minde to be merry he will get a Punch-house, and very good fellows. I hope in a little time I shall want nothing but the company of the prettie Girls, to all whom, who retain any remembrance of me, Let my service be remembered, and to all friends. I long exceedingly to hear from you, but more to see you:

we had many difficulties at our entrance, and in our first indeavours, But when you come, I hope they shall be prevented by

Your affectionate Commorad
Thomas Fullerton."

(25) A Letter from James Johnstone of Spotswood, to Alexander Henderson, writer in Edinburgh, dated the 9 of March, 1685, from his Plantation at the blew Hills in East Jersey in America.

" Kind Commorad.

These are to present my best wishes to you, and all acquaintances, if any injoyment could make up the want of your company, I should not complain here ; what else can contribute to profite or pleasure, being here to be had : neither is there any thing here to discourage us : Quakers are not numerous : Wolves are so far from troubling men, that if a man should lay a Glove upon a Carcass or their prey, they will yell, but not come nigh it : You cannot come nigh a rattle-Snake, but they will rattle with their taile, whereby a man is advertised either to kill them, or go by them : they frequently charm the Squirrels, or other little Beasts off the tops of the Trees unto their mouth, and that without touching them with their teeth ; which if they did they would poison themselves. There is a Flee by the Salt Marshes most troublesome in Summer, but is not in the uplands. I am mightily well satisfied with my coming over, neither do I think I could live again in Scotland. In the Summer there is plenty of Fruits, Peaches, Walnuts, Chesnuts, Strawberries, and another berry like Currants ; Vines as good as any where. I and all who have come over, have kept our health very well ; our food hath for the most part been Venison we got from the Indians, which I like exceeding well. The Indian Corn, Indian Beans and Pease, are pleasant Grains : we have very good fishing. Present my service to all Friends, and believe me to be ever Sir,

Your obliged Servant,
James Johnstone."

(Scot's *Model*, pp. 263-264 : " Sir, I nothing question but by the perusal of the above written Letters, you are abundantly satisfied, that East Jersey as to all things necessary will accommodate our present design. But if some (Malevolent Persons) who because they have not the courage nor resolution to adventure upon such an undertaking themselves, do cavill at the design in others, may insinuate that the greatest part of these Letters being written by Gentlemen, it may be presumed, interest may oblige them to represent thing otherwise than they are, to the advantage of the place. This is easily answered, that there are severall persons in this Town, who have perused all their Letters, and declare they find nothing contained therein, that they can contradict. But as for a further proof thereof, I have though fit to conclude with a letter from a Mason, sent over as a Servant by Captain Hamilton : he being a plain Countreyman, it is not very probable he can have any design. I had the Letters from his said Master as followeth :) "

(26) A Letter from James Cockburn Mason, Servitor in East Jersey in America, to Captain Hamilton, at the Ship tavern in Edinburgh, dated the 12 of March 1685, to his Uncle James Brown, Shoe Maker in Kelso.

" Uncle

this few Lines do testifie that I am well and in good health, blessed be God for it, desiring to hear the like from you, for I am very well in this land of America. We lake neither wild nor tame to eat : the most part of our drink is Rumm, Cyder, and Beer ; such as have these to sell drives a very good Trade. I am working at my work daily, in good weather, and have very good encouragement among the old Planters. If my Sister Katharin inclines to come over, she may have good service here, and Francie also ; it is better to be bound some few years, than come free, except they have a good stock ; it is dear living here the first year or two. The Indians are a harmless People, and very kind to us ; they are not a hairie People as was said to us in Scotland. A Shoemaker would live very well here, if he brought any store of Leather with him ; the Shoes are five or six shillings a pair; there is nothing discourages us more than want of Ministers here, but now they have agreed about their Stipends; there is one to be placed in New Perth, Piscattaway, Woodbridge, and Elizabeth Town; they have a mind to bring them from Scotland, Uncle I hope you will let me know of your welfare, and how the Town is repaired again, and so I rest your Nephew unto death

JOHN COCKBURN."

(27) Another from the same hand to George Fal Mason in Kelso, from New Perth in America the 20 of March 1685.

" Cusin.

These are to show you that I am in good health, blessed be God for it, wishing to hear the like from you. We had a long Voyage, but we came very well to our Harbour in this place off America within a stone cast of my Masters Lott: it is upon the very Harbour. This Town is scituate betwixt two great Rivers, the one called Rariton, the other Hudsons. It is a very pleasant Countrey and good for all Tradesmen; you was angry with me for coming away, but I repent nothing of it myself, for I have abundance of Imployment. I am at the building of a great Stone house in New Perth, with another Scotsman. They build most with Timber, but are beginning to build with Stone: there is as good stone in this Countrey as in Scotland, if they were at the pains to find it out: there are not many of our trade in the Province. Any who hath a mind to come here will get good wages; these who have a mind to come here will do far better than in Scotland. I have no more desire to my Native Countrey than I had never been in it; they had better be bound some years with a good Master, than come over free, for it is dear living at first here. The Natives of this land are a harmless People, they do wrong to no man; they are very kind to us; tell my sister if she pleases to come over, she may have good service here: Remember me to all Friends, and Comorads in Kelso, and so I rest your Cusin, while I live,

JOHN COCKBURN."

APPENDIX F

Proposals

By Walter Gibson, Merchant in Glasgow, to such persons as are desirous to Transport themselves to America, in a ship belonging to him, bound for the Bermudas, Carolina, New Providence, and the Cariby Islands, and ready to set Sail out of the River of Clyd, against the 20 of February in this instant year, 1684.

[Broadside—*Tracts of Lord Fountainhall*—Advocates Lib. AAA 77, No. 54.]

I. To such as are willing to Transport themselves, with design to settle in Carolina, if they be able to pay for their Passage and Entertainment at Sea, and making the Voyage: The said Walter Gibson is content to Transport them at the rate of five Pound sterling for each man or woman, and fifty shillings Sterling for every child, from two to fourteen years of age: and those under two years of age for nothing. And the Persons that are thus Transported, when they come to Carolina, are to have from the Government there, settled upon them and their heirs for ever; if they be Masters, seventy Aikers of ground for themselves, and as much for every Child and Servant they take over with them, paying one Penny Sterling per annum for every Aiker: The Payment of which Rent is not to begin till September 1689, till which time they are to pay nothing. And the Servants such Masters take over with them, after they have served four years, are to have from the Government, to them, and their Heirs: for the like Quit rent per annum fifty Aikers to each of them.

II. To such as are desirous to transport themselves to the

said Colony of Carolina, and are not able to pay their Passage: If they be Tradesmen, who have past their Apprenticeship in any Handy-craft: The said Walter Gibson is content to Transport them on his own Charges, they obliging themselves to Serve him three years, during which time he will furnish them sufficiently with Meat, Cloaths, and other necessares. At the issue of the time of their Service, they are to have settled upon them and their Heirs from the Government, each of them fifty Aikers of Ground, they paying one Penny Sterling per Aiker yearly as above. And all other, Men or Women, from eighteen to fourty-five years of age, they obliging themselves to Serve him four years; and those under eighteen years of age, they serving him five years: at issue of which, they are to have each of them fifty Aikers of Ground ut supra, and their Meat, Cloathes, and other Necessaries, during the time of their Service.

III. The said Walter Gibson will give his best advice to all such as will Transport themselves, anent these things, which will be necessary for them, to carry alongst with them; and hath at Glasgow Patterns of some Tools which are used there, which shall be showed to them. And these who go in this vessel will have the occasion of good company of several sober, discreet persons, who intend to settle in Carolina, will dwell with them, and be ready to give good advice and assistance to them in their choice of their Plantations, whose Society will be very helpful and comfortable, especially at their first settling there.

INDEX

Abercrombie, Sir Ralph, 40.
Aberdeen, 11, 12, 164-166, 176, 234, 255.
Acadie, 3, 4, 22, 54, 70, 80, 127.
Act of East Jersey Assembly prohibiting carrying of swords, pistols and other arms, 152.
Acts of Scots Parliament for encouragement of trade, 128-135.
Alexander, Sir William, Earl of Stirling, 3, 8, 39 et seq., 77, 85, 89, 90, 110, 214-226.
Alexander, Sir William, the younger, 78, 79, 80, 84, 214-226.
America, Treaty of, 187.
Andrews, Professor C. M., quoted, 2, 3, 121.
Anstruther, 34.
Aragon, union of, with Castile, 22.
Arcadia, Sir Philip Sidney's, 43.
Argall, Captain Samuel, destroys French settlement at Port Royal, 56; troubles Dutch settlers on Hudson, 153.
Argyll's Rising, 171, 172.
Ashley, Lord, Earl of Shaftesbury, 187; liaison officer between Scotland and Carolina, 189.
Auchleuchries, General Patrick Gordon of, 9, 10.
Ayr, 176.

Bacon, Sir Francis, 33.
Bahamas, 3, 125.
Bairnsfather, Captain Bruce, 14.
Balboa, Vasco Nuñez de, 5.
Barbados, 114, 122, 123; correspondence, 292-232.
Barclay, Colonel, 146.
Barclay, David, 163, 238, 240, 247, 254.
Barclay, Robert, the Apologist, 145 et seq., 156-158, 233-237.
Baronets, Nova Scotia, 63-65, 214.
Basse, Jeremiah, Governor of East Jersey, 180, 181.

Bermuda, 2.
Berkeley, Lord, 2, 153, 154, 168.
Bishops' Wars, 113
Blackness Castle, 112.
Blackwood, William Laurie of, trial, 190-191.
Boston, 22, 191, 192.
Bothwell Bridge, 113.
Bristol, 33, 52.
Buccaneers, exploits of, 120, 121.

Cabot, John, 17.
Caledonia Bay, 5, 119.
Calvert, Leonard, 2.
Campbell, Captain, of Fonab, 5.
Campbell, Sir George, of Cessnock, 191, 194, 195, 197, 200.
Campbell, Lord Niall, 163 n, 171-173, 174, 175, 179.
Cape Breton Island, 3, 4, 92 et seq., 221, 222.
Cardross, Lord, 202-205, 207-208.
Caribbean Islands, 2, 5, 120, 121.
Carolina Project, origin of, 190-191; connection with Insurrectionary Plot, 192-193, 199-201.
Carstairs, William, 201, 202.
Carteret, Sir George, 2, 153, 154, 168.
Cartier, Jacques, 22.
Cary, John, 140-142.
Castile, union with Aragon, 22.
Champlain, Sieur de, 4, 22, 54, 71, 75.
Child, Sir Josiah, 137-140.
Clarendon, 138, 187.
Clyde, Firth of, 18, 81; cruising in, 203.
Cochran, Sir John, 191-195; flight of, 200.
Columbus, 22.
Committee of Trade of Scots Parliament, 128, 129; of Scots Privy Council, 132.
Connecticut, 2, 23.
Cortés, 22.

280

INDEX

Covenanters, 2, 22, 113, 115, 188-211.
Cromwell, 2, 22, 114, 120, 137.
Cupid's (or Cuper's) Cove, Newfoundland, 33, 36.

Danby, Sir Thomas, 138.
Darien Scheme, 4, 5, 10, 11, 22, 119, 120, 126, 144, 211.
Darien Scots at Jamaica, 123; at New York, 119, 120.
Davenant, Dr. Charles, 138, 139.
Daniel, Captain, of Dieppe, 107 *et seq.*, 222.
Drumclog, 113.
Drummond of Hawthornden, 43, 44.
Dumbarton, 66-69, 73, 214.
Dumfries, 176.
Dunbar, 113, 114.
Dunlop, Principal William, 146, 162, 201-204, 208.
Dunnottar Castle, prisoners in, 173, 174, 178.
Dunoon—"people taking extraordinary prices at," 203.

East New Jersey, 2, 114, 119, 127, 128, 143, 145 *et seq.*
East New Jersey in America, Brief Account of, 142, 155.
East New Jersey, Model of the Government of, 142, 155.
Edinburgh, 34, 35, 36, 64, 162, 170, 176, 238, 255, 258, 263.
Erskine of Carnock's *Journal* quoted, 24-26, 172, 203, 204.

Farrand, Professor Max, quoted, 16.
Ferguson the Plotter, 199.
French Kings, Scots Guard of, 6, 7.
Fundy, Bay of, 3.

Georgia, 3.
Gibson, Captain James, 204.
Gibson, Walter, 115, 165, 203, 278, 279.
Gilbert, Sir Humphrey, 32.
Glasgow, 9, 126, 142, 157, 165, 176, 201, 202, 203, 278, 279.
Golden Knights, Order of, 62.
Gordon, Charles, "his head-akes and coughs," 170; letters from, 254-259, 270-271.
Gordon, John, Doctor of Medicine at Montrose, 170, 234; letter to, 270-271.
Gordon, Sir John, of Durno, 156, 164, 173.
Gordon, General Patrick, of Auchleuchries, 9, 10.

Gordon, Sir Robert, of Gordonstown, 63, 65, 145, 146.
Gordon, Sir Robert, younger, of Gordonstown, 173.
Gordon, Sir Robert, of Lochinvar, 10, 58, 91 *et seq.*, 110.
Gorges, Sir Ferdinando, 2, 38, 48, 51, 52.
Greenock, 198, 203.
Groome, Samuel, Receiver and Surveyor-General of East Jersey, 156.
Guard, Scots, of French Kings, 5-7.
"Gunning for Deer and Turkies" in East Jersey, 242, 249, 260, 262.
Guy, Alderman John, of Bristol, 33.

Hakluyt, Richard, 13.
Halyburton, Andrew, 17.
Hamilton, Andrew, Governor of East Jersey, 179-181, 185.
Herries, Lord, 100.
Home of Eckills, Sir George, 81, 84, 216, 217.
Hudson River, 153, 182.
Huguenots, 137, 186, 219.

Indians, from Acadie, 80; of New Jersey, 169; in S. Carolina, 209, 210.
Insurrectionary Plot, connection with Carolina Scheme, 192-193, 199-201.
Irvine, 176.

Jamaica, 2, 120, 122, 123, 141; Darien Scots at, 123.
Johnstone, James, of Spotswoode, 236, 251; letters from, 242, 253, 275.
Johnstone, John, "Drugist at the sign of the Unicorn," 176; inherits Pitlochie's prisoners, 178; in East Jersey, 179, 185; letter to, 242.

Keith, George, 171.
Kelso, 236, 277.
Ker, Colonel Gilbert, 24.
Kilmarnock, 176.
King's Lynn, 34.
Kirkcudbright, 3, 58, 101 *et seq.*, 176.
Kirke, Captain David, 4, 75, 78, 79, 83.
Knights, Order of Golden, 62.
Knox, Andrew, Bishop of the Isles, 19, 34.

Largs, 81, 82, 226.

La Rochelle, 17, 73, 218, 219.
La Tour, Sieur de, 76, 79, 80, 83.
Lawrie, Gawen, 157, 162, 163.
Leith, 157, 165, 174, 176, 178.
Lescarbot, Marc, 55, 67.
Linlithgow, Provost of, 126, 127.
Lochinvar, Sir Robert Gordon of, 10, 58, 91 et seq., 110.
Lockhart, Sir George, 188, 190, 196.
Lyly, John, 13.

Maine, 2.
Mackay, Sir Donald, first Lord Reay, 8, 68.
Mackenzie, Sir George, 192, 193.
M'Ward, Rev. Robert, 26.
Maryland, 2, 167, 245.
Mason, Captain John, 2, 19, 20, 31, 33 et seq.
Maxwell of Pollok, Sir John, letter to, 218, 219, 226.
Memorial concerning the Scottish Plantation, 124 et seq.
Menstrie, House of, 40, 44; Goodman of, 45.
Middle Shires, 27, 28.
Monts, Sieur de, 22, 54.
Montrose, 147, 148, 157, 165, 171, 176.
Morgan, Sir Henry, 121.
Mudie, James, letter from, 259.

National Covenant, 113.
Navigation Act, English, 117.
Navy, Old Scots, 21.
Netherlands, Scots Brigade in, 7, 8.
Netherlands, Scots trade with, 20, 21.
New Amsterdam, 2, 143, 153.
New Edinburgh, 5.
New England, 51-54, 140, 141.
Newfoundland, 3, 17, 31 et seq.
New Hampshire, 118.
New Jersey, 2, 152-185.
New Perth (Perth Amboy), 156, 237, 238, 240, 242, 256, 259.
New York, 119, 127, 182-185, 193; Darien ships at, 119, 120.
Nicolls, Colonel, Governor of New York, 153, 154, 167, 182.
Nova Scotia, 3, 49-90, 78, 214-226.

Ochiltree, Lord, 3, 4, 79, 80, 104 et seq., 221, 222.
Oglethorpe, James, 3.
"Old Buckskin Planters," 114, 256.

Paterson, William, 81, 136, 145.
Peckham, Sir George, 32.

Peden, Rev. Alexander, 23.
Penn, Admiral, 2.
Penn, William, 143, 149.
Pennsylvania, 3, 118, 143, 149.
Pentland Firth, 34.
Perth, Earl of, 151, 160, 163 n.
Pilgrim Fathers, 2.
Pizarro, 22.
Plymouth Company, 51.
Popham Colony, 51.
Port Royal in Acadie, 3, 4, 54-56, 69, 70, 76, 79, 80, 85-88, 221-226.
Port Royal in South Carolina, 161, 186, 187, 206, 207, 210.
Poutrincourt, Sieur de, 55, 56.
Prisoners, gifts of, from Scots Privy Council, 173-178.
Proclamations of Scots Privy Council regulating trade, 132-135.
Puritans, 22, 23.

Quakers in Scotland, 146-149; in East Jersey, 244, 275.
Quebec, 4, 75, 78, 88, 89, 220-224.

Razilly, Chevalier de, 72, 89, 112, 145.
Reed, John, "who was gardener to the Lord Advocate," 167, 169; letter from, 238.
Rhode Island, 2.
Richelieu, Cardinal, 71-73, 107.
Rotterdam, 25, 26.
Rudyard, Thomas, Deputy Governor of East Jersey, 155, 156, 163.
Rullion Green, 113.
Rutherford, Rev. Samuel, 23, 24.
Ryswick, Peace of,

Sagamore Segipt, 80, 86.
St. Augustine, 50, 186, 187, 206, 209, 211.
St. Germain-en-Laye, Treaty of, 3, 89.
St. Kitts, 120.
St. Lawrence, 4, 22, 71, 75, 78, 89, 225, 226.
St. Malo, 17.
St. Martin, 120.
Salem, 2, 23.
Sandy Hook, 156, 250.
Santa Cruz, 120.
Santa Catalina, Puritan outpost on, 23.
Santa Catalin, mission station in Florida, 210.
Santa Maria River, buccaneers on, 121.
Sawkins, Captain, 121.
Saybrook, 23.

INDEX

Scot, George, of Pitlochie, 142, 145, 155, 159-162, 171, 175-179, 188.
Scott, Sir John, of Scotstarvit, 36, 145.
Scott, Sir Walter, quoted, 5.
Scots Brigade in Netherlands, 7, 8.
Scots Guard of French Kings, 5-7.
Scots Navy, 21.
Seafaring, 11-21.
Sea fisheries, 16-20.
Sea poetry, 12-15.
Sidney's, Sir Philip, *Arcadia*, 43.
Smyth, Sir Thomas, Treasurer of Virginia Company, 28, 29.
Solemn League and Covenant, 113.
South Sea, 5.
Star Chamber, 27.
Stevenson, R. L., quoted, 162.
Stirling, 40, 176, 177.
Stirling, Earl of, *see* Alexander, Sir William.
Stuart's Town, South Carolina, 4, 23, 112, 143, 145, 161, 186-211.

Stuyvesant, Governor, 117.
Swinton, John, 146, 147.

Tadoussac, 71, 76, 77, 223, 225, 226.
Thetford, 34.
Thirty Years' War, 8.
Thomas, Dalby, 138, 139.
Tillières, Comte de, 70, 212-213.
Toubacante, storming of, 5.
Turner, Sir James, *Memoirs* quoted, 8.

Ulster, Plantation of, 57, 63.

Vaughan, Sir William, 64.
Virginia, 2, 3, 28, 264.
Virginia Company, 28, 29, 50, 51.

West New Jersey, 3, 127, 143.
Willoughby, Lord William, Governor of Barbados; letter from, 230; dispatch from, 231.
Worcester, 113, 114.

www.ingramcontent.com/pod-product-compliance
Lightning Source LLC
Chambersburg PA
CBHW030135170426
43199CB00008B/74